D1302160

# PUBLIC MANAGEMENT IN LEAN YEARS

Withdrawn
IOWA STATE UNIVERSITY
of Science and Technology
Library

# PUBLIC MANAGEMENT IN LEAN YEARS

## Operating in a Cutback Management Environment

### JAMES L. MERCER

QUORUM BOOKS
Westport, Connecticut • London

**Library of Congress Cataloging-in-Publication Data**

Mercer, James L.
    Public management in lean years : operating in a cutback
management environment / James L. Mercer.
        p.    cm.
    Includes bibliographical references and index.
    ISBN 0–89930–357–9 (alk. paper)
    1. Public administration. 2. Government productivity. 3. Budget
deficits.    I.    Title.
    JF1351.M388    1992
    350—dc20            92–15782

British Library Cataloguing in Publication Data is available.

Copyright © 1992 by The Mercer Group, Inc.

All rights reserved. No portion of this book may be
reproduced, by any process or technique, without the
express written consent of the publisher.

Library of Congress Catalog Card Number: 92–15782
ISBN: 0–89930–357–9

First published in 1992

Quorum Books, 88 Post Road West, Westport, CT 06881
An imprint of Greenwood Publishing Group, Inc.

Printed in the United States of America

The paper used in this book complies with the
Permanent Paper Standard issued by the National
Information Standards Organization (Z39.48–1984).

10 9 8 7 6 5 4 3 2 1

For
Karolyn,
Theresa,
Betty,
Tara,
Kurt,
Ethan
Jim,
Angela
and Timothy

# Contents

# Acknowledgments

"It was the best of times, it was the worst of times . . . we had everything before us, we had nothing before us."
— Charles Dickens, 1859

Special acknowledgment goes to my brother-in-law, J. C. Rogers, who, as did I, grew up in southwestern Oklahoma. He graduated from Oklahoma State University and was the agriculture teacher in Sayre, Cheyenne and Erick, Oklahoma, before retiring. Among other things, J. C. is famous around those communities for the stories he tells and, more important, for the length of time it takes to tell them. The significance of what I have learned from J. C. really didn't hit me until the snowy day after Christmas, when I was having a breakfast of eggs, sausage, hash browns, biscuits and gravy (all low calorie, of course), in a local cafe in the Texas panhandle city of Plainview. As I was eating, I couldn't help but overhear the conversation of two local ranch hands in the next booth who were telling one seemingly concocted story after another and having a great time doing it.

Western Oklahoma and the Texas high plains can be big, endless and lonely places. If one isn't careful, one can become very depressed in such places. To overcome boredom and loneliness, many local residents have become great story tellers. They've brought such stories almost to an art form and in so doing, they have risen up to cope with their circumstances in whatever way they could.

People, and particularly Americans, are very adept at coping with circumstances of many kinds. So, the fact that state and local governments are facing difficult times may challenge our ability to cope effectively with a new set of negatives. If people can tell stories to cope with loneliness or boredom, surely state and local government managers can find ways to manage in a reduced revenue environment.

I would also like to acknowledge the work on cutback management done by Marvin Townsend, Gary Gwyn, John Harrison and Ron Cox, all previous or present Texas city managers, and the early work on cutback management done by Bill Donaldson and Charlie Levine (unfortunately, both of them are now deceased) with me at the University of Michigan. Thanks, too, to the National Science Foundation and to Porter Homer and Ron Philips at Public Technology Inc., for the opportunity to develop and manage the Urban Technology System, where considerable information on cutback management was developed. Appreciation is also expressed to Ed Ungar, formerly vice president of Battelle Memorial Institute and presently president of Taratec Corporation, and to Don Grace, Rudy Yobs, Dave Clifton and Cliff Bragdon at Georgia Tech where many cutback management and employee involvement ideas were spawned, nurtured and, in come cases, tried out in workshop settings.

Thanks, too, to the International City Management Association, the Kentucky Municipal League, the Florida League of Cities, the Texas Municipal League, the Pennsylvania State Association of County Commissioners, the Minnesota City and County Management Association, and others for giving me forums or publishing articles on cutback management or employee involvement processes.

Appreciation is also expressed to Mai Watlington for getting me involved in the University of Michigan's seminar series on Managing with Reduced Revenues, and to Susan Woolston for helping me prepare for them.

Finally, high praise is in order for Dianne Narten, who did a super job of typing the manuscript for this book, and to Tom Gannon at Quorum Books who continues to be patient with me regarding deadlines.

# 1

# State and Local Government Trends for the 1990s and Beyond

"If we can know where we are and something about how we got there, we might see where we are trending—and if the outcomes which lie naturally in our course are unacceptable, to make timely change."
                                        —Abraham Lincoln

The sixties was the decade of federal largesse with expanding revenues, responsibilities and opportunities for state and local governments. The seventies was a transitional decade when reality, primarily in the form of inflation, energy and citizen cynicism, began to constrain state and local government resources. During that decade, there was a move to suburbia and exurbia by a large portion of our population, partially due to industrial expansion in rural areas that may have now gone to foreign countries. Expectations about what government might accomplish not only stopped growing, but to some extent, these expectations reversed themselves. Citizens began to perceive government negatively, as part of the problem.[1]

During the 1980s, there was a migration to urban areas by a large percentage of our population. By 1990, 75 percent of the U.S. population lived in urban areas. In early retrospect, the eighties was the decade of new federalism, when state and local government administrators faced circumstances of constraint wholly different from conditions they operated under during the past two decades. This was a boom decade economically (except for the oil patch), but it was also the decade when the federal government off-loaded more programs and less funding on state and local governments, and the demand for services increased. Federal government growth virtually stopped during the 1980s.

As a result, economic development became the highest priority to produce revenue with which to operate state and local governments, create jobs and stimulate lagging economies. Revenue shortages meant that infrastructure began to be neglected, the drug problem got out of control, AIDS was widely recognized, the plight of the homeless became more acute, health care costs became staggering, gang violence increased and concerns about the environment mounted. It was also a decade when political barriers to international cooperation broke down, allowing for more sharing of state and local government solutions to problems. In the western states, the latter part of the decade was one of serious drought and critical water supply problems. Worldwide, the move to democracy became a stampede.

For state and local government administrators, the 1990s will mean exacerbation of the cost/revenue squeeze in which they currently find themselves, and the resulting need to manage with reduced revenues and resources. This is no small challenge. What are some of the trends and pressures that will influence state and urban strategies for the 1990s? The following are fifteen that state and local administrators ought to be thinking about.

*1. The conflict between economic development and environmental protection will intensify.* As a result of programs carried out during the past two decades, substantial progress has been made in water and air quality improvement and in recycling. Continued pressures for development to spur the lagging economy threaten to stop and maybe even reverse this momentum. Environmentalists will let this occur, however, only after extensive media, legislative and legal battles. State and local government administrators will be caught up in this maelstrom.

The competition for economic development among states and cities will intensify, and the temptation will be there to increase incentives for expansion or relocation of industry and other economic stimulators. Care will need to be exercised to keep from giving away the legacies of future generations by today's actions. More imagination and creativity will be required of state and local government administrators in this area.

With regard to land use, state and local governments will have to evaluate the economic consequences of new development to see if it can pay its own way. State and local governments will look more closely at encouraging growth in and around declining center cities and close-in suburbs, although such economic development plans may make the attainment of federal clean air standards more difficult.

There will also be increasing concern for world environmental conditions such as global warming, depletion of rain forests, drought, depletion of the ozone layer, more extensive recycling and so forth and what states and cities should do as their part in facing these problems. Further, economists project another energy crisis by 1995, a harbinger of what we found during the 1970s.

2. *The state and urban financial crisis will continue.* Some states are cutting welfare payments, recession is rampant and taxpayer frustration with government all indicate more, not less, financial distress for states and cities in the 1990s. As a result, the nineties may become the decade of the user fee.

State and city accounting practices must be improved so that managers can clearly see what revenues are coming in, what is being spent and how wide the gap is between the two. The public in the next decade will demand such information. Cash accounting does not allow for sound financial planning. It does not provide any basis on which to project what labor negotiation and capital improvement decisions arrived at today will actually cost in future years and whether future revenues will enable these obligations to be met without further borrowing.

A related problem is state and municipal pension fund accounting. Few states and cities even know what future costs will be, let alone whether revenues will be adequate to pay pensions owed to today's employees. State and city financial management is also hampered by the existence of many disparate funds, a lack of attention to the depreciation issue and inadequately managed transfusions of meager federal funds or, at the local level, state and federal funds.

At a minimum in the 1990s, the responsible state or local administrator will need to make sure that an accurate and updatable picture of the state or local government's finances exists and that financial procedures conform to Governmental Finance Officers Association (GFOA) guidelines. Disclosure of a true picture of a state, city or county's condition to the public as soon as possible may make citizens more understanding when times get harder and the budget-cutting choices become more limited and more painful.

The emergence of "edge cities" such as Perimeter Center in Atlanta and those in the Dallas–Forth Worth area have siphoned off city revenue and may require taxpayer bailouts in the 1990s if the glut of unused office space continues.

Internally, there will be continuing pressures for downsizing, cost reduction and abandonment of non-legislatively mandated programs. More tools such as strategic planning and total quality management will be borrowed from the private sector in efforts to increase productivity and reduce costs. Employees will also be asked to pick up a greater share of health care and other benefit costs as these costs continue to rise.

3. *The post–World War II "baby boom" has reached middle age and the impact on states and cities will be dramatic.* There were really two post–World War II baby booms: between 1946 and 1954 and between 1955 and

1964. The former "leading edge boomers" have reached middle age and the "trailing edge boomers" are not expected to achieve the same standard of living as their predecessors.

The proportion of the elderly in U.S. society has increased substantially during the past decade. This, plus the increase in working women, declining birth rate and changes in traditional family households, signals that public services and facilities will need to be altered accordingly. Recreation and health services, for example, may take precedence over law enforcement as the teenage population declines. Private companies are already planning to meet these trends; state and local government should do the same. One of the problems faced by many elderly, for example, is difficulty in obtaining transportation to get to health care centers.

Fewer people are entering schools and colleges, but the demand of middle-aged working men and women for adult education, both career related and non-career related, may redirect usage of such facilities. Increasing leisure and high education levels of working adults in the 1990s may combine with longer lives and less mobility due to fuel prices to enhance radically the role of community colleges as providers of nearby, relatively inexpensive "enrichment" courses. These may range from physical fitness to languages to a rekindling of interest in the arts and crafts of earlier decades.

Also, the increasing age of our population has produced shortages in service establishment labor, and those shortages will become more acute in the 1990s. Even the shakeout from the early 1990s recession will not measurably increase the pool of unskilled labor.

An older population will change many state and local government service priorities because of its influence on politics and the fact that a higher percentage of older people go to the polls to vote. This will give their wants and needs considerable influence on state and local decision making.

*4. In the 1990s, the "water crisis" will be widely recognized.* Water is being wasted and polluted at an alarming and increasing rate. Several hundred billion gallons a day are currently consumed in the United States, compared to about 40 billion gallons in 1900. In some places, underground sources are being depleted so fast the land is sinking. The big users of water are large-scale agriculture and industry, the latter mostly in cooling processes. Domestic uses such as home plumbing and yard care consume only about 9 percent of the water used daily. Nevertheless, these activities are being carried out with little interest in conservation because water is underpriced. The parallel with petroleum is obvious.

Water problems for the 1990s and beyond include those of water rights, particularly in the West, energy development (synthetic fuels production requires massive amounts of water), pollution and treatment, regional shortages, reclaiming of water, and the safety of drinking water. State and local governments will need to inventory water supplies. Measures to stop waste should focus on innovative agricultural practices that conserve water. Technology is available for water recycling, but there is little demand for these systems, except perhaps in areas of the West. Local governments should consider whether municipal water charges reflect the finiteness and potential scarcity of the commodity.

Because almost every plan to increase the water supply in one city, state or region would result in a decrease in some other city, state or region, intergovernmental negotiation and cooperation will be crucial when the water crisis arrives. The enormous growth of southern California could not have happened without the Colorado River water. Phoenix is blooming in a desert because of borrowed water. What will happen when the rivers have no more to give? Although there is a need for national attention to this issue, the answer is not a new Department of Water in Washington eager to regulate, ration, misallocate and pontificate. The lead should be taken locally.

5. *Infrastructure maintenance will be a principal focus of state and local government activities.*[2] As the International City Management Association's Committee on Future Horizons concluded several years ago, "The continual, and expensive, maintenance of water and sewer lines, bridges, power plants, utility connections must continue. Deferred costs of maintenance, repair and replacement are simply additions to the mortgages of the future." Infrastructure maintenance will be even harder due to cutbacks in federal and, at the local level, state aid. More and more, managers will have to develop accurate, inexpensive ways of assessing regularly the conditions of streets, traffic lights, bridges and so on. The most efficient repair schedules should be developed, and strategies such as recycling asphalt and buying longer-lasting street striping materials should be employed. Provision of infrastructure through privatization will increase in the 1990s and beyond.

6. *State and local government activities will have more international aspects.* State and urban management efforts in states such as California, Texas and Florida have been affected for decades by the presence of undocumented workers. Similar problems are now occurring in states, cities, counties and towns in various parts of the country where Southeast Asian refugees are being resettled. As the economy worsens and competition for jobs intensifies, the resulting conflicts will add to the burdens of state and local governments.

A different type of international impact involves the increasing interest of foreign companies in investing in the United States. This is due to the size and attractiveness of the U.S. market and this country's political stability. As economic development becomes more and more important as a means of generating state and local government revenues, the competition for foreign plant locations will increase in the coming decade. Numerous states have economic development offices in Europe and Japan. The skills of people charged with attracting foreign investment are quite different from traditional local or state administrative skills. Cities can work with states to enhance the "package" of overseas investors.

Availability of energy and transportation, the quality of labor, the proximity of markets and suppliers and tax incentives are the criteria for foreign investment decisions. The Japanese Sony Corporation of America built a $50 million, 800-employee factory in Dothan, Alabama, because that city was geographically convenient for its South American markets, because Sony wanted to get away from states with high tax rates and because it was enthusiastically welcomed by city and state officials. The Michelin Tire Company of France opened an 1,800-employee plant in Dothan as well. The state of South Carolina has attracted several billion dollars in foreign investment, making cities such an Spartanburg and Greenville high growth areas.

Promotional advertising by local and state governments might seem incongruous in an era of cutback but in reality may reflect sound strategy with major long-term payoffs.

The breakdown of communism also has provided opportunities to share state and local government successes in Eastern Europe and the former Soviet Union, an opportunity thought beyond reach in the last decade. The challenge is how to turn this opportunity into a net revenue generator for state and local governments in the United States.

7. *The need for productivity improvement through the introduction of new technologies and innovative management techniques will continue to be acute.* In the 1990s, state and local governments will need to make more and better use of new scientific and technological products and processes with money savings and improved operations as a result.

Techniques for improved productivity can come from the use of new technology that substitutes capital for labor, by the use of more effective management systems and industrial engineering techniques or by humans. The longest lasting, most effective approaches come from the involvement of people in the process.

8. *Automation, information and telecommunications technology advances will dramatically affect state and local government operations.* In the 1990s, almost all large state and local governments will utilize a computer to carry out some functions. Typical uses are recordkeeping, calculating and maintaining payroll. More sophisticated uses will be computer programs for developing optimal routes for refuse collection or snow removal equipment, locating new public facilities, developing air quality models and projecting land use patterns. There will also be increasing use of microcomputers as their power and functionality increase.

State and local government office operations will become automated to a much greater extent. New technologies in the form of high-end work stations, desktop publishing, electronic customer service, integration of voice and data (using fiber optic networks), high-definition television and so on, will be utilized in offices to control high labor intensiveness and rising costs of operations. Alternatives to paper creation, reproduction and storage such as the use of electronic storage will come into much greater use. New technologies such as advances in video supercomputing, artificial intelligence, networking, and for-fee-services such as public access, word processing, reprographics, conferencing, geographic information systems and teleprocessing will become commonplace. The impact of these technologies on people (ergonomics) will also come under much greater scrutiny.

Telecommuting will become a more common way for many workers to do their jobs. For example, in San Diego County, about 10 percent of the 900 Public Works Department employees now telecommute one to three days each week. To make telecommuting even easier, the county is planning to build several satellite centers in outlying areas complete with FAX machines. San Diego County has found that telecommuting improves work performance by forcing supervisors to define job tasks more clearly. Telecommuting is expected to make considerable inroads in state and local government customer service functions during the next decade. It also reduces air pollution by keeping cars off the road, reduces parking and office space costs, decreases dry cleaning and gasoline costs for employees, increases productivity, reduces absenteeism and traffic-related stress for employees and reduces traffic gridlock during rush hours.[3]

*9. Citizen and media pressure will increase for areawide service delivery.* The cost of the balkanization of government will be more widely recognized. Citizens are looking more and more into all facets of government, beginning at the local and state levels. There will be hard questioning of the costs of proliferating special districts, as well as the duplication resulting from several towns, cities or counties providing similar services in a relatively small geographical area.

Theory and practice offer a vast array of alternative local government structures for delivering services and exercising regulatory control. Topologies are almost as numerous as the authors and articles addressing the subject. Academically, there is little agreement on the types and even on the definition of a type. In many ways, the array of alternatives exists as a continuum ranging from a multipurpose, singular entity to specialized, multiple governmental entities.

Comprehensive alternatives include the following:

#### 1. Consolidation of City and County Governments

• One or more cities merges with the county government

• Plan often features merger of only the principal city with the county

**2. Strong Urban County/Limited City Government**
- County assumes role of a central metropolitan government
- Governmental functions are transferred to county level
- County and the municipalities are not merged

**3. Multiple Use of Single-Purpose Metropolitan Authority**
- May involve coordination of several single-purpose agencies
- Reflects desire to return decision making to city and county officials

**4. Multipurpose Service District**
- To provide/finance services across a metropolitan area
- To reduce need for multiple, single-purpose, regional or special authorities
- To span one or more counties and include a number of cities

**5. Metropolitan Council with Policy Making and/or Veto Powers**
- May serve as regional planning/general purpose planning body
- Has authority to veto plans/projects of single purpose special districts
- May have authority to review land use plans

**6. Voluntary Council of Governments**
- Beyond planning and coordination functions
- Added responsibilities of coordination and/or service delivery

**7. Non-Voluntary Council of Governments**
- Requires memberships and/or financial contributions
- Tends to have more formal powers

**8. Privatization**
- Total abandonment (or sale) to the private sector

Limited alternatives include the following:

**1. Functional Consolidation**
- Offers function-by-function form of city-county consolidation
- Provides for consolidation of certain activities/services without total consolidation of governments

**2. Transfer of Services**
- "Permanent" shift of service provision between governments
- Shift usually from city to county
- Permanent transfer

**3. Interlocal Contracting**
- Purchase of government services by two or more local jurisdictions
- Forms: single contract, jointly performed service by two or more local governments or jointly created separate organization

**4. Annexation**

• Urban-type services are provided to all or most of the territory of a county

• County government can concentrate on judicial/recordkeeping and selected area-wide functions

**5. Contracting Out**

• Government retains responsibility for service, but contracts function to private company

Albeit there are numerous choices, three distinct types of structures are often identified as most appropriate: (1) full consolidation, (2) metropolitan government and (3) partial consolidation. The factors used to distinguish between these are the number and type of entities merged. Full consolidation results from merging all, or almost all, of the governmental entities into a single entity. Metropolitan government involves creating another entity to oversee and provide certain services. Partial consolidation has a variety of forms usually based upon function or geography and may involve continuation of all existing entities, expansion of the role and powers of existing entities or reduction in the number of local government entities.

*1. Full Consolidation.* Full consolidation into one metropolitan entity is the most extensive governmental reorganization that could occur. This could conceivably take the form of all governmental and quasi-governmental units in a county being merged into one entity. Such an extensive consolidation, however, has not occurred in this century.

More typically, the largest municipality and the county government merge. From 1921 to 1978, there were eighty-eight major attempts to consolidate cities and counties submitted to voters. Since that time, several more have been attempted—Louisville-Jefferson County, Kentucky (for a second time); Asheville-Buncombe County, North Carolina; Salt Lake–Salt Lake County, Utah (for a second time); Charlottesville-Albemarle County, Virginia; Staunton-Augusta County, Virginia; Dublin-Pulaski-Pulaski County, Virginia; St. Louis–St. Louis County, Missouri; Clifton Forge–Covington-Allegheny County, Virginia; Wilmington–New Hanover County, North Carolina; Augusta-Richmond County, Georgia; Athens-Clarke County, Georgia; and Conyers-Rockdale County, Georgia, to name a few. All of these have failed, except Athens-Clark County, Georgia, which passed in 1990 and is currently being implemented. Although this data is not presented to dismiss full consolidation as a viable option, it does suggest that a full consolidation through local referenda may be difficult to achieve.

Although there is no substantive data on the number of attempts versus successes, there have been ten instances in which full consolidation was mandated by state legislature. In one instance, Las Vegas–Clark County, Nevada, the state supreme court voided the consolidation. There are at least twenty-seven fully consolidated governments currently in the United States, the majority of which are in Virginia. There is only one full consolidation in Florida: Jacksonville-Duval County. At least ten full-consolidation attempts have succeeded during the past twenty-one years, and several others are currently under consideration.

Warren J. Wicker, assistant director emeritus of the Institute of Government at the University of North Carolina at Chapel Hill, states that the major reasons the attempts have failed were fear of increased taxes by residents outside the city, fear of being overwhelmed by city concerns, ethnic representation concerns and no compelling reasons to make changes in the existing service delivery structure.

In many instances, the argument that consolidation leads to cost savings through economies of scale does not appear strong enough to overcome voters' reluctance to change the status quo. But the results have certainly been cost savings coupled with service enhancement.

For example, in Nashville-Davidson County, Tennessee, the merger was considered very successful by most analysis. A public survey showed an 88 percent approval rating eight years after merger. Public services have been expanded and improved, and costs have been reduced for some internal, administrative departments.

In Jacksonville-Duval County, Florida, the quality and quantity of services provided since consolidation have increased, and the tax rate has decreased from 0.22 per $100 valuation to 0.12 per $100. There have also been workforce reductions through a ten-year attrition program. For example, the Finance Department reduced its staff size from 125 to 75.

*2. Metropolitan Government.* The second most comprehensive form of consolidation is to establish a third entity in the form of metropolitan government. The purpose of this entity would be to consolidate certain services presently offered by the county and municipalities, and possibly other jurisdictions in the county. These would be services that could be offered most cost-effectively on an areawide or regional basis. Although these services may be related functionally (water and wastewater, for example), the key is that the metropolitan entity is multipurpose or delivering more than one service.

Water, wastewater and solid waste services are often provided by these metropolitan entities. Some depend on user fees and some on a combination of fees and taxes. With one exception, these metrogovernments emphasize direct service delivery. The Metropolitan Council of the Twin Cities, Minnesota, is an interesting example of a comprehensive planning and coordination agency, providing oversight and coordination in a number of service areas, but not direct delivery of services. The Portland, Oregon, Metropolitan Service District, the Municipality of Metropolitan Seattle and Metropolitan Dade County, Florida, are examples of metropolitan governments. In terms of results, Seattle METRO has been extremely successful in providing regional wastewater disposal service and in providing a regional public transportation system.

*3. Partial Consolidation.* Of the various forms of consolidation available, partial consolidation takes place the most frequently. It is a very general term that can refer to any number of service delivery approaches. Generally, it involves having one entity deliver a particular type of service(s) throughout an area. This functional consolidation is usually accomplished by transferring service delivery responsibilities from one entity to another, or by creating a new entity to provide a single service throughout the area.

An example of this type of consolidation is the creation of geographic service zones. Under this scheme, one governmental unit provides services in one geographic area and another unit provides the same services in the remaining area. Geographic service zones can be used to allocate public resources more efficiently by establishing "natural" service areas; for example, in road maintenance, fire protection and law enforcement.

Geographic service areas have been established in fully consolidated, metropolitan and partially consolidated local governments. In addition to rationally allocating local government services, geographic service areas enhance general tax equity by ensuring that one geographic area does not subsidize service delivery in another geographic area. Geographic service areas are related to, but distinct from, differential tax zones.

It is important to note that partial consolidation can be achieved in many service delivery areas without confronting major legal constraints. Some examples of partial consolidation include the following: St. Paul and Ramsey County, Minnesota, have established a Joint Purchasing Office; Hamilton County and Cincinnati, Ohio, have established a joint computer center for use by the city, county and the local law enforcement district; and Payne County and Stillwater, Oklahoma, share a single jailing and intake system.

As has been discussed, the need for greater cooperation and consolidation of government is a growing concern in many communities, particularly in light of the current fiscal crisis most local governments face. In recent years, there has been an increasing tendency to create additional governmental entities, particularly in the form of special districts. Although this specialization may be desirable, the potential for consolidating activities, particularly those of an administrative nature, still exists. Services of a governmental entity can also be performed by another organization through contractual arrangements. This same perspective has encouraged the move toward privatization of governmental activities, as well. Consolidation and privatization are similar in that a governmental entity may, in both cases, contract with another entity to provide services. Both can result in cost savings as well as increases in the efficiency and effectiveness of a service.

Keys to successful governmental consolidation include a driving force for merger and cohesive governmental leadership. Persons supporting consolidation usually see it as a way of improving political clout and planning, providing equitable services, reducing cost, improving efficiency, controlling urbanization, improving the local economy and bringing equity to pay and tax structures.

Opponents cite higher taxes in unincorporated areas, loss of municipal identity, loss of local political power, increased costs, loss of jobs, loss of sovereignty and uncertainty associated with change.

The extent to which political, business and community leaders are open to a proposed merger will also impact its chances of success. Support need not be (and virtually never is) unanimous among these groups. However, experience with past consolidations in the United States has shown that efforts fail unless support, or at least open-mindedness toward the proposal, is displayed by some prominent political and community leaders in the effected jurisdictions.

Political feasibility is often dependent upon community attitudes and openness to change. In the absence of other factors that would negate the political feasibility, this is an issue that is best resolved at the ballot box rather than being second-guessed. However, there are common factors that come into play as voters contemplate the relative merits of such a change. Being able to address these issues from a historical perspective is useful in responding to common community concerns. These factors include the following:

- *Loss of identity*. This has been an issue in virtually every consolidation attempted in the United States. What is known about successful consolidations can help ease this common apprehension. Past experience has shown that short-term concerns about loss of identity are quickly replaced by a new sense of identity—and by a special sense of pride in being part of a consolidated government community. Citizens of consolidated government by large majorities are happy with the new community created, according to a 1987 study by Research Atlanta.

- *"If it ain't broke, don't fix it."* This has been among the most oft-repeated phrases among opponents of past consolidation attempts. Without "red flags" or "hot buttons" to motivate voters, the natural tendency for many is to remain with the status quo. At the same time, the most aggressive—and effective—proponents of past consolidations have not been the naysayers who tear down the existing community and government structures. Rather, they have often been supporters and defenders of their respective communities who saw consolidation as a progressive continuation and improvement of sound fiscal government, and as a means of strengthening and solidifying the prevailing "sense of community."

- *Cost effectiveness*. People are naturally concerned about taxes and want to know what impact consolidation will have on taxes and on service delivery. Historical data is significantly more positive than negative. One 1982 study compared per capita costs of ten consolidated governments with the per capita costs of similar sized non-consolidated governments. The finding was that six of ten merged governments operated less expensively per capita than comparable unconsolidated jurisdictions. Another analysis found that property tax rates fell in three of four consolidated governments studied. Further, "the most consistent result of consolidation has been improved and expanded public services," according to the 1987 study by Research Atlanta. "The reorganized governments were able to fund service extensions and capital improvements and resolve jurisdictional disputes."

- *Job security*. There is always concern in a consolidation attempt about whether people will lose their jobs. Although it would be up to the local jurisdiction, layoffs do not generally result from consolidation. Typically, consolidated governments have relied on attrition and job reassignments to eliminate duplicated functions.

- *Closeness of government*. Typical in consolidation efforts is concern among citizens that they will lose access to, or closeness with, their local government. What little information is available on the effects of consolidation on citizen-government interaction is actually encouraging. The issue has been addressed from three perspectives: (1) actual level of participation in government, (2) existence of institutional opportunities for such involvement and (3) citizens' beliefs about government responsiveness. Studies of four consolidated governments (Lexington and Fayette County, Kentucky; Nashville and Davidson County, Tennessee; Jacksonville and Duval County, Florida; and Indianapolis and Marion County, Indiana) found that all reported varying measures of apparent increased involvement among citizens in government and civic affairs.

Many consolidation charters have provided institutional opportunities for involvement to safeguard against an erosion of involvement due to the government's increased jurisdiction. Such measures as creation of one or more citizens' advisory commissions and creation of a special office to handle citizens' needs (ombudsman function) are examples of provisions that have been written into consolidation proposals to encourage community involvement.

Limited public opinion surveys have been done on citizens' feelings about government responsiveness after consolidation. Though results have been mixed, a majority of survey results have indicated that most citizens actually believed that the consolidated government was more responsive. As mentioned earlier, consolidation has had the result of bringing different elements of a metro community together, generating a new shared identity and sense of purpose and pride.


None of this is to say that winning public approval of a merger proposal is easy. Consolidation has occurred in at least twenty U.S. communities since World War II. Merger proposals have been defeated by voters at least twice as often.

Traditional citizen resistance to areawide service delivery may erode when inflation and cutbacks dictate that a service can be provided only on an areawide basis or not at all. Annexation laws may be liberalized or proposed in states where they do not now exist. City-county consolidation proposals will reappear. At a minimum, state and local governments should experiment with interlocal contracting and pooling of equipment and personnel when appropriate.

*10. Transportation decisions of the 1990s will be more complex and difficult than ever before.* Transportation and land use are closely intertwined. Local officials control land use decisions; many transportation decisions, however, are made by the states and the federal government. Because of this, solving state and urban transportation problems in the 1990s will become harder and harder.

Automobiles, the epitome of consumer goods and the bedrock of American belief in individual freedom and mobility, are not going to go away. Technology will eventually make them operable without gasoline. The nation's highway investment will continue to need maintenance. It is likely that more people will try to live closer to their places of work; public policy should make this as easy as possible.

State and local government officials should recognize the future role of the automobile but also consider other possibilities. For example, aeronautical technology advances will make possible a new generation of cleaner, quieter, safer, fuel-efficient commuter aircraft and helicopters. Such aircraft have a potential role in taking the pressure off overcrowded hub airports, expanding the use of secondary airports in less urbanized areas (a prospect with major economic development effects) and reducing congestion and ground-based urban transportation modes. Although these aircraft won't be available until nearer the end of this century, state and urban policymakers and planners should take these possibilities into account in planning land use decisions. Secondary airports, for example, should not be closed but should be considered as possible key elements in regional development strategies.

In transportation, as in so many other public sector activities, good solutions are always interjurisdictional and funding is almost always intergovernmental. Not only do public administrators have to evaluate the technical and social (efficiency/equity) merits of their decisions, but they also have to recognize that the multigovernment coordination aspects may be equally important or even override the other aspects in determining the success of strategies chosen. This ability to recognize the intergovernmental element as that which will determine the execution of specific functional responsibilities is one of the true challenges of the 1990s from many perspectives.

*11. Privatization will become an increasing alternative to the delivery of public services.* We are living in an age of privatization. All over the world, the private sector is assuming functions that were once the purview of government. Some factors fueling this shift include increased need for cost effectiveness, union issues, insufficient capital resources, excessive demand for government services, and the inability to attract qualified staff at government salaries.

Various forms of privatization are being implemented in Canada, Mexico, the Netherlands and other European countries. The recent events in Eastern Europe are in great part a privatization movement. Even the former Soviet Union is experimenting with it. In the United States, federal, state and local governments are involved as well.

The privatization trend has affected specific U.S. industries through deregulation or discovery on the part of the private sector of opportunities for financial gain. Examples include infrastructure, postal delivery and rehabilitation services.

A recent survey of privatization practices in twenty-two state government rehabilitation agencies, for example, indicated that 91 percent were engaged in some form of privatization. The methods of privatization being employed vary. Some types were being used more frequently than others. "Contracting out services" was the most frequently mentioned form. It was being employed by 95 percent of the responding agencies. More than one-half were using volunteer personnel (65 percent) and promotion of consumer self-help (55 percent). The major reasons cited for privatization included cost reduction, policy changes encouraging privatization and the opportunity to make use of other organizations with new or enhanced capabilities. Eighty percent saw privatization as a part of their future.[4]

A similar survey of 120 cities, counties and special districts in 34 states and 30 recognized privatization experts indicated the following:[5]

- Virtually all local governments surveyed contracted out at least one service to a private company. The vast majority of respondents had contracted out engineering and management consulting as well as major construction. More than half the surveyed cities also contracted out food services, often in the form of vending machines and concessions; counties and special districts frequently contracted out legal and architectural services as well. Some 26 percent or more of the respondents were likely to have contracted out janitorial services, solid waste collection, building maintenance, security services, towing services, management and maintenance of parking garages and grounds maintenance. At least one-quarter of surveyed counties also contracted out some human resources services, landscaping and parks maintenance, food and medical services, services for the aging and special consulting, landfill, data processing and wastewater services.

- The results of privatization have been overwhelmingly positive. That's the word from 97 percent of the cities, 99 percent of the counties and 81 percent of the special districts that have tried it. Financial savings were reported by 100 percent of the participants, and quality of the work was cited as a positive factor by 45 percent of respondents. Other factors contributing to success are a contractor's past experience; ability to follow specifications, to be flexible, and to get the job done on time; and the extent of political awareness.

- Specific sources of cost savings have been reduced personnel and equipment needs, the capacity to pay only for work done, more work for the same dollars, no start-up costs, reduced internal workload, and generally fewer service problems.

- More than half of all cities and three-quarters of all counties that contract for services have encountered some problems. Cities, counties and special districts all say that obstacles from employees and unions head the list. Citizen opposition and opposition from elected officials were also cited frequently.

Future trends include these:

- Increased use of privatization at the state and local government levels as the need to manage in a reduced revenue environment continues.
- More use of the privatization concept in infrastructure areas such as wastewater treatment and facilities. Also, private companies building infrastructure (e.g., toll roads) on a lease-back or pay-back concept will increase.
- Some use of reverse privatization (i.e., selling public services to raise revenues, such as excess data processing capacity or crime lab use to neighboring jurisdictions) will increase.

Contracting out and privatization present a means of providing services at lower cost and the potential for increases in the level of service quality. Many local and state governments and special districts are utilizing the practice based on the apparent cost efficiency inherent in contracting out of services.

*12. The drug problem will continue to be with us through the next decade.* There appear to be no easy solutions to the problem of illegal drugs that pervade our society. Unfortunately, the problem seems to be not solely one of apprehension and prosecution but also that a large number of people have "dropped through the cracks in our society." We may need somehow to resocialize a sizeable portion of our population, and the task associated with that is extremely complex and difficult. Until this problem is solved, however, we can continue to see the dehumanizing effects of drugs on our youth and on adults and of the other crime problems associated with drug use and abuse.

On the positive side, there seems to be an upward trend in the recognition of the negative effects of alcohol on humans and a concomitant reduction in its use. This trend should continue to be positive in the decade ahead and could have spin-off benefits for helping solve some portions of the drug problem as well.

*13. Changing values and diversity in the workplace will present considerable challenges in the 1990s and beyond.* Over the past three decades, the American state and local government workplace has changed. It now contains more women and more minorities, particularly blacks and Asians. This increased workforce diversity presents new challenges to state and local government administrators in how to create and maintain the most effective work environment and provide opportunities for all staff to reach their full potential.

In addition, employees' values have changed. Whereas it had been commonplace to dedicate oneself totally to one's work at the sacrifice of everything else, that is no longer the case. Although the present approach taken by many employees is perhaps healthier in that a better balance between work and leisure time is being struck, there are also some disturbing trends.

Many employees today seem to lack commitment to the organization and its managers. On closer examination, they say that "the organization is not committed to me, because if times get bad I'll get laid off, so why should I be committed to the organization?" Also, many schools and universities are not properly preparing new employees with basic skills needed in the workplace, and many employees must be retrained or further trained at the expense of the state or local government.

Continued changing values and greater diversity in the workplace are expected to be the norm in the decade of the 1990s and beyond. The most effective state and local government administrators will recognize this trend and create a work environment conducive to all employees' reaching their full potential.

*14. The plight of the homeless will continue to draw the attention of state and local government officials.* The boom times of the eighties have resulted in a severe housing shortage for poor people. As more money went to build houses for the upper and middle classes, the supply of low-rent housing fell to its lowest point in twenty years. By 1989, there were 4.1 million more poor people than affordable housing units.[6]

In a related matter, the lack of health care that now affects about 35 million Americans is up by 1.3 million in the past year. The effects of this trend on the elderly and the homeless could place a higher social burden on taxpayers in the years ahead.

All one has to do to see the plight of our increasing homeless population is to travel to any large urban area in the United States. This is particularly true of sunbelt communities where the weather is more conducive to outdoor living. In some cases, public facilities such as parks in Santa Monica, California, and Miami are being heavily used. Sanitary conditions are being overloaded and, in some cases, real or perceived security is being breached.

Whole communities of shacks have sprung up under bridges and viaducts to house the homeless, and soup kitchens of non-profit agencies are being overburdened. In some instances, hate groups are retaliating against the homeless by burning their meager shanties. Also, some local governments are increasingly enforcing panhandling ordinances and have enacted legislation to prevent loitering by the homeless in certain business sections of cities because of their feared impact on business.

There doesn't seem to be an easy answer to the problem, and it is expected to exacerbate during the first half of the next decade. A few things are being done, for example social service agencies are already making greater use of computers to help find the homeless a bed, a meal or a hot bath. To increase awareness of an involvement in the homeless problem by younger people, San Francisco State University is offering classes in the homeless and bringing homeless people in to talk about their plight and their needs to students. Another possible area of assistance is through creation of a land bank authority that can be empowered to take possession of foreclosed and tax-delinquent property in a community, forgive the taxes and place it in the hands of non-profit housing groups.

The plight of the homeless is a growing national problem, but its solution will most likely have to come from state and local leadership during the coming decade.

*15. There will be a decreasing ability of the U.S. private sector to assist in meeting state and local needs.* The unprecedented changes occurring among major corporations and their fallout effect on the economy in general, and on state and local governments in particular, are enormous. Restructuring at IBM, bank mergers, airline failures, downsizing at General Motors, and so on all make for less support to state and local governments from strong private financial corporations. Loaned executive programs may be harder to come by in the future and the alternative of private providers of certain social services may all but dry up by the end of the decade. This creates a new challenge to state and local leaders to make it on their own as best they can in the decade to come.

## NOTES

1. James L. Mercer and Susan W. Woolston, "Urban Strategies for the 80's," *Western City*, October 1980, pp. 12–14, 16.

2. "Excerpts from the Report of the International City Management Association's Committee on Future Horizons," *National Civic Review*, vol. 19, no. 2 (February 1980), p. 73.

3. David Beasley, "On the Job, Yet Right at Home," *The Atlanta Journal/The Atlanta Constitution*, December 16, 1991, pp. C1, C7.

4. James L. Mercer and Roxan E. Dinwoodie, *Study of Privatization Practices in State Rehabilitation Agencies: Executive Summary* (Atlanta, Ga.: Georgia Division of Rehabilitation Services, 1990), pp. 1–9.

5. James L. Mercer, *The Mercer Group, Inc., 1990 Privatization Survey* (Atlanta, Ga.: The Mercer Group, Inc., 1990), pp. 1–46.

6. Gregory H. Nobles, "The Homeless Become Target of Scapegoating," *The Atlanta Journal/The Atlanta Constitution*, December 17, 1991, p. A25.

# 2

# Cutting Back in the Face of Restrained Revenues

"I cannot imagine any condition which could cause this ship to founder.
I cannot conceive of any vital disaster happening to this vessel."
—E. J. Smith, Captain of the *Titanic*, 1912

A majority of U.S. state and local governments have been faced with some form of tight financial situation for many years. In the past, this circumstance was brought about by difficulty in generating new and additional taxes and other revenues and, concomitantly, by increased demand for services and by increased construction, material, energy and labor costs. Presently, the financial plight of state and local governments has deteriorated dramatically due to the most recent recession. As a result, the average political leader or manager is striving even harder to develop budgets to meet service demands. In many cases, to achieve minimum annual operating budget levels, this has meant postponing needed capital expenditures and infrastructure improvements until some future date. A significant, added difficulty facing state and local governments is the downturn in economic activity. Robust economies have been the major revenue-enhancing resource for state and local governments, particularly in high growth areas such as Florida and California. As a result of the slower economic activity, some state and local governments may be forced to take drastic measures, such as employee layoffs, to operate with reduced revenues. Other governments in areas in which economic growth has only slowed may be somewhat more fortunate. In any event, the challenge for elected and appointed state and local government officials will likely be to find ways out of this malaise without sacrificing needed public services.[1]

The purpose of this book is to assist state and local government administrators to grapple with strategies to deal with the impacts of the "cost/revenue" squeeze that they have been with for some time. Unfortunately, this squeeze has exacerbated as we enter the 1990s, and it is expected to continue to be with us in the rest of the 1990s and beyond.

This book contains general information about the trends impacting state and local governments and gives a number of practical, down-to-earth suggestions about approaches that might be used for both cost reduction and ways to involve employees at all levels in the organization in decisions that affect them. By using such techniques and others, state and local administrators should be able to find solutions to some of the more difficult problems that they face now and later in this decade.

## EFFECTIVE MANAGEMENT WITH SCARCE RESOURCES

To deal with the issues of effective management within a resource-scarce environment, state and local government officials should recognize two sides of the financial picture: They can address the revenue side and the expenditure side. The revenue objective is to increase revenues by raising the traditional sources in amount, by spreading them over a wider base and/or by finding new alternative sources of revenue. The following methods are perhaps most realistic as ways to increase income in today's state and local government climate:

- Provision of services for a fee
- Selling services to others: public entrepreneurship
- Franchising: public/private partnership
- Leveraging higher economic activity: another public/private partnership

Each of these methods will be discussed more fully below.

### Provision of Services for a Fee

Over the years, and especially during good times, state and local governments may be providing activities and services that no longer serve large segments of their community or state. If you accept the original purpose of state and local governments as entities to provide those services citizens could not logically provide for themselves, for example, protection, water, streets and so on then the myriad of state and local government activities being provided today is obviously considerably expanded. Expanded services include swimming opportunities, tennis courts, golf courses, art pavilions, other recreation opportunities and many more. Many of these "enhanced services" are paid for by taxes.

At all times, and especially during lean times, state and municipal officials should continually and carefully examine their array of delivered services and programs to determine:

- If the services or programs they are providing are required by their citizens. In other words, what could you stop doing?
- What things they might get others to do for them (other levels of government, non-profits, the private sector).
- Where they can use low-cost or no-cost labor.
- What services or functions they can pool with others to reduce costs (local or state governments, non-profits).
- Where they can substitute capital (or technology) for labor.
- Where they can ration services or reduce demand.

Although not all of the above will be net revenue producers, they can have an impact on state or local government bottom-line costs.

For those services that are not mandated by law, a realistic cost for providing the service should be developed and an evaluation should be done for providing the service on a user-fee basis. Continuation of the services for a fee in legally mandated enterprise fund areas, such as solid waste collection and disposal, sewage treatment, water and so on should be maintained as well. Realistic financial contributions by these enterprise funds need to be made to the general fund for administrative and overhead costs. In addition, a careful evaluation of costs of internal or staff services, such as informational bulletins and risk management programs, may be found less costly if supplied by other providers. True costs in these areas are often not allocated properly by state and local governments.

### Selling Services to Others: Public Entrepreneurship

Another often overlooked area of potential state and local government revenue is selling services or excess capacity to other governments, private industry, non-profits and so on. Such public entrepreneurship might include anything from renting extra office space, selling excess computer or word processing time, renting specialized equipment or training facilities to public and private organizations, to providing fire and police protection or purchasing services to neighboring states or jurisdictions. This area is limited only by state and local laws and the imagination of public officials. In a free enterprise economy, it is always difficult to determine how far local or state governments can go in this area without appearing to be unfair competitors with private providers of such services. In most instances, however, room for expansion in this area still exists. Examples include user fees to tap into development or court system data bases and so on.

### Franchising: Public/Private Partnership

Additional state or local government revenues may also be generated by allowing private operators to run park and recreation and similar concessions on a franchise basis. This is a form of public/private partnership. It might include anything from refreshment stands to full-fledged amusement parks, to parking garages, to cafeterias, to more exotic franchises such as cable television. Although this practice is now being used by many state and local governments, continuing evaluation, realistic pricing and negotiating of franchises, and expansion of franchises into unexplored areas of state and local government are potential new sources of needed revenue. This area, too, is limited only by the imaginations of state and local government officials and by possible legal constraints, some of which could be changed.

### Leveraging Higher Economic Activity: Another Public/Private Partnership

State and local governments can also increase revenues by using a small amount of public dollars to leverage private investment that will pay off in more jobs, higher taxes, higher user fees and overall increased economic activity. This is the more traditional public/private partnership. One approach to this concept might be the provision of enterprise zones where public land is made available at a reduced cost. Taxes and user fees are abated or reduced during early years to stimulate growth or to nurture business enterprises within a governmental jurisdiction. Although most state and local governments are seeking new industry to spur economic resurgence, many are overlooking the fact that the vast majority of new industrial growth and jobs comes from the expansion of present business and industry. This often neglected sector of our economy needs to be courted and assisted.

These are just a few of the approaches state and local governments might take to reduce the effect of the current cost/revenue squeeze by increasing revenues. The next section will address the cost reduction side of the ledger.

## IMPROVING PRODUCTIVITY

Improving productivity is a topic that has been written about and talked about more than perhaps any other subject in recent years. Before state and local government officials can come to grips with improved productivity, they must first develop a definition of productivity that best meets their needs. Engineers often define productivity as output per unit of input. Others include factors of quality, services and image in the definition. A definition that seems to fit well in the state and local government environment is that productivity is equivalent to quality goods and services produced per person hour. This, of course, is a measure of labor productivity and overlooks some aspects of totally automated operations in which human input is minimal. There aren't many of these in typical state or local government settings, however.

There are a number of things that state and local governments can do to improve productivity. An illustrative list follows:

• Substitute technology for labor
• Streamline administrative, operational and service delivery systems
• Involve humans in decisions that affect them (e.g., improve decision making)
• Adjust policies, plans, procedures, budgets and controls
• Change managerial and supervisory attitudes and approaches
• Alter work methods
• Provide awareness and training for staff in productivity concepts
• Alter working hours (i.e., institute flextime)
• Provide a sense of ownership
• Develop teamwork

Of these, the largest payoffs come from improving technology and systems, and properly handling human resources. A study conducted a few years ago by the U.S. Department of Labor determined that the effective use of technology contributed more to improved productivity (by a factor of 72 percent) than any other element, because it basically substitutes capital for labor.

Decisions concerning the size, form and location of new state and local government facilities are made at a fast pace. Water pollution control projects, transportation control plans, solid waste management schemes, disposal of hazardous wastes—these programs call for daily decisions of enormous, longstanding implication. Yet typically decisions about these projects are made with limited scientific and technical information, almost no knowledge of imminent breakthrough in the state of the art, and very limited understanding about possible long-term implications and about impact on the public, such as expenditure levels.

Technology is an underutilized source of assistance for state and local governments trying to improve operations and reduce costs. Technology can make a difference in public service performance and delivery. The problem has been that most state and local governments do not have staff members who are familiar with what science and technology can offer or who know where to turn to find information on technical innovation that could help them solve problems.

Some local governments that have had local technological expertise in the past achieved some significant cost reductions by using better technological approaches. These include the following:

1. In Little Rock, Arkansas, there was a sanitation workers strike. The workers were dissatisfied with existing methods for work assignment and what they perceived as their lack of input into the decision-making process. A city technology agent acted as a go-between for labor and management. He opened up lines of communications while suggesting new techniques for improved equipment utilization and route balancing. As a result, grievances were reduced from ten a month to none. Absenteeism went from 20 percent to only 5 percent. Citizen complaints dropped from one hundred to seven per day. Savings in Little Rock, validated by the city manager, came to about $300,000 per year. The methods used to improve solid waste collection in Little Rock are adaptable to any jurisdiction with similar levels of manpower and equipment.

2. An example involving another major local expenditure area is a fire service innovation instituted in St. Petersburg, Florida. The problem was the high cost of fire protection service. The city technology agent reviewed all aspects of its fire services and decided it would be cost-effective to organize mobile firefighting squads. This provided faster responses and allowed maximum use of equipment and manpower. Estimated cost savings for this readily transferable innovative concept were $500,000 per year.

3. In Akron, Ohio, there was a parks management problem. The city needed to determine the optimum allocation and mix of maintenance resources (mowers, trucks, laborers, etc.) for seventy parks. The technological solution was the development of a mathematical model to allocate resources optimally and to project the impact of any changes in equipment, manpower and so on. A local university helped develop this model, which resulted in the identification and elimination of bottlenecks and equipment constraints.

Technology might include a new computer application to reduce the labor intensiveness of an operation. It might also include the use of new office technology, such as word processing and group training sessions that use teleconferencing techniques to reduce the cost of travel and per diem expenses. Technology might also include an electrostatic paint system that increases adhesion and reduces paint overspray in the sign shop, or it might include sophisticated water and sewage remote monitoring systems using telephone lines that substitute capital for labor.

What should state and local government administrators do immediately to find ways technology can help solve their jurisdiction's problems? Here are a few suggestions:

1. Recognize that sources of information and help are readily available. You might, for example, obtain the technical briefs on successful problem solutions that have resulted from the Urban Technology System and the Urban Consortium for Technology Initiatives Program to see if any are applicable. These briefs are available from Public Technology Inc., in Washington, D.C.

2. Retain an expert or team of experts to provide advice on how new methods and technology would improve various phases of your operations.

3. Contact your state and/or national city, county management association to see what information it can provide on science and technology.

4. Approach nearby resource institutions for assistance. Such institutions could be technical. For example, a university or the research department of a local company might be interested in a public service project that could be jointly developed. Or approach a local private foundation concerning financing a productivity or management improvement project you have developed in conjunction with a research or consulting organization.

5. Appoint a committee of citizens who are technical experts by profession (engineers, scientists, professors, systems analysts, for example) to volunteer advice on technical state or city problems and to help develop research projects.

6. Appoint an interested staff member to act as an "ad hoc technology agent" to frame problems and research needs in technical terms, to ask department heads for their ideas on what is needed to cut costs or improve productivity.

In summary, the public has every right to demand that state and local government, and government at all levels, be as efficient as possible while at the same time provide them with an adequate level of services. It is naive to expect technology to be either a panacea or a "quick fix" to longstanding, complicated public problems. There is, however, a growing body of documented proof that technology, when applied selectively and with careful attention to the people who will be involved in the changes it will produce, can help state and local governments do more with less—in effect, begin to outwit the cost/revenue dilemma. This summarizes succinctly why state and local governments need to incorporate science and technology into their decision-making and program activities.

Management systems and industrial engineering approaches might include computerized, optimal routes for solid waste vehicles, resource allocation models for park maintenance activities, or better office layouts that increase the proximity of workers who interact frequently. Also included might be more systematic approaches to setting priorities and making decisions under conditions of uncertainty, or more sophisticated energy audits to find ways to reduce consumption. In addition, these approaches might include more systematic ways of vehicle repair and maintenance, equipment modifications to improve efficiency, or more efficient ways to process solid waste to remove precious metals, extract heat and reduce environmental damage.

Besides new products, software improvements, especially management decision-making tools, have great potential to help boost state and local productivity. A large number of local governments have made use of a mathematical model to help them determine optimal fire station locations on the basis of response time, area population and buildings, instead of just number of blocks. This has provided better fire protection at lower cost. Pasadena, California, instituted a citywide productivity improvement program. In the first year, recommendations for the program led to reorganization of the finance department, improved city accounting procedures, and implementation of a management information system resulting in an annual savings of $200,000. This program also contributed to the city's ability to hold its tax rate constant for a fourth straight year.

In the human resources area, perhaps more can be done to increase productivity and cut costs than in any other place. The old adage is true: "You can't do the job without people." We know, for instance, that money is still a strong motivator of people, particularly at lower levels in the organization. However, through setting goals, measuring employee performance and providing regular feedback on that performance, increases of 15 percent to 18 percent in group productivity have been achieved. Through rigorous employee job enrichment efforts, 10 to 20 percent increases in productivity have resulted. It is a proven fact that employee reward and incentive systems work!

One typical approach that administrators often take during tough times is to recentralize decision making in the office of the chief executive and insist that all decisions be made at the top. Such an approach is often a mistake. The person on the firing line is far better equipped than anyone else to make decisions that will increase his/her productivity or cut costs. Those people should be systematically involved in the decision-making process.

Employee participation programs such as Quality Utilizing Employees, Systems and Technology (QUEST) and gainsharing hold much promise for productivity improvement. Unfortunately, too many top officials are looking at productivity teams as panaceas for solving all their productivity and cost-reduction problems. They are not cure-alls, just as management-by-objectives and other processes haven't been.

All these elements—technology, management systems and human resources—contribute to improved productivity and reduced costs, which helps us manage better in lean years.

## PRIVATIZATION

Privatization[2] occurs when a public sector organization entirely abandons providing a service, leaving it to be operated by the private sector on a contract basis. Most of the time when people are talking about privatization, they really mean contracting out. Virtually, every service provided or function performed by state and local governments could conceivably be contracted out. Of course, some activities like planning, zoning and environmental management are emotionally charged and are therefore more difficult to divest. Others, like police and fire protection, are perceived as basic services that government should not abandon. Still, they aren't impossible to spin off; Scottsdale, Arizona, for instance, contracts out its fire protection services and thereby saves $1.6 million a year.

To get an idea of the process that leads a municipality to contract for a service that it had always done itself, let us look over the shoulder of the city manager of Little Rock, Arkansas, as he prepares his budget. Because of inflation, higher wage rates, low labor productivity, and higher costs of supplies, expenditures for City Hall custodial services had risen steadily to an annual figure of $60,000. At the same time, revenues to pay for these services were being squeezed tighter each year. A study by his technical advisor shows the city manager that the fourteen public sector custodians are working at about 45 percent efficiency, at a cost per work unit of $9. He reviews bids from outside contractors to provide these services for the coming year. The qualified low bidder, a medium-sized company head-quartered in Little Rock, has bid $31,000. The cost per work unit of this bid would be $2.50. A memo attached by the advisor notes that this contractor can provide the services at half the current cost to the city. One factor is economies of scale; the company is performing similar work in nearby buildings and could use its equipment more efficiently. The city manager decides to proceed with a contract to this low bidder.

Since that day several years ago, Little Rock has continued to have City Hall custodial services handled in this manner. The quality of service has not deteriorated and the city has saved money. This example is not unique. Other examples include the following:

- The City of Butte, Montana, has contracted with a company to operate a municipal hospital. The annual saving, compared with the cost when the city ran the facility, exceeds $600,000.

- A small public relations firm handles the public relations for Cleveland Heights, Ohio, for $8,000 a year less than the expenditure when the function was handled in-house.

- Garden Grove, California, saves $55,000 a year by contracting out administration of its health insurance services.

- A large company operates the wastewater treatment plant in Great Falls, Montana, saving the city an annual $170,000.

- A small company delivers paramedical services to Hawthorne, California, for $35,000 less than the sum the community had spent by delivering these itself.

- One-third of the refuse produced in Newark, New Jersey, is collected by a company at a saving to the city of $200,000 a year.

As these disparate examples show, local governments are turning to the private sector for the provision of many services that public employees traditionally have performed. With costs rising and tax and other revenues having difficulty keeping up, the private sector is likely to find many more

**Exhibit 2–1**
**Fast-Growing Service-Contracting Areas**

| Service or Function | Examples |
|---|---|
| Municipality contracts with an entrepreneur to be its city manager. Contractor is free to do consulting or teaching or operate another business. Contractor provides own fringe benefits, pays own taxes. | Brea, California (saving, $12,000 a year) |
| Small local government units that do not need a full-time manager contract jointly with an entrepreneur to be their city manager on a part-time basis. Contractor provides own fringes and can contract with as many towns or counties as can be effectively served. The communities save because they pay only for whatever they need. | Georgetown and Superior, Colorado; Sanborn, Walnut Grove, Wabasso, Lucan and Milroy, Minnesota; Girard, Girard Borough, Springfield Township, and Platea Borough, Pennsylvania |
| City or county contracts with a company to operate its computer center. | Orange County, California (first-year saving, $1.6 million) |
| Consultants work with municipal or county hospitals on a full-time or part-time basis. The goals are to reduce current costs, avoid future expenses, improve quality and improve productivity. | Beaufort County, North Carolina; Lee County, South Carolina; Cocke County, Tennessee; (saving, from several thousand to several million dollars) |

opportunities in the years ahead to do work for state, municipal and other local governments.

Although such "privatization" is growing rapidly, there is still plenty of room for further expansion. Exhibit 2–1 shows some services and functions that seem to have the greatest potential for contracting outside.

According to the Governmental Finance Officers Association, full-time public employees working in labor-intensive functions still perform about three-fourths of the work of the 37,000 U.S. local government units. Naturally, because they lack the facilities, equipment and manpower, small local authorities do more contracting for services than larger ones.

As you might expect, cost reduction is usually the reason for privatization. The expense of refuse collection, the function perhaps most often contracted out, can drop as much as 40 percent when done by private organizations. Economies of scale and other efficiencies drive the price down. Companies are freer to buy advanced equipment and use specialized technology, which reduces the labor intensiveness of many functions. Moreover, by contracting with entrepreneurs, state and local governments often escape union pressures and the difficulties of firing unproductive workers.

When deciding whether or not to contract out a service, state and local governments should use the following criteria: cost reduction, quality, enabling legislation, control, in-house and external capability, flexibility, liability, union pressures, number of potential providers, community attitudes and personnel. A variety of factors arising from the particular circumstances should also be considered.

Besides the negotiation of a fair and equitable agreement, a key to a successful contractual relationship is an understanding about how performance is to be measured. The governmental unit should define the method planned for measurement in its request for bids. The method should include, when possible, quantitative measures of performance, such as sanitation routes operated per month per dollar value. It is important to include a gauge of effectiveness, such as "with no more than X complaints per 100 households."

When quantitative measures are difficult or ineffective—which happens more often nowadays as privatization spreads—it is important to establish a qualitative yardstick, such as "belief that service has improved." Performance can be measured with some degree of confidence by comparing a baseline "customer" survey, taken before the contract was reached, with the results of the survey done six months or a year later. By definition, the results are subjective, so rigor must be applied to make the analysis effective. Other factors also should be considered, such as political perceptions by public officials, citizens and community leaders.

It is important that public authorities set objectives at the outset with the contractor. The two parties must specify goals and target dates and agree to quantitative and qualitative methods of measuring their attainment. One way to stimulate good performance is to contract out only a portion of the service (when feasible, of course). As an example, Phoenix has only part of its refuse collection handled by a private firm. The city believes that its mixed system keeps the contractor honest and encourages good performance from both public and private employees.

In recent years, privatization has extended to computer services such as data and word processing. These can pose measurement problems because performance often breaks new ground. Prince George's County, Maryland, faced this difficulty when it entered into a five-year agreement with a company to run the county's data-processing operation. The contract includes incentives to reward performance exceeding the agreed-on obligations. To check progress, the county maintains a five-member "contract administration" unit.

Companies wishing to bid for a service that has always been performed by a state or local government often find it difficult to assess the true cost of the service, thus making guesswork out of the bid preparation. Government cost accounting systems often do not accrue all costs, such as overhead and internal service costs such as accounting, purchasing, data processing and so on.

Moreover, the politics of a state or community may outweigh considerations of economy and efficiency. A few years ago, the city council in a

Georgia community decided to contract out its fire protection services. This move galvanized the fire department staff into an effort to gain community support for a city council recall. In the face of that effort, the council cancelled the proposal. Of course, it's up to the public officials involved to generate support for a contracting proposal at the grass roots and among state or community leaders. Once a decision is made, the two parties should collaborate on a transition plan that involves the affected public employees. Additionally, the wise contractor will give continual feedback on progress to elected government officials and leaders of interest groups.

Contractor responsiveness, quality of service, efficient performance and attention to detail will help state and local governments and the contracting companies overcome politics, union pressures and tradition. The pressures on local governments' budgets will create more privatization opportunities in the decade ahead as tax reduction movements spread.

If privatization is to work, a non-adversary partnership between the contracting company and its client must be developed and fostered. Both parties want a businesslike relationship that is fair to all concerned. The local authority wants the provision of effective service for a better price than it could achieve by doing the work itself. The contractor wants a fair return on its investment, a satisfied customer, an untarnished reputation, and few hassles.

For those state and local governments considering it, a checklist for privatization is provided below:

(√) Understand concept

(√) Clarify process

(√) Assess opportunities

(√) Select function(s)

(√) Conduct cost/benefit analysis

　　　—Determine cost of in-house provision

　　　—Determine criteria for successful provision

　　　—Assess outside contractors

　　　—Determine scope of function(s) to be contracted out

　　　—Prepare request for proposals

　　　—Evaluate proposals and price

　　　—Compare with in-house provision

　　　—Decide on in-house versus outside

(√) If outside, select contractor and negotiate contract

(√) Execute agreement

(√) Implement approach/monitor

(√) Evaluate results

(√) Evaluate process/adjust as necessary

(√) Repeat cycle

## PAYING FOR INFRASTRUCTURE MAINTENANCE

One of the results of the state and local government cost revenue squeeze and the cutbacks in federal programs has been the inability of many state and local governments to pay for new or improved infrastructure or public works projects. This is one area of the state or local government budget that can sometimes be delayed in the short run, but one for which delays will most assuredly have long-term negative consequences. To meet this need, state and local governments will, in many cases, have to turn to complex and creative financing. One of the ideas being used in this area is the establishment of a statewide infrastructure bank. This bank would not be another bureaucracy but would be a financing instrument within the existing structure. It would require a partnership between business and government. The basic concept would be to establish a bank that is usually operated by a state municipal league (e.g., the Georgia Municipal Association is developing one) or county association to agglomerate funds to pay for public facilities. These funds would be turned into low cost loans that local governments could repay.

Another possibility is the creation of an urban service tax district within a specified area of a municipality or county. If the citizens in that area require additional infrastructure, such as tennis courts, swimming pools or road maintenance, they pay higher taxes and/or user fees. This concept has found practical use in Florida and a few other states where existing legislation permits it.

Another approach is the concept of payments in lieu of taxes. In other words, industry X pays for Y road improvements if its taxes are reduced or abated. The problem is that you are often robbing Peter to pay Paul when this concept is used.

There are few panaceas in this area, but the urban service tax district idea holds some promise for slight alleviation of a portion of the cutback management problem.

## CONCLUSION

What can state and local government administrators do today to reduce the impact of the cost/revenue squeeze? The following are some general suggestions:

1. Investigate the use of new technologies and better techniques that can increase efficiency and productivity in government services and functions

2. Seek ways to reduce the labor intensiveness of certain functions

3. Develop new cooperative partnerships with other state and local governments to reduce service duplication and achieve economies of scale

4. Develop new working relationships with universities, local industries, research and development (R&D) and other organizations to develop jointly better methods and products

5. Seek out alternative non-local sources of funding

Finally, make a strong effort to hold down and reduce costs in all areas. Marginal or the least used services will need to be cut back or eliminated. Middle management may have to be trimmed.

As state and local governments experience additional belt tightening in the years ahead, a number of different approaches can be used to help alleviate the cost/revenue squeeze. These include effective management of scarce resources, provision of services for a fee, selling services to others, franchising, leveraging higher economic activity, improving productivity, privatization and new ways to finance infrastructure improvements. Few panaceas exist. The challenge is to find effective approaches that work. The best methods are those that achieve concurrence at all levels of the state or local government organization.

Before any cutback management approach begins, the organization needs to examine its environment and set a direction for the future. The next chapter on strategic planning will assist state and local administrators to set a direction for the future of their organizations.

## NOTES

1. James L. Mercer, "Cutback Management, Florida Style," *Quality Cities*, February 1991, pp. 28–31.

2. James L. Mercer, "Growing Opportunities in Public Service Contracting," *Harvard Business Review*, vol. 61, no. 2 (March/April 1983), pp. 178, 186, 188.

# 3

# Strategic Planning as a Direction-Setting Tool

"In the long run, men hit only what they aim at."
—Henry David Thoreau

or

"Engage the enemy and see what happens."

—Napoleon

The two views of the future expressed above are obviously diabolically opposed. Most state and local governments choose the former because they cannot abide the latter.

As budgets continue to be tight and economic conditions continue to be bleak, there are an increasing number of state and local government problems that might be alleviated through the appropriate application of strategic planning[1] and management. This should then be followed by selected cost-cutting strategies. Such approaches should be the first step in an effective state and local cutback management program. Albeit a strategic planning approach starts as "top-down," to be truly effective, it must evolve into a "bottom-up" approach.

Such planning and strategic thinking can lead to an increased ability of state and local government managers to carefully evaluate, select and implement alternative approaches to the financing and delivery of needed public services. Such application of strategic planning, thinking and management—drawing upon the available vast assistance resources of a variety of organizations and institutions—can have significant positive impacts upon the efficiencies of state and local government, the improvement and simplification of selected service delivery functions and the resultant financial viability of individual agencies and jurisdictions.

To deal with the trends of the future, state and local government leaders need to develop a clear direction and improved options and strategies that will assure the best possible futures for their state, agencies, cities, counties or special district. Economic and social changes are forcing state and local leaders to think strategically about the future of their agencies, jurisdictions and communities. Often, they must reconsider the major roles of their organizations/communities and some of their current policy directions. Strategic planning will provide a major leadership and directional mechanism for state and local governments to think and act strategically about how they deliver and finance their services, build the state and local economy and improve the quality of life in the coming decades.

## STRATEGIC PLANNING CAN HELP

Strategic planning is meshed and interwoven with the entire process of management. Thus, all managers should understand the nature of strategic planning and how to utilize it as a managerial tool. In its most elementary sense, the objective of any strategic planning process is to increase organizational performance through an examination of service needs, establishment of a vision or mission and the identification of steps necessary to achieve that vision or mission. Strategic planning concerns itself with establishing the major directions for the organization (e.g., What are its purpose/vision/mission, major clients to serve, major problems to pursue and/or major delivery approaches?).

## STRATEGIC PLANNING: A WAY TO SET DIRECTION

Perhaps the most effective view of strategic planning is as a process that allows decisionmakers to view directional alternatives and scenarios. In the public sector, a one-time, all-encompassing plan does not recognize the reality of the political process and the fact that public sector organizations require an ability to continually re-examine their strategic options. An effective strategic planning process facilitates the examination of questions such as these:

- What business is the state or local government in? What should it be in? To whom does it provide services? Who is paying for them? Who should pay for them?
- What are the alternative revenue strategies? What should the government system look like in response to the alternatives?
- What are the alternatives and realistic economic development possibilities and the effects on services and infrastructure?

- Are there major reorganizations to be considered?
- What service delivery issues deserve priority (i.e., What is the impact if there is a focus on economic development, public safety?).

In terms of economic development, targeting growth industries and businesses is a must these days for states and communities that want to be competitive. What are the economic trends in the United States that affect development opportunities in states and in urban communities? What are the prospects for the manufacturing and service sectors as sources of economic and job growth in the 1990s and beyond? What are the opportunities for improving the state and local business climate? And how can one plan a development strategy that works? These are some of the questions that effective strategic planning will help answer.

### Strategic Planning as a Process

Strategic planning is primarily a process rather than a set of specific products. It is often short term to midterm in time frame rather than long term, such as long-range planning. It is not systematic zero base; planning, programming, budgeting systems (PPBS); performance or program budgeting. However, strategic planning is linked to these budgeting processes by providing an approach for clarifying goals necessary for carrying out any performance-oriented mission.

Strategic planning provides direction and identifies desirable outcomes and paths that hold the most promise for accomplishing them. As a process, strategic planning helps to avoid the problem of "It makes no difference which path you take since you don't know where you're going!" Public sector strategic planning combines at least four elements:

1. The evaluation of the total external and internal environment within which the state, community and organization exists
2. The identification of major threats and opportunities facing the state, the community or the organization
3. An assessment of the strengths and weaknesses of the organization and the community or the state
4. Development of a concentrated strategy enabling the entity to harness effectively all needed resources and operate within its environment

Although strategic planning has become the hallmark of well-managed organizations, managers are often skeptical about its usefulness and how it should be done. Some managers argue for a comprehensive, rational approach that lays out a course of action for five years or so. On the other hand, managers should develop resources to face an uncertain future and react to opportunities and threats as they arise with these resources. The purpose of this chapter is to lay out the formal steps to strategic planning and then present the options available for adapting them to your own organization.

## The Responsibility of Senior Management

The above elements together create the principal responsibility of senior management and policymakers of state and local government. It is their responsibility to evaluate the economies and the environment within which the organization operates, and they should arrive at an understanding of existing and potential opportunities and threats confronting the organization, the community or the state. At the same time, the community, the organization or the state should be examined to ascertain strengths and weaknesses in such areas as organizational structure, finance, productivity, service delivery capability, community involvement and understanding, and overall management capacity. Finally, through a systematic meshing of external opportunities and perceived threats with institutional strengths and weaknesses, the governing body and senior management can establish specific directions and then develop the strategies, policies and control mechanisms that are most likely to contribute to the achievement of the entities' vision/mission.

### Relationship to Budgeting

An effective strategic planning process must be based on, and tied directly into, a strong budgeting system. Although a budgeting system by itself can overlook strategic issues, a strategic planning process unrelated to the budget is without substance. An effective strategic planning process should be an important link between comprehensive planning and the annual operating and capital budgets.

### Strategic Planning: A Buzzword?

Strategic planning has become a catchy buzzword with obvious benefits, less obvious pitfalls and a variety of meanings. The area of complexity, importance and expense it has assumed through popularization also might confuse or discourage public officials. There are almost as many definitions of strategic planning as there are persons talking about the subject. When one definition spans both the private and public sectors of the economy, the meanings become even more broad and varied.

### What Is Planning?

At least three decades ago, Peter Drucker defined planning as actions taken *right now* to reach tomorrow's objectives. His definition still holds;

planning means deciding what has to be done to prepare the organization for the future. It implies that managers need to work now to make the future happen. So a plan that puts a decision off until next year isn't a plan at all—it's procrastination.

It is just as important to remember what planning isn't. Most importantly, planning is not the latest fad or technique pushed by consultants. A forecast is not a plan either. Forecasts focus on trends that will continue into the future and are inputs to the planning process. Most importantly, plans don't eliminate risks. Instead, good plans highlight those risks and spell out the options for minimizing their effects on the organization.

Planning is deciding in advance what to do, how to do it, where to do it, who is to do it and when to do it. Planning denotes organizational relationships and personnel needs. It determines the types of controls to be applied as an organization proceeds with its plan. Planning is the function of all managers. The alternative to planning is "management by crisis"!

Planning bridges the gap from "where we are" to "where we want to go"! It makes it possible for things to occur that would not otherwise happen. In an overall managerial sense, planning is a function that is intellectually demanding and the most basic of all managerial functions. Planning should logically precede the execution of the management functions of organizing, staffing, directing and controlling. It is a function of management that is unique in that it provides direction for all group efforts.

### The Relevance of Planning

As we are all aware, change is the important reality of our time. The key to organization effectiveness and success is to manage change properly by utilizing pragmatic planning approaches. Now that strategic planning and its concepts are becoming more widely utilized and accepted, public sector organizations will increasingly adopt these concepts as effective approaches to managing in the turbulent, uncertain and complex environment of the 1990s and beyond.

### The Purpose of Strategic Planning

The purpose of strategic planning is to provide management with a framework on which decisions can be made and that will have an impact on the organization. A conscious effort to systematize the process and to manage its evolution is preferable to an unmanaged and haphazard evolution. The basic planning problem being faced is how to allocate the organization's limited resources across a set of services and demands for those services. The major benefits to be expected from planning include improved sense of direction for the organization, better performance, increased understanding of the organization and its purpose, earlier warnings of problems and the achievement of more effective decisions.

### What Is Long-Range Planning?

Long-range planning is most often an extrapolation of the present. It answers the question "How can we get the job done?" For example, if you (as a city department head) plan to provide the same services with the same frequency to an expanded city, that is long-range planning.

### What Is Strategic Planning?

Strategic planning began as a military discipline and, in modern times, became a private sector discipline. It was started in the U.S. private sector in the mid–1950s and early 1960s by the General Electric Company. It achieved widespread adoption by the end of the decade of the 1960s, and it quickly spread to other private companies as well.

Strategic planning has many definitions. It basically answers the question in an organization "*What* shall be done?" Strategic planning is a leadership instrument and a process. It begins with establishing organizational aims and purpose, followed by formulating ways and means to achieve that aim or purpose and providing direction for implementation of operational or tactical planning.

Strategic planning is a process for setting future direction, a means to reduce risk and a vehicle for training managers. It is also a process for making strategic decisions, a way to develop consensus among top managers, and a means to develop a written long-range plan. Strategic planning can be defined as a method of guiding managers so that their decisions and actions affect the future of the organization in a consistent and rational manner, and in a way desired by top management.

Strategic planning involves those choices related to overall organizational purpose, oriented toward the future, and importantly involving uncontrollable environmental forces. Strategic choices are those that emphasize future missions and future generations of service outputs and resource inputs. In contrast, the organization's day-to-day operating environment emphasizes current objectives and the existing generation of outputs and resources.[2] Or strategic planning is a decision process that defines the business the organization is in and that identifies the opportunities and constraints that face the organization as it attempts to be successful and lays *out* a plan of action for goal attainment. Another definition of strategic planning is "the process by which the guiding members of an organization envision its future and develop the necessary procedures and operations to achieve that future."[3]

State and local government strategic planning is the process by which the governing body and top management of a state, city or county envision the organization's future and develop the necessary organization, staff, procedures, operations and controls to achieve that future successfully.

### Four Fundamental Strategic Questions

Although strategic planning has become a very sophisticated function in many organizations in recent years, particularly in the private sector, the basic questions that strategic plans should answer haven't changed. These are the following:

1. What are our services now?
2. What should our services be?
3. What will our services be if we keep on the present track?
4. If we didn't possess a monopoly in our service area now, would anyone procure our services?

The following sections of this chapter provide the information and analytical techniques needed to answer these questions in your own organization.

### Key Parts of a Strategic Plan

Effective strategic plans include five key elements:

1. A *vision/mission statement* that defines the place where the organization wants to be or the fundamental purpose of the organization and its boundaries
2. An *environmental scan* (situation analysis, SWOT analysis, or size-up) including an examination of both external and internal factors apt to be encountered as you try to achieve the vision or carry out the mission
3. A *set of strategic objectives* indicating what you will do to carry out the mission or achieve the vision
4. *Tactics* or short-term operating plans for meeting objectives
5. *Controls*, measures and evaluation steps to determine how well the strategic plan is progressing

All organizations may not use these same labels and may not go through all these elements in exactly this order, but every good strategic plan has all five parts built in—these five elements are the essence of strategic planning. The parts are arranged in hierarchical order from very general, policy board and top management issues to more specific, lower-level operating issues. Ideally, the plan at each level is tied to a higher level in the organization helping to achieve overall consistency and unity of purpose.

### Levels of Strategic Planning

A strategic plan may be statewide, regional, community based or organizational. Depending on the size and complexity of an organization, two levels of strategic planning are also possible: (1) overall organizational strategic planning and (2) functional, departmental or programmatic strategic planning. Functional/departmental/programmatic strategic plans deal with what to do to operate a specific organizational component in a specific overall organization. Issues such as technology and service changes, location of new facilities and expansion to serve newly annexed areas are examples.

Overall organizational strategic planning is conducted at the next higher level and is concerned with the overall organization. Issues such as new services, consolidations, joint agreements and major reorganizations of departments are examples.

### Summary

Strategic planning is not dreaming, nor futuristic thinking, but is an example of process versus substance. Strategic planning is the process that creates a balance between "what is desired!" versus "what is possible." Strategic planning enables managers to distinguish truly important decisions from other decisions and to build a strategic agenda. It is a process that deals with interdepartmental issues and allows the organization to develop synergy among functional components. It is a process that helps managers deal with turbulent, complex and influential environments. It helps to identify critical success factors or key result areas, to avoid incremental thinking and to develop the organization in such a manner as to deal effectively with change.

Strategic planning often leads to serious organizational change. If you undertake it, you must be able to address these questions: Can you accomplish the change? Can you sustain the change?

Strategic planning is increasingly a line management function versus a staff assignment. It is a line management function that is necessary to the effectiveness of any organization.

### DIFFICULTIES WITH PUBLIC SECTOR STRATEGIC PLANNING

Public sector strategic planning difficulties include a lack of strategic planning management skills and a lack of time to devote to the process. Other difficulties include a lack of dollars to spend on the process and constraining regulations and laws. Other difficulties include constant fiscal crisis of governmental organizations and frequent elections.

## OPERATIONAL (TACTICAL) PLANNING

Operational (tactical) planning includes those actions to be taken to put strategies into effect. This type of planning answers the question "How can we get the job done?" It often consists of specific objectives accompanied by short narrative action plans.

## STRATEGIC MANAGEMENT

Strategic management may have two diametrically opposed definitions. One is that it is the overall encompassing effort for total management of the organization; another is that it is merely a portion or "tool" of strategic planning. An older school definition is that strategic management is the day-to-day implementation of an organization's strategic plan. It is important to choose and properly communicate one of these definitions throughout the organization. The first definition has been adopted for this book.

## STRATEGIC THINKING

Strategic thinking can be of three types: (1) as-it-is, dealing with immediate concerns as you perceive them; (2) reductionist, starting with immediate concerns and breaking them down into component parts for solution; and (3) expansionist, which means starting with the immediate concerns and expanding to find creative solutions. As managers, we are apt to deal with a strategic issue in one of the first two ways, but we are often not skilled in the expansionist approach. A really effective strategic thinker should consider the third alternative, as well.

Some people consider strategic planning really to be strategic thinking. In this context, the process is paramount because it expands your mind beyond the present.

## DOES PLANNING PAY OFF?

This is a tough question. It depends on the time frame with which plans are judged, how "payoff" is measured and all kinds of controllable factors such as new technology, federal and state regulations and the general economy. Generally, most studies find that formal planning (making a conscious effort to cover most of the planning basics) has a positive payoff. Putting resources into a planning effort should result in more knowledge for decisions and, therefore, higher organizational performance. So, another way to phrase the question is "Can planning hurt us in any way?" If you've never done planning before, the answer is an obvious "No."

## A STRATEGIC PLANNING MODEL

A comprehensive model for state and local government strategic planning encompasses the following nine steps:

1. Preparing to plan
2. Developing a vision/mission statement
3. Performing an environmental scan
4. Listing strategic issues
5. Identifying critical strategic issues
6. Developing strategic objectives
7. Internally assessing ability to carry out the plan and resultant gap analysis
8. Tactical planning
9. Obtaining feedback, evaluation and follow-up

## NOTES

1. James L. Mercer, *Strategic Planning for Public Managers* (Westport, Conn.: Quorum Books, 1991), pp. 1–28.

2. William R. King and David I. Cleland, *Strategic Planning and Policy* (New York: Van Nostrand Reinhold, 1978), p. 15.

3. J. William Pfeiffer, Leonard Goodstein, and Timothy M. Nolan, *Applied Strategic Planning: A How to Do It Guide* (San Diego: University Associates, 1986), p. 1.

*4*

# Organizing Around Critical
# Success Factors

"... organizations are creatures of habit just like people. They are
cultures, heavily influenced by the past."
—Robert H. Waterman, Jr.

During the 1990s and beyond, state and local governments will face a
continuous, dynamic and ever-rapidly changing environment. This environment will be replete with threats and opportunities that policymakers
and managers must deal with. A few select strategic issues (or critical
success factors) will need to be addressed if appropriate positive results
are to be achieved. Successful managers will need to focus their organizational components around these critical success factors. These factors
will also change from time to time as the environment changes. Therefore,
they must be constantly monitored to determine when directional changes
should occur.[1]

## DIRECTION SETTING

The great hockey player Wayne Gretzky has said that the secret of his
success is that he skates to where he thinks the puck will be. To achieve
success, state and local government policymakers and managers need to
focus the direction of their organizations on a course of action that will
most likely take them to a place that they wish to be in the future. Most
should adopt Wayne Gretzky's view of how to achieve success because
they can't afford the significant risks associated with a more risky view.
As discussed in chapter 3, the best approach to achieving success (or

hitting the desired spot in the future) is through the use of a valuable organizational transformation and renewal tool called strategic planning. In its simplest sense, strategic planning is a direction-setting technique. It is not necessarily time related, nor does it answer the operational planning questions of "how," "who," "where" and "when." It answers the strategic question "What shall we do to achieve our stated mission or vision for our organization?"

## STEPS IN ORGANIZATIONAL STRATEGIC PLANNING

At a minimum, seven key steps are necessary to the development of a state and local government organizational strategic plan. These follow:

1. Mission/vision
2. Environmental scan
3. Identification of strategic issues
4. Defining critical success factors
5. Setting strategic objectives
6. Developing tactical plans
7. Monitoring and feedback

Each of these steps is briefly explained below.

1. *Mission/vision.* A statement of desired state of being, or purpose and organizational direction. Answers the questions: "What do we want to be?" "What business are we in?" "What business should we be in?"

2. *Environmental scan.* An assessment of the external and internal trends influencing an organization, the opportunities and threats created by the external and internal environment and internal strengths and weaknesses to respond. Also called situational analysis, size-up, environmental analysis, SWOT analysis, and so on.

3. *Identification of strategic issues.* The issues that will be identified in the environmental scanning process that must be addressed as the organization tries to be successful in carrying out its mission or achieving its vision. Not all of these will be absolutely critical to success, but they are issues that will be encountered along the way.

4. *Defining critical success factors.* The key elements that are crucial to success in carrying out the mission or attempting to achieve the vision. Also called key result areas or critical issues.

5. *Setting strategic objectives.* The milestones to be accomplished from a strategic standpoint as the organization moves to try to carry out its mission or achieve its vision. These answer the question "What do we do to carry out the mission or achieve the vision?"

6. *Developing tactical plans*. The short-range operating plans to carry out the strategic plan. Tactical objectives that are specific, measurable, assignable, realistic and time related need to be set.

7. *Monitoring and feedback*. The signals that are put in place to determine changes in the environment that may affect the strategic direction or the mission/vision of the organization. Feedback is then provided to the strategic planning process so that it can be changed to meet the new direction that is needed.

In addition, proper preplanning and assessments of organizational ability and resource availability are necessary.

## Identifying Critical Success Factors

As the environment is scanned, a number of issues that need to be addressed will be identified if the organization is to be successful in achieving its stated mission/vision. Some of these issues are critical to success; others are less important or peripheral. The important thing is for the organization to focus on the five to seven critical factors, which, if managed effectively, will lead to mission/vision accomplishment. These must be the factors that are on the critical path to success.

## Organizing around Critical Success Factors

Once the five to seven critical success factors have been identified and further scanned and evaluated, the components of the organization need to be realigned around the most optimum approach to their accomplishment. As the organizational arrangement is considered and adopted, the tendency among conservative managers will be to overlay it upon the present hierarchical organizational structure. That will be a mistake because if the mission/vision and appropriate five to seven critical success factors have been identified, then no other organizational arrangement (except perhaps support functions to the five to seven critical success factors) will be needed. This is where the gut-wrenching decisions of organizational transformation and renewal will come into play, because the traditional organization will have to be scrapped and realigned, and it may not all fit the required mode. Here a transformation will be required. Once the new organization is in place, then appropriate staffing, direction, control and evaluation can be implemented as well.

## Cruciality of Monitoring

If such an organizational arrangement is to work effectively and produce appropriate results, the organizational external and internal environment must be constantly monitored to ensure that the precise five to seven critical success factors are selected and that they continue to be the correct ones to pursue relative to the organizational direction established by the mission/ vision statement. Changes must be made swiftly as environmental forces produce altered dynamics and require the selection of altered critical success factors.

To ensure this attenuation to the pulse of the environment, key members of the management team must be assigned specific elements of the environment for monitoring (e.g., the strategy surrounding state or communities as related to economic development). These signals need to feed changes into the strategic direction that may alter strategy, reassessment of mission/vision and/or selection of alternate critical success factors.

### Summary

These concepts may sound radical, but they are regularly being employed in the private sector. Elements of them are also already in place in progressive state and local governments. Focusing on a clear mission/vision and organizing around a select group of critical success factors will begin to become an accepted approach that public managers of the 1990s and beyond will use to achieve their aims and purposes. Being sure the mission/ vision is correct and that the right five to seven critical success factors are selected and maintained are central to achieving positive results with this methodology.

If pursued properly, this approach will set the stage for significant organizational transformation and renewal. It will also lay the foundation for other innovative management and leadership approaches for the future, such as self-managed teams and strategy development at all levels of the organization.

### ORGANIZING FOR EFFECTIVENESS: A CASE STUDY

The organizational structure of the city of Hampton, Virginia (population 130,000) was developed while the city was in a cutback environment, with three assistant city managers supervising groups of departments and making many day-to-day operational decisions. This slowed down response to problems and underutilized the resources of department heads and other employees.[2]

In the fall of 1984, the newly appointed city manager, Robert J. O'Neill, Jr., asked a committee of department heads to review the city structure and make recommendations regarding its effectiveness. Out of those discussions came the current organizational structure, which is essentially flat with all department heads reporting directly to the city manager. Assistant city managers were taken out of the direct chain of command and their focus brought to bear on the major issues impacting the city's future: financial management, human resources, economic development and quality of life. Department heads are asked to join one or more operational task forces that are facilitated by a member. Facilitators are rotated on an annual basis. Each task force generates its own annual priorities, shares resources and solves problems through consensus and cooperation. Currently, operational task forces are functioning in the areas of infrastructure, public safety, management resources and community services. The task force system has been used throughout the organization in an effort to involve as many employees as possible in the design of work, the decision-making process, and the encouragement of creativity and innovation.

Department heads and employees are empowered to make decisions and demonstrate a personal commitment to the organization's success and are encouraged to share information freely with peers and subordinates. At the end of FY 1988, more than forty task forces, problem-solving groups, special project committees, and other similar efforts were identified with memberships in these groups reaching more than 900. This has been accomplished in a work force of slightly more than 1,200 employees.

## LINKING EXECUTIVE COMPENSATION TO THE ORGANIZATION'S MISSION: A CASE STUDY

The city manager of Hampton, Virginia (population 130,000) wanted to develop a way to link the performance of the city's key executives—assistant city managers, department heads and related managers—directly to the organization's mission and to reward executives based on their specific contributions.[3]

On July 1, 1987, the city implemented a new executive compensation program, $p^2$ (an acronym for performance planning), which took all of the city's department heads and assistant city managers out of the general compensation system and gave the city manager greater flexibility to reward executives based on individual performance contracts. The plan contains no salary ranges, allows for cash bonuses for outstanding performance, and grants flexibility for the department head to receive his/her salary in a combination of monetary and non-monetary forms. The executive compensation program is one component of a citywide performance planning process that functions like a series of building blocks in the development of an integrated approach to municipal government. Beginning with the city council's mission statement, "to establish Hampton as the most liveable city in Virginia," council established critical success factors for the organization—those key areas having the greatest impact on the accomplishment of the city's mission. The first year, critical success factors were economic development, physical appearance, communications, leisure, fiscal health and transportation. Performance indicators were then developed for these factors. Department heads are asked to develop annually critical success factors, performance indicators, goals, objectives and strategies for their departments, which are placed in a formal performance contract. Progress is reviewed six months into the fiscal year and a formal evaluation is done at year-end. Compensation is set based on accomplishments.

The final product is a work plan for the city containing measurable objectives and task assignments. Each department head is evaluated by the city manager relative to the accomplishment of his/her agreed-upon objectives and overall contribution to the organization's success. The results of this evaluation convert into executive rewards based on individual performance contracts. This provides every department head with a clear understanding of his/her accomplishments and contributions relative to achieving the organization's mission.

## NOTES

1. James L. Mercer, "Organizing Around Critical Success Factors: The Structure of the 1990's and Beyond," *Texas Town & City*, March 1991, pp. 10–11, 40.

2. Tharon J. Greene, "Organizing for Effectiveness," City of Hampton, Virginia, January 1990, p. 1.

3. Tharon J. Greene, "Linking Executive Compensation to the Organization's Mission," City of Hampton, Virginia, January 1990, p. 1.

# 5

# Techniques for Improving Employee Productivity

"I keep six honest serving men (they taught me all I knew); their names
are what and why and when and how and where and who."
                                                    —Rudyard Kipling

A number of approaches have been found to be effective in increasing
employee productivity, including goal and objective setting (management-
by-objectives), employee involvement processes, gainsharing programs,
job enrichment, task forces, employee incentives, management-by-walking
around, and QUEST. These techniques, the attributes of which are described below, can be effective in a cutback management environment.

## MANAGEMENT-BY-OBJECTIVES (MBOs)

It is a proven fact that individuals and organizations accomplish more
and achieve higher degrees of satisfaction if they establish operating goals
and objectives and if they are regularly monitored relative to how they are
progressing in light of a goal and its related objectives. The validity of this
principle reaches from athletes and athletic teams to state and local governments.

An effective approach to establishing a management-by-objectives program in local government, for example, is to begin with the city council
or other governing body. This can be done at a retreat such as those recently
conducted by the cities of Tyler, Texas; Atlanta, Georgia; and the Bir-
mingham–Jefferson County (Alabama) Transit Authority; or by asking the
council to write its goals, as did the city of Fairborn, Ohio.

Once the governing body has established annual or longer-term goals for the local government, then the city manager or chief administrator should require the various department heads to develop specific objectives to carry out each goal. Each objective should meet at least five criteria, including being specific, measurable, tied to a specific time frame, realistic, and assigned to a specific function or individual responsible to see that it is met.

After objectives have been set, the process should be delegated to lower levels within the organization to delegate authority properly and develop organizational and individual accountability for the accomplishment of objectives to meet overall goals. To be most effective, individuals within the organization and the organization itself should be held accountable for establishing objectives and achieving them as part of their regular performance review process. The most difficulty in effectively carrying out management-by-objectives programs has been in not properly involving lower levels and individuals within the organization in helping to attain overall organizational goals, or in making the process so extensive that it becomes "process oriented" versus "results oriented."

Individuals within an organization find greater satisfaction from their work when they know that their work is important to the organization and that their contributions are being measured.

**EMPLOYEE INVOLVEMENT PROCESSES**

Employee involvement processes such as self-managed teams, cost-reduction teams, Quality Circles and so on involve employees voluntarily making decisions and solving problems in their jobs. Such approaches are based on the assumptions that employees want to contribute to the betterment of their work, that their expertise can be tapped, and that this can result in better decisions and actions for them and the organization. Employee involvement processes can be of significant value in increasing morale; enriching jobs; increasing quality, productivity and motivation; and tapping employees' unused knowledge.

Employee involvement processes function to identify and analyze causes of problems affecting the team members' work place, to determine appropriate solutions to these problems, to recommend solutions to management, and when possible, to implement approved solutions. Management commitment and proper planning and training are crucial to the development and implementation of an effective employee involvement process.

Employee involvement processes are not panaceas for solving all of the organization's productivity or cost-reduction problems. Nor do the form and structure of such processes necessarily have to follow a textbook example, but they can be adapted to fulfill a state or local government's particular needs. The state of Florida; Dallas, Texas; Fort Collins, Colorado; and Pensacola, Florida, are examples of state and local governments that have effectively utilized employee involvement processes.

## GAINSHARING PROGRAMS

Gainsharing programs are designed to obtain more work output with the same level of labor input. Gainsharing attempts to motivate working harder and working smarter. Therefore, good gainsharing systems do not, by definition, sacrifice quality for quantity. For a gainsharing system to be totally effective, it must be designed, developed and executed as an integrated system.

The basic concept of gainsharing is to share monetary gains achieved from a predetermined work effort with individual or group contributors to that effort. For example, if a manager wanted to improve the employee productivity of the fleet maintenance operation, he/she could establish a cost savings target with all employees of the department, communicate how cost savings are to be measured, and once achieved, agree to split say 50 percent of the savings as a cash bonus to be shared equally by departmental employees.

Among the gainsharing programs available are the Scanlon Plan, the Rucker Plan, and Improshare. These plans have similar administrative aspects in that they are individual employee cost-saving suggestion systems tied to monetary rewards. The Rucker and Improshare plans are registered trademarks, meaning that, if used, a state or local government would be obligated to pay a royalty to the developer of the plan. More about group gainsharing programs will be discussed later in this chapter.

## JOB ENRICHMENT

People who have been in jobs for some time often get stale, or even burned out. In addition to the objectives of revitalizing the humdrum existence or monotonous routine for each employee is the desire to add something new to the job or otherwise to change the makeup of the work. This can be done through a variety of methods, including training, cross-training and added or changed responsibilities. Care has to be exerted so as not just to add more work but to change the makeup of the work creatively in a way that motivates higher productivity and increases morale, worker involvement and higher quality.

## TASK FORCES

Another approach to improving employee productivity and finding new ways to cut costs that works effectively with managers is the use of task forces as opposed to more traditional employee involvement processes and gainsharing approaches. These management teams are usually formed and appointed by state or local government executives or department heads for specific purposes and for finite periods of time. They have a limited life span and are to achieve specific accomplishments by defined target dates.

For example, the city manager of Hampton, Virginia, appointed a number of key management task forces to address a variety of organizational and council-related issues. One task force is assigned to the area of human resources and is responsible for the development of new ways to involve employees in decision making and improved productivity and quality through training and new approaches. Task forces seem to work more effectively with managers as ways to improve morale, productivity and quality, as opposed to more traditional employee involvement approaches and gainsharing approaches, which work more effectively with non-managerial employees.

## EMPLOYEE INCENTIVES

Most organizational development researchers have concluded that there are four primary methods of motivating employee performance. These are money, goal and objective setting, participation and job enrichment. A fifth area, behavior modification, has been identified as well, although most researchers include it within the other four. Money was identified as an important motivator by Frederick W. Taylor, the acknowledged pioneer of scientific management. Since then, social scientists have downgraded its value as a motivator. Money can still be a strong motivator, however, especially at lower levels within a state or local government.

Several forms of employee involvement and participation have already been discussed. Others include various Japanese management practices such as early morning employee "jumping jack" or exercise sessions to foster teamwork, programs such as Tommy Lasorda's "Dodger Blue," instilling greater pride via organizational teamwork and non-monetary reward systems. In this latter regard, former Cincinnati, Ohio, and Tacoma, Washington, City Manager William Donaldson made it a practice to offer non-monetary rewards to managers who exceeded performance expectations. These included such rewards as a new microcomputer for the department or a trip to visit another innovative city.

## MANAGEMENT-BY-WALKING AROUND

The Hawthorne experiments at Western Electric proved many decades ago that productivity increases when managers pay attention to employees. Although today's employees have changed dramatically over the years, and their motivations for work have changed as well, the philosophy of "management attention" still has value as a way of improving employee productivity.

The most highly regarded current management books support this concept. The basic concept of "management-by-walking around" is for the top managers to make a regular practice of paying visits to the levels and personnel within the organization that produce the services. But to be effective, these cannot be just casual visits to "shoot the breeze." They must be planned, well thought-out and executed by executives and managers in such a way that quality, work-related discussions are held with employees at all times within the organization on a regular basis. In addition, since management-by-walking around creates expectations on the part of the employee, management is obligated to provide employees with feedback on issues that they discuss.

## QUEST

Many managers have been able to incorporate employee involvement processes and gainsharing techniques individually into their organizations to improve quality and productivity. A new approach successfully combines the positive attributes of these established productivity and quality improvement concepts in a system called QUEST (Quality Utilizing Employees, Systems and Technology). QUEST is a process that utilizes the formal training, reporting and evaluation format typically found in more traditional employee involvement processes, with the financial incentives associated with gainsharing programs. Since there are currently strong budgetary pressures at all levels of government, the challenge for managers and administrators today and in the 1990s and beyond is to demonstrate that through the use of productivity and quality improvement techniques, the total cost of providing products and services can be reduced and ultimate results can be enhanced.

QUEST is designed to maximize productivity and quality in any organization. There are also secondary benefits such as increased employee morale, attitude and job commitment; increased concern for safety in the workplace; cost reduction and quality control; increased communication and teamwork; and decreased absenteeism and abuse of sick leave.

The reason many government officials have not used employee involvement approaches to productivity and quality improvement in the past is that there are a number of issues that make such processes and gainsharing programs, when used independently, less effective in the long-run. In the QUEST system, there is an inherent structure that provides tangible and intangible gains through the use of both employee involvement and gainsharing techniques. On the employee involvement side, most of the immediate gains to the employee are intangible (i.e., attitude, morale, producing a better quality service and meeting hierarchical needs), and the government entity initiating the system receives enough immediate tangible cost savings to more than offset the cost of the process. In gain-sharing, both the employee and the employer receive immediate tangible (financial) gains through participation in the program, and it has been argued that monetary gains offer the highest degree of motivation to in-crease productivity by an employee, particularly at lower levels of the organization. By combining the two techniques, QUEST allows a manager to implement a system that will improve quality and productivity with benefits to workers, the organization, and the users of its services.

## SUMMARY

To be most effective in improving employee productivity and cutting costs, state and local managers must commit to a course of action, must properly prepare for the course, must communicate it effectively to em-ployees and must stick with it long enough to reap the rewards. As a wise advisor once said: "Do not follow where the path may lead. Go instead where there is no path and leave a trail."

The most effective managers of the 1990s and beyond will be those who systematically involve employees at all organizational levels in decisions that affect them. This should be done both operationally and tactically as pointed out in this chapter, and strategically as pointed out in chapter 3.

In general, these approaches have included other revenue sources, cost reductions, productivity improvements and future cost avoidance.

## ACHIEVEMENT AWARD PROGRAM IN HAMPTON, VIRGINIA: A CASE STUDY

The city of Hampton, Virginia[1] (population 130,000), needed to develop a program that would encourage and reward employee involvement, in-novation and problem solving. The city's management philosophy is based on the knowledge that its employees are its greatest resource and supports the involvement of employees in shaping the quality of their work lives.

Each city department was given responsibility for developing written performance criteria and corresponding incentives and rewards. Employees were encouraged to become involved in the development of their depart-ment's system. Achievement awards are expected to relate to special ac-complishments above an individual's or group's normal scope of activity and to meet at least one of the following criteria: (1) save the city money, (2) improve services to the community or (3) enhance the city's image with the public.

Understanding that people are motivated by different needs, managers may use monetary and non-monetary incentives. Types of achievement awards include monetary—up to $1,000 or 10 percent of annual cost/benefit of the activity, if appropriate—or non-monetary—paid time off, commemorative gifts, special training, designated parking space, gift certificates and so on. When awards are given, their documentation is made a part of the employee's personnel record.

Since its inception in 1985, 331 employees have submitted ideas or accomplished activities that resulted in city savings of approximately $825,000. Monetary awards in the amount of approximately $82,000 have been given, as well as a great variety of non-monetary awards. Typical award winners include a $5,900 savings generated by two employees who designed a more efficient hydraulic system on a refuse truck and an administrative "how to" handbook developed by five employees across department lines that outlined the administrative procedures throughout the workforce.

## NOTE

1. Tharon J. Greene, "Achievement Award Program in Hampton," City of Hampton, Virginia, January 1990, p. 1.

# 6

# Success Through Shared Values

"The only way to get this country back on track is to return to good old-fashioned horse sense. We've got to start with the basics: how we raise our kids, how we care for our sick and homeless, what it is each of us truly believes. And we've got to remember what America stands for, so that we can take our tarnished values and make them shine again."

—Lee Iacocca

An understanding and consideration of the underlying values of a state, a community or an organization and its related culture are essential to successful strategic planning and cutback management efforts. There is a need for congruence between the entity's values and its strategic efforts. Strategic plans and cutback management efforts that do not take values into account will be in trouble and may even fail.

For example, a full-service city with a 135,000 population recently began its first strategic planning and cutback management process. The newly appointed city manager was thoroughly committed to the process and arranged for an outside consultant and trainer to impart the basic skills to city departments and division heads. The consultant was also asked to provide facilitation assistance during the initial one-year effort to develop the strategic plan and its related cutback management strategies. The training and facilitation efforts were completed for both top and middle management and the initial strategic plan was developed. More progressive members of top and middle management became deeply involved in and committed to the strategic process and saw the benefits in dynamic thinking and needed organizational change that could result from the effort. Some other, more entrenched top and middle managers grumbled that the process would never work but said they would go along with it if the new manager wanted to do it. Some said privately, however, that they had "seen managers come and go" and that they would "outlive" this city manager as well.

Sure enough, the new city manager came to cross-purposes with the city council over a political issue and was asked to resign about six months into his second year on the job. His successor was appointed from within the organization and was a long-term employee of the city and a local native. The strategic direction process faded away quietly under the new manager. The moral of this story is obvious: Get the total organization committed to the process!

## VALUES DEFINED

A value is an enduring belief that a specific mode of conduct or result is personally or socially preferable to an opposite or converse mode of conduct or result. Simply stated, a value is the strongly held belief that one approach or result is preferable to another. These beliefs or values determine what individuals, groups, organizations or communities consider to be appropriate and inappropriate behavior. They are the determinants of norms or standards of acceptable behavior.

Values lie at the heart of almost all organizational decisions. When managers say that a particular manager always can be counted on to fulfill his/her promises or that the water department would never sell unsafe water because it is a highly ethical department, they are explaining those organizations' behaviors in terms of their value bases.

### Influences of Values

Values assist in the design of an organization and in its greater attention to issues. They assist in making down-the-line decisions and in determining who reaches the top in the organization. In addition, they assist the organization in its public relations.

### Sources of Values

Our personal values are heavily influenced by families, friends, religion, school system (teaching techniques: "how to think" versus "what to think") and media (particularly electronic, e.g., music, television). A significant emotional event (SEE) can change basic values after the age of twenty. Examples include death of a loved one, marriage, divorce, religious experience and so on.

## Levels of Values

Values may be measured in at least four levels in a state or local government environment. These are at the individual, work group, organizational or community levels.

### Individual Values

Our individual values are shaped by the world context that existed when we were developing our value system. Individual values tend to be shaped mostly from the ages of five to nineteen years. Basic values are more or less locked in by the time we are twenty years old and are heavily influenced by our generational grouping. On the basis of generational groupings, four basic value groups tend to be represented in organizations today:

- *Traditionalists*. Born prior to about 1935
- *In-betweeners* (or *"Tweeners"*). Born between about 1935 and about 1948
- *Rejectionists* (the *"Now Generation"*). Born between about 1948 and about 1960
- *Synthesists*. Born after about 1960

Another group that will be those persons born after 1980 is now forming and may be referred to by a new title.

The traditionalist is most often characterized by the following set of values:

- Conformity
- Sacrifice
- Formal views
- Strong work ethic
- Social order based on arbitrary distinctions
- Sensitivity to organizational position
- Sense of loyalty
- Looking to individuals in positions of authority for direction
- Material things
- Problem-solving orientation
- Resistance to change

In-betweeners are a compromise group, value-wise, between traditionalists and rejectionists. Tweeners' values tend to be based on the premise of working together as a team. The closer the birthday to 1935, the more traditional the orientation. The closer the birthday to 1948, the more oriented toward rejectionist's values. The Tweener is characterized by the following:

- Strong team orientation
- Sense of "we" or unity
- Achievement orientation
- Ability to pull resources together or solve problems
- Inconsistency as perceived by others

Rejectionists represent those individuals who are programmed to question and challenge tradition. Their values are represented by the following:

- Strong "I" or individualist orientation
- Questioning or challenging ideas
- Experimentation
- Informal approach
- Self-expression
- Sensual orientation
- Balancing of life between work and personal goals
- Loyalty to peers rather than the organization
- "Cause" rather than "solution" orientation
- Strong participation in decision making

*Assessing Personal Values*

There are several techniques for assessing values on the individual level, as follows:

- One-on-one interviews conducted by a process consultant
- Ranking personal values listed in columns
- Diagnostic instruments
- Writing down values or beliefs

A simple exercise for assessing personal values is shown in Exhibit 6–1.

**Exhibit 6–1**
**Personal Values Exercise**

Please rank from 1–10
  1 = Most important to you personally
  10 = Least important to you personally

1. Getting along with colleagues
2. Professional reputation
3. Achievement of organizational goals

4. Excitement

5. Leisure time for family or fun

6. Material wealth

7. Respect of peers

8. Contribution to society

9. Pleasing others

10. Accomplishing personal goals

### Group, Organization and Community Values

For a state or local government organization to be successful with strategic planning and cutback management, some sense of the shared values of groups within the organization, of the organization as a whole and of the community as a whole is important. A "values audit" is a good tool to determine these shared values. Methods that can be used to assess group and organizational values include group process techniques, such as nominal group, Delphi and so on; use of diagnostic instruments; and comparisons with stated values from sources such as Tom Peters' book *In Search of Excellence*.

## STATEMENT OF VALUES

An example of a statement of values follows:

"To Be the Best City of Our Size in America by 1994"
—City of Fort Lauderdale, Florida

One way of testing values is to determine to what degree the stated values differ from the actual behavior in an organization.

## SHARED VALUES

Every organization has shared values.[1] These shared values may be grand in scope or narrowly focused. They can capture the imagination or they can simply drive. If they are strong, they can command everyone's attention. If they are weak, they may often be ignored.

In the past, managers rarely paid much attention to values. Values are not "hard," like organization structures, policies and procedures, strategies, systems or budgets. Often values are not even written down. And when someone does try to articulate them in a formal statement or organizational philosophy, the output often bears an uncomfortable resemblance to the Bible.

Yet "hard" or not, shared organizational values powerfully influence what people in an organization actually do. They should, therefore, be a matter of concern to public managers. Excellent performers among successful organizations seem commonly to have highly focused and widely shared values and to work hard at keeping them intact. This suggests that senior managers who aim for outstanding performance can ill afford to neglect the task of shaping and sustaining the values of their organizations.

### Shared Values Do Make a Difference

A management consultant characterizing one of his favorite high-performance organizations remarked, "They're just turned on, up and down the line!" The phrase rings a bell. All of us have at some time seen this phenomenon. Most people in each "turned-on" organization share a common belief about the distinctiveness of their organization. An example includes the values that the mayor, city council and city administration of Defiance, Ohio, developed in a group session to be a part of their strategic plan. These initially brainstormed values are as follows:

- Honesty
- Dignity
- Credibility
- Pride
- Integrity
- Responsibility
- Dedication
- Sensitivity
- Conscientiousness
- Flexibility (open to change)
- Loyalty
- Self-discipline
- Integrity, morals—"belief in system"
- Team worker

- Hard working
- Accepting of responsibility
- Perceptive
- Efficient use of time, people, resources
- Service that sacrifices individual interest
- Personal drive—personal mission
- Innovativeness
- Mutual consensus
- Pride in performance
- Objective standard—not subjective/ consistent judgment
- Teamwork—community

These were later refined into a smaller group that captures the shared values of the city leaders.

Mediocre organizations present a different picture. Although their senior managers often point to values they regard as characteristic of their organizations, one finds that these values are less strongly held and that the sharing is confined to a limited group of top management. There is no real sense of everyone pulling together, no clear evidence of managerially established patterns in the flow of decisions and actions. Below top executives, motivation and identification with the organization are relatively low.

## The Underlying Theory of Shared Values

Reviewing the shared values of outstanding organizations produces a simple, central insight: For those who hold them, shared values define the fundamental character or corporate culture of their organization—the attitude that distinguishes it from all others. In this way, shared values create a special sense of identity for those in the organization, giving meaning to work as something more than simply earning a living. Shared values are a reality in the minds of most people throughout the organization. Sometimes managers refer explicitly to one or another of these values in providing guidance to subordinates. They are embodied in the organization's folklore. New people may be told stories about the heroes of the organization and of the organization's past that underline the importance of these values to the organization. People interpret these values in the context of their own jobs. These values guide behavior.

As we have already seen, shared values define a state or local government organization's view of itself in relation to the outside world—notably to citizens in the community. But they do not deal only with an organization's relationship with the outside world. Within an organization, they also govern "the way we do things around here." For example, they indicate what matters are to be attended to most expeditiously. They suggest what kind of information is taken most seriously for decision-making purposes. And they define what kind of people are most respected. "The way we do things around here" is also part of the distinctive character and culture of an organization.

Other shared values may be less directly linked to the basic concept of the state or local government organization. For example, some organizations are ardently committed to equal opportunity for employment and advancement; others place little value on it. Some seek leadership in environmental protection whereas others consciously let developers defer compliance until the last possible moment. These, too, are shared values so long as they really do influence behavior in the organization—especially managerial behavior.

Shared values, when strongly held, tend to establish the strategic ground that the organization will occupy. This gives much room for initiatives, but it also sets the bounds of the strategic alternatives that an organization is likely to generate, and of those that its people are likely to implement successfully. Deeply held shared values are hard to change. Hence, although they provide a source of clear, common understanding in an organization, they also constitute a constraint. When an organization with strongly held values finds that it has lost ground to other states or communities of economic relevance, it generally has great difficulty adjusting successfully.

### Determining Organizational Performance with Shared Values

How do shared values actually help to determine state or local government organizational performance? In broad terms, they act as an informal control system that tells people what is expected of them. At one organization, the new administrator actually threw out piles of policy manuals when he became chief executive, preferring to rely on the guidance of shared values. More specifically, shared values affect organizational performance in three main ways:

1. *Managers and others throughout the organization give extraordinary attention to whatever matters are stressed in the organization's value system.* This, in turn, tends to produce extraordinary results. For example, one community provides services much more efficiently than others because efficient operation is what it values and what its managers concentrate on. Another organization values financial management most highly; accordingly, its managers worry less about service and concentrate instead on squeezing every cent of potential revenue from their enterprise operations.
2. *Down the line managers make marginally better decisions, on average, because they are guided by their perception of the shared values.* When a manager is confronted by a close question, for example, making a particular investment in increased productivity versus one in new service development, he/she is likely to opt for productivity.
3. *People simply work a little harder because they are dedicated to the cause.* "I'm sorry I'm so late getting home, but a citizen had a problem and we never leave a citizen with a problem."

### The Role of Leadership

Shared values are not timeless. They do not come into being spontaneously, and though durable, they are not immutable; on the contrary, they are perpetually subject to modification or reinforcement. As unfashionable as it may be to say so, the driving force behind shared value creation, maintenance and change seems to be nothing other than top management leadership. This is clear in the case of the city of Fort Lauderdale, Florida, under the leadership of its former City Manager Connie Hoffman:

We all have our own personal values, most of which we acquired from our family as we grew up. These values define who we are and what we believe in. Our City organization is a family, too, and we have values that need to be defined.

The Department Heads... and I spent two days recently talking about what "being the best" means, how we can make the City the best, and defining what was important to us. The results of our work are the six value statements listed below:

1. We treat each employee and citizen with honesty, consideration and respect
2. We are committed to keeping taxes and service charges reasonable
3. We always look for a better way
4. We know that an active partnership with the community is vital to our success
5. We know that the City is in the business of customer service and the citizens are our shareholders
6. We realize that laws and regulations are necessary for citizen protection and we apply them fairly and reasonably.

Sounds great, doesn't it? But can we live up to the ideals expressed in these statements? We have to, if we want to achieve our mission of being the best City of our size in America in 1994 and to be recognized as such.

We realize that we've got a way to go before we can say that we live and breathe the beliefs expressed in those six statements. Like our mission, the values are something that we have to work toward. But we've taken an important step in getting there by stating in black and white the ideals that should influence and guide our day-to-day activities.

What's the next step? The values need to be refined and action plans developed for making them the guide by which we do business. We need your input. What do the values really mean? How will they affect the way we do our jobs? Are they something that you personally can believe in and be proud of? Your department director will be working with you in developing the answers to these and other questions over the next few months. Speak up and don't be shy. If you think that we do conflict with these values, tell us. Remember, it's a part of making this the "best City of its size in America."

## Creating and Instilling Values

A strong set of shared values seems always to come initially from a forceful leader who is bent on their establishment. A model for this conclusion is the South Carolina Budget and Control Board. Its organizational shared values were inspired by its executive director, Dr. Jesse Coles, as shown in Exhibit 6–2.

**Exhibit 6–2**
**South Carolina State Budget and Control Board Statement of Values**

**Professional Competence**

• We expect of ourselves a high standard of performance that reflects a personal commitment to excellence
• We accept personal integrity and ethical behavior as an intrinsic part of our job performance

**Pride in Group Success**

• We believe in teamwork and that the success of any part of the organization is a success for the entire organization; conversely.

• The success of the organization is the result and reflection of the individuals who are part of the team

**Quality Work Produce**

• The outcomes of our work efforts are products that are consistently superior
• The products of our work effort establish for the Budget and Control Board an identification and expectation of quality

**Dedication to Service**

• The way we serve our clients conveys the Budget and Control Board's commitment to professionalism, excellence and moral behavior
• By serving agencies well, we enhance our ability in turn to provide quality services to the people of the state

**Dependability**

• Our work is thorough and reliable; those we serve have confidence that our services and products can be trusted
• We accept change as part of our daily working environment by adapting not only to changing technologies and opportunities, but also to the changing needs of those we serve

## SUSTAINING AND MODIFYING VALUES

Given that shared values stem from a leader's initiative, what keeps them fresh and vital in a state or local government organization over long periods of time? Certainly one key is continuing, explicit management attention. In general, the primary stimulus and example for constant reinforcement of values continues to come from the chief executive. People pay attention to what he/she says, and even more attention to what he/she does. They read the patterns of decisions emanating from the executive floor to figure out what *really* counts with top management. When the chief executive's statements and actions remain consistent with the established values of the organization, people remain oriented to those values. When the pattern of his/her actions begins to diverge from those values, people become confused, their own focus dissolves, and the drive born of the sense of shared values may simply evaporate.

Other senior managers, as well, help to reinforce (or weaken) the shared values of the organization through their words and actions. It could be said, in fact, that the mark of a senior management team, as opposed to that of a disparate collection of individuals, is coherent support for common values—despite possible differences over policy and practice.

### Organization Supports

More than persistent senior management attention is needed, however, to sustain a strong set of shared values in a large and complex organization.

In addition, the values must be reflected in several other key features of organizational life. Perhaps the most important of these is the process of assimilation or "socialization" of new employees.

As one New England public official, Ron Zemke, said, "The top people can agree on the goals and values and set a vision, but that has to be communicated to the organization, people have to be given an opportunity to accept that vision, to become aligned with it."

### Assimilating New Hires

The first one or two years on the job are crucial for the instilling of value systems in new employees.

### Rewards and Recognition

In outstanding organizations, personnel systems typically support the shared values in several ways. Virtually all promotion is from within; this minimizes dilution of the organization's value system and enables it to guide communication and behavior throughout the organization. Promotions tend to go to those with outstanding achievements of the sorts prized by the organization's value system. Fast-track people are often channeled into jobs that make them proselytizers for the value system, and thereby deepen their commitment to it.

Informal personnel rewards are equally important. It is natural that top managers should more readily lend an ear to people whose behavior is attuned to the organizational value system. These are the people whose accomplishments are most likely to be publicly recognized, and who are most likely to be favored with privileges such as attendance at conferences. Many organizations even structure these informal rewards: providing special titles, on-the-spot bonuses and various other kinds of recognition. To the outsider, such rewards may appear hollow, but those on the inside really aspire to win them.

### Organizational Folklore

People in the organization are consistently trying to interpret why it is the way it is. One of the most common ways of doing this is by telling stories that capture important aspects of its character. The thesis that folklore makes an important contribution to an organization's shared values is supported by recent academic research.[2] A study contrasting two organizations found employee commitment higher in the one in which employees could tell a lot of organizational stories.

### Structure and Systems

Organizations that are guided by strong shared values also tend to reflect these values in the design of their formal organization. The most readily recognizable case is the organization oriented to tight control of costs. Generally, its finance officer will be a leading member of the top management group. Almost always, its dominant management systems will be those for budget development and operational control, and even its long-range planning will be geared to the needs of financial control.

By and large, the most successful managers are precisely those who strive to make a mark through creating a guiding vision, shaped shared values, and otherwise providing leadership for the people with whom they work.

### Risks and Pitfalls

The power of values is that people—at least some people—care about them. This power can be a problem as well as a source of strength. If a manager chooses to build or reinforce the shared values of the group of people he/she works with, he/she had better recognize the risks being assumed.

Although there are serious risks in tampering with the shared value system of a state or local government, there are also rewards if it is done right. Organizations with strong shared values seem universally to be outstanding performers as long as the values are relevant to environmental conditions. Those with the strongest track records, in fact, seem to be just the organizations whose operative values are most directly relevant to the performance of key competitive functions. When the environment changes and the objectives of the key functions change, the shared values can get in the way until they are reshaped.

### Deciding Priorities

If shared values influence behavior as powerfully as we have asserted, then managers can hardly afford not to be concerned with them. All the same, it is clear that the task of shaping shared values can't always head the top manager's agenda. When should the values get special priority? Experience suggests at least four situations in which top management should consider shaping shared values as something close to its most important mission:

- When the environment is undergoing fundamental change and the organization has always been highly value driven
- When the situation is highly competitive

- When the organization is mediocre or worse
- When the organization is truly on the threshold of becoming the very best

## PURSUING A VALUE-SHAPING PROGRAM

If a top manager decides to place the value-shaping task high on his/her list of priorities, how should he/she pursue it? Today's manager knows how to control operations, how to evaluate a capital improvement proposal, how to recruit fresh management talent and how to deal with regulatory agencies, but what does he/she do to shape values? To begin with, the manager gives it as much attention as any other truly top-priority task—which is to say, a lot. He/she puts shared values at the center of the agenda and consciousness, not in the "get-to-it-as-soon-as-possible" category.

Often the first step a top manager takes to shape shared values is to begin talking about them with closest colleagues. He/she explores with them the role shared values can play in an excellent organization, the state of the organization's current values and the ways in which they need to be reinforced, reinterpreted or reviewed. These conversations have two aims: to gain collective commitment to the idea that a strong set of shared values is to be a principal legacy of this particular top team and to forge a common understanding of the specific values to be pursued.

Soon after taking this first step, value-shaping top managers look for ways to reach down into their organizations to establish the importance of the chosen values. Almost invariably, they spend an unusually high proportion of their time "in the field" making contact with as many people as possible in the organization. In addition, many look for relatively structured devices for focusing attention on shared values. For example, an executive might conduct a series of seminars for down-the-line managers—several levels down—to demonstrate the economics underlying the overriding need for cost control, particularly as expressed in high staff utilization and low support costs, and describe the implications of these values for everyday management practice and for tough decisions.

Special management initiatives such as this go a long way toward dramatizing the values that a management team aims at establishing or reinforcing, but they are not enough unless the day-to-day behavior of the value-shaping manager reflects his/her concern with the importance of key values. People are interested by what a person says he/she values, but they are really convinced only by what he/she does. What counts is rarely the single dramatic act but the consistency of a pattern of behavior over time.

Down-the-line managers are constantly analyzing the behavior of their superiors, and their peers, for that matter, to figure out what they really care about, what they really expect, and what they really will accept. The manager who would shape values turns this reality into his/her advantage.

All this is to say that top managers who would shape values must consistently and continuously regard themselves not only as deciders, controllers or doers, but also as symbolic leaders, sending signals by their behaviors. This view of the manager's job flies in the face of much current management mythology, but it is consistent with the realities that have been observed: the reality of followers who continuously scrutinize and interpret top-management behavior, and the reality of successful value-shaping leaders.

## SUMMARY

Shared values are powerful influencers of organizational performance, and determined manager-leaders can shape and reinforce them in important ways. One reservation, however, may remain. Our society today suffers from a pervasive uncertainty about values, a relativism that undermines leadership and commitment alike. Who today really does know what is right? On the philosophical level, we find ourselves without convincing responses. But the everyday state or local government world is quite different. Even if ultimate values are ephemeral, particular values do clearly make sense for specific organizations operating in specific circumstances.

Choices must be made, and values are an indispensable guide in making them. Moreover, it is equally clear that actual organizations have, in fact, gained great strength from shared values. Perhaps because ultimate values seem so elusive, people do respond positively to practical values that give life in the organization some sense of meaning. And that considerably eases the task of value-shaping managers as they strive to "make meaning" for the employees in the organization. Instead of encountering resistance, they can usually expect to meet with respect and support as contributors in some distinctive way to the larger society.

## NOTES

1. Julian R. Phillips and Allan A. Kennedy, "Shaping and Managing Shared Values," Staff Paper, McKinsey & Company, United Kingdom, December 1980, pp. 1–55.

2. Alan Wilkins, "Organizational Stories as an Expression of Management Philosophy," Ph.D. dissertation, Stanford University, Palo Alto, California, 1978.

# 7

# Employee Involvement Processes

"None of us is as smart as all of us."

—Anonymous

Employee involvement processes are approaches for voluntarily involving people at all levels in an organization in decisions and problem solving, often in their normal workplace, that will contribute to better quality, more productive work and cost-reduction ideas. Employee involvement processes are not panaceas for solving all of an organization's productivity, cost savings or quality problems. They can, however, be of significant value in increasing morale, enriching jobs, motivating people, tapping people's unused knowledge, increasing quality and productivity at work and reducing costs.

Employee involvement processes in the form of Quality Circles were invented in the United States in the 1950s, but at that time, they were never utilized to any significant extent. They were first adopted in Japan in 1962. Their first major implementation in the United States was in 1974 by the Lockheed Missiles and Space Company in Sunnyvale, California. As Terry Brandt, assistant city manager/municipal services, Laguna Beach, California, has said: "Other countries are now passing us by in terms of real productivity growth, which should provide the impetus for a close look at our current management practices. By no means are Quality Circles the answer to all of our problems, but the evidence is there to justify attempts to apply the concepts."

This chapter will define and describe employee involvement processes. It will also discuss their use in a typical organization and discuss the results achieved by them in a few organizations that have already implemented them. The use of one type of employee involvement process, Quality Circles, increased significantly among many organizations, both public and private, during the 1980s, as the need to reduce cost and increase productivity in the American economy became more pronounced. They were followed in the late 1980s by self-managed teams, cross-functional teams, total quality management (TQM) and flatter organizations. They will most likely be followed in the 1990s and beyond by the adaptive organization in which most employees will be regularly brought together in task teams to deal with problems or accomplish tasks.

## BACKGROUND

There has been a history of "bottom-up" employee involvement starting as early as 1890 when the German optical company Zeiss involved employees in problem-solving groups in its optical manufacturing organization. This was followed in the 1920s by the Hawthorne studies at the Western Electric Company, which proved that paying attention to employees, not increases in lighting, affects productivity in a positive fashion.

These efforts were followed in the 1930s with work simplification and in the 1940s with statistical quality control. In the 1950s, Abraham Maslow's work indicated that it is important to deal with employees' needs. In the 1960s, Frederick Herzberg said that it is important to deal with employee dissatisfiers. Rensis Likert said that participative managers achieve higher productivity and have a more highly motivated workforce.

In the 1970s, quality of work life programs were implemented and in the 1980s, Quality Circles and Deming's methods became the approaches most used to involve employees in increased productivity. As previously mentioned, the 1990s will be the decade of self-managed teams; toward the end of the decade and beyond, the adaptive organization will come into vogue. Most of the recent heavy emphasis on employee involvement has come from the impact that Japan has had on the U.S. public and private sectors and on American management practices. As Pogo has said, "We have met the enemy and he is us!"

## WHAT ARE FOREIGN MANAGERS DOING THAT WE AREN'T DOING?

What are private and public managers in foreign countries, specifically Japan, doing differently than American managers? Why are their operations consistently more productive than ours?

During the 1960s and 1970s, a number of new theories of management were being espoused by a group of management theorists known as "behavioralists." This group consisted of such individuals as Douglas Mc-

Gregor, Rensis Likert, David McClelland, Frederick Herzberg, Abraham Maslow, Warren Bennis and others. The management theories that these individuals recommend systematically and realistically involve employees at all levels in an organization in significant decisions affecting their organizations. Some of these theories were applied in practice in managerial situations, and, in most cases, significant positive results, including improved productivity, were achieved. As is true of many things developed in this country, foreign managers, particularly the Japanese, took many of these behavioral management concepts and applied them in their countries most effectively.

The concepts included Maslow's Needs Hierarchy, Herzberg's Two-Factor Theory about employees' attitudes toward their jobs, McGregor's Theory X and Y, and Likert's Systems 1–4. A brief explanation of some of these managerial theories follows.

*Theory X*: Assumes that the average human has inherent dislike for work and will avoid it if possible.

*Theory Y*: Assumes that

- Expenditures of physical and mental effort is as natural as play and rest
- External control and threat of punishment are not the only means for accomplishing organizational objectives
- Commitment to organizational objectives is a function of the associated rewards
- Average humans learn to accept and seek responsibility
- Capacity to exercise imagination, ingenuity and creativity is widely distributed in the population
- Intellectual capabilities of humans are only partially being utilized

According to Douglas McGregor, "Theory Y people are fundamentally hard-working, responsible and need only to be supported and encouraged."

Rensis Likert's approach was to identify management practices as Systems 1–4, with System 1 being very autocratic and System 4 being participative. Likert's research concluded that American business and government organizations are both currently operating on the average at System 2.5. He also concluded that an organization can gain productivity improvements of 10 percent to 40 percent as it moves closer to System 4 from System 2.5.

Another theory of management being espoused in the 1980s was "Theory Z." It is described in the book on Japanese management practices authored by William Ouchi.[1] According to Ouchi, Theory Z is a special way of managing people, a style that focuses on a strong organizational-entity philosophy, distinct corporate culture, long-range staff development and consensus decision making. Results that have been achieved via the use of Theory Z management include lower employee turnover, increased job commitment and dramatically higher productivity.

According to Ouchi, there are separate and distinct organization types A and J. Type A equates to the typical American organization. Similarly Type J is equivalent to the typical Japanese organization. Type A organizations are represented by heterogeneity, mobility, individualism, people linking tenuously to each other and intimacy rarely being achieved. In a typical Type A organization, top management may be heavily committed to long-term organizational goals, but that commitment may decrease markedly as one moves downward in the organization to middle management and to rank and file employees.

Type J organizations, on the other hand, are represented by homogeneity, stability, collectivism and individual behavior meshing intimately together. In a typical Type J organization, personnel at all levels throughout the organization are frequently just as heavily committed to the overall goals of the organization as is top management. The contrasts between Type A and J organizations are presented in Exhibit 7–1.

**Exhibit 7–1**
**Contrasts between Japanese (Type "J") and American (Type "A") Organizations**

| (Type "J")<br>*Japanese Organizations* | (Type "A")<br>*American Organizations* |
|---|---|
| Lifetime employment | Short-term employment |
| Slow evaluation and promotion | Rapid evaluation and promotion |
| Promotion from within | Hiring from outside |
| Non-specialized career paths | Specialized career paths |
| Implicit control mechanisms | Explicit control mechanisms |
| Collective decision making | Individual decision making |
| Collective responsibility | Individual responsibility |
| Holistic concern | Segmented concern |
| High concern for quality | Allowance of "acceptable quality level" and planned obsolescence |

Essentially, foreign managers consistently

- Display significant determination
- Demand responsibility from their employees up and down the line
- Provide "continuous learning" opportunities for all employees
- Provide realistic ways for employees to be involved in decision making (e.g., employee involvement processes)

- Structure employee benefits according to need
- Take more seriously the value of product or service to the customer
- Systematically and purposefully abandon the old, the outworn and the obsolete (including plant and equipment, as well as ideas, practices and attitudes)
- Clearly separate for measurement areas of short- and long-term results
- See themselves as national policymakers

Japanese workers are so highly motivated that they often run physically from work position to work position and to and from work breaks.

German managers make effective use of a highly skilled senior worker or "meister" as a teacher, assistant or standard-setter instead of "boss." The biggest single factor in the foreign manager's phenomenal success, however, is the realistic and systematic involvement of employees at all levels in decision making affecting their organization.

## IMPROVING PRODUCTIVITY AND REDUCING COST

In his book *Improving Total Productivity*, Paul Mali says that mathematically there are only five ways to increase productivity:

1. Doing more with the same resources
2. Doing the same with less resources
3. Doing more with less resources
4. Doing considerably more with slightly more resources
5. Doing slightly less with considerably less resources[2]

We also know that there are only two ways to reduce cost: reduce present cost and/or avoid future cost. We know that greater productivity contributes to a better standard of living, enhances ability to compete in a world economy and leads to a strengthened national currency position. Lower productivity, on the other hand, contributes to inflation, a less competitive economy and a weakened national currency position.

Business, labor and government have all played a part in poor productivity performance. Public and private sector managers have the greatest purview for improving productivity, but not nearly enough is currently being done.

### How Do We Improve Productivity and Reduce Cost?

There are no "snake oils" or "magic elixirs" that will help improve productivity or reduce cost in the American economy and there are few quick processes for correcting such a long-evolving situation. (TAN-STAAFL—"There ain't no such thing as a free lunch!") The "old shoes are comfortable" attitude won't get it anymore. Sure, we can stick our heads in the sand like an ostrich and hope the problem will go away, or we can say BOHICA (Bend over, here it comes again!) and take our punishment like we did when we erred in elementary school. It is always tougher to fight back, but it is one of the best techniques for building strength, character and, in turn, better managers. As Robert Frost said, "Selecting the road less traveled by made all the difference."

In terms of increasing productivity and reducing cost, there are three approaches that can be used by state and local governments. These are (1) the selective use of technology, (2) better management systems and industrial engineering techniques and (3) more effective utilization of human resources. All of these approaches are interdependent.

Technology contributes more to improved productivity and reduced cost by a factor of 72 percent than any other approach. This is because it basically substitutes capital for labor. Technology might include the selective use of robots in areas that are hazardous to humans, new computer applications or word processing systems. Management systems and industrial engineering approaches might include energy conservation techniques, alternative work methods or optimal routing of service vehicles. But in the 1990s and beyond, the real productivity and cost reduction payoff for state and local governments may be in the human resources area. Finding new ways to enrich jobs, motivate people, involve them in decision making and, through these approaches and others, increase human productivity may be the most effective approach.

There are four assumptions that can be made about people in their workplace: (1) people want to contribute, (2) people are experts at their own jobs, (3) their expertise should be tapped, and (4) if they are properly tapped, better decisions and actions will result.

Money is still an important motivator of people, particularly in lower levels of an organization. However, realistically setting goals with subordinates and providing them with regular feedback can increase productivity (on the average) by 15 to 18 percent. Enriching employee jobs can increase the productivity of a group by 10 to 12 percent. Combining these approaches with a realistic employee group participation program can increase productivity 20 to 50 percent. If these impressive gains are combined with the selective use of technology and management systems, enormous gains in productivity in selective operations may be possible. But if state and local government management is to be effective in the human resource area during the next decade, archaic attitudes need to be changed, and behavior at all levels within the organization, including management levels, may need to be modified. As one witch said to another, "I'm giving up spells and going into behavior modification."

Any improved human resource program must be designed to overcome employee mistrust. Four proven techniques for management to use in overcoming employee mistrust include (1) consistent approach, (2) sharing information, (3) honest involvement, and (4) goal setting and feedback.

The most important single element in any plan to improve organizational productivity and achieve cost reduction, however, is top-management commitment. If improved productivity and cost reduction are to be achieved on a consistent and long-term basis, management must "pay the price" by significantly committing itself to such a clearly defined goal.

## QUALITY CIRCLES: AN INTRODUCTION

As has been discussed, a systematic approach that worked well in the 1980s for involving employees in decisions affecting their workplace is the concept of using Quality Circles.[3] Quality Circles have been extensively used in Japan where millions of workers participate in them. In fact, they are being used so extensively in Japan that it is estimated that four of every five Japanese worker participates in them. During the 1980s, Quality Circles gained widespread acceptance in American industry, business and government as ways of improving productivity and quality in diverse organizations. Much was learned from them to propel us into a new wave of employee involvement processes in the 1990s and beyond. Therefore, it is important to understand them.

### The Quality Circle Approach in Japan

The quality circle process in Japan was developed and aimed specifically at the foreman and production-worker levels. The Japanese started the first circle in 1962. Today, more than 11 million people in Japan are actively involved in Quality Circles, and, because not all Quality Circles are registered as they originally were intended to be, this estimate may, in fact, be conservative.

The growth of Quality Circles outside Japan and their development in the West were fairly slow. One main reason for this was that people in the West tended to believe that Quality Circles reflected something very unique to Japanese culture and, therefore, wouldn't work outside Japan. Another reason was the communications barrier. Not very much had been written about Quality Circles, and what was written was in Japanese and was not translated.

In addition, industry outside Japan did not regard the Japanese as significant competitors in the world market. The Japanese had been brushed aside because of their previous reputation for poor quality goods and because of their virtually having to start production from scratch after the Second World War. No one was concerned about Japan until the Japanese started making inroads into the world market. Now, of course, the reputation of Japanese goods—at least in certain areas—is excellent. Such products as Sony televisions are regarded as top quality, the best available in the world. This did not happen overnight; it took much training and education.

### Implementation of Quality Circles in the United States

The Lockheed Missiles and Space Company in California was the first U.S. company to use Quality Circles, beginning in 1974. Lockheed sent people to Japan to study the concept and how the Japanese were doing their work. These individuals returned, having decided that Quality Circles did have possibilities outside Japan and could work at Lockheed.

Between 1974 and 1979, the use of Quality Circles grew slowly. By 1979, approximately 150 U.S. companies had developed them. At the end of 1980, perhaps 300 to 500 companies had ongoing Quality Circle processes, and current estimates are that ten to twenty times that number are in place today.

Quality Circles may be described as

• Effective concepts for improving quality and/or productivity in any work environment
• Employee-involvement processes and philosophies
• Participative management approaches
• Problem-solving techniques

Quality Circles consist of people who contribute intelligence and creativity to solving problems affecting the work they do. For their efforts, employees receive training in the operation of Quality Circles, recognition and trust of their management and a greater awareness of the importance of their work to the organization as a whole.

### Objectives of Quality Circles

Quality Circle processes may have several objectives, including improved productivity, improved quality of products and services, improved people development approaches, participative management promotional techniques, improved quality of work life, improved relations between management and labor, improved decision making and improved communications throughout the organization.

Almost any activity in which group problem solving can be of value can be an objective of a Quality Circle process. The only caution is to be certain that Quality Circles are being utilized to their fullest positive potential, rather than as a means of facilitating something questionable that management wants to drive home with employees.

## What Constitutes Quality Circles and How Are They Organized?

As was mentioned earlier, a typical Quality Circle consists of a small group of volunteers, ideally seven to eight persons; it could consist of two to fifteen persons. The size of the circle will probably depend upon the size of the organization, the nature of the work being performed in the area in which the circles are to be implemented, the size of normal work groups and other factors. The circle should consist of persons who perform similar work such as might be found in a typical accounting office, work crews, a maintenance shop, and so forth. The Quality Circle concept is flexible enough, however, that it can be used with management personnel or with personnel from diverse groups.

Quality Circles should meet regularly and on state or local government time. If the circles must meet during off-hours, overtime or compensatory time should be paid to circle members. In the beginning phases of a Quality Circle process, the circles should probably meet weekly. Later on, after a number of problems have been solved, it may be more appropriate for them to meet less frequently, perhaps biweekly or monthly. The circle leader may be the group's normal work leader, such as a foreman or supervisor. It is also possible for circle members to select their own leader from among their group. This could be accomplished by a vote of the circle members.

One of the most important aspects of Quality Circle activity is the training circle members receive in problem analysis, solution development, management presentations and solution implementation. To be truly effective, this training must be in-depth and continuous.

## What Do Quality Circles Do?

Quality Circles basically have four main functions:

1. To identify and analyze causes of problems affecting the circle members' workplace
2. To determine appropriate solutions to these problems
3. To recommend solutions to management
4. To implement approved situations when possible

Quality Circles are just as effective in service or governmental organizations as they have been in industry. They are also equally as effective in the maintenance department, as the office, with white-collar or blue-collar employees and with sophisticated or unsophisticated organizations.

### What Are Quality Circles Called?

Do Quality Circles always have to be called "Quality Circles"? Not at all. They have been and continue to be called by other names such as teams, inner circles, management committees, employee involvement groups, productivity teams and problem-solving teams or groups. The most important thing is not so much what you call a Quality Circle process but that it really is a Quality Circle process. It should have all of the elements of a true Quality Circle process. It cannot be an employee suggestion program that one renames or an altered scheme that fits the needs of management.

### What Are the Major Elements of a Quality Circle Process?

There are at least five, and possibly six, major elements of any good Quality Circle process, depending on the size and level of sophistication of the organization contemplating its use. Each of these key Quality Circle components is described below.

1. *Circle members*. From two to fifteen employee volunteers who normally work together on a day-to-day basis and who meet regularly to identify, solve and implement solutions to problems affecting their workplace.

2. *Circle leaders*. The employees' normal work leader, such as a foreman or supervisor, or any other person elected by the circle members themselves or appointed by management. The circle leader is responsible for the operation of the Quality Circle and for continuous training of circle members. The leader must be trained in various elements of leadership and must work very closely with the facilitator.

3. *Facilitator(s)*. In the early stages of implementing a Quality Circle process, the facilitator may be an outside consultant or an in-house training officer, personnel director or staff or line person who has been charged with the responsibility for the Quality Circle facilitation role. After the Quality Circle process is operational, the facilitator role should definitely shift from an outside consultant to an in-house individual. The facilitator is responsible for maintaining Quality Circle process operation, working closely with the steering committee to receive its policy direction and to keep it informed of the circle process, training circle members and leaders, coordinating circle operations, providing coordination between circles and other elements of the organization and maintaining records of projects, meetings and circle activity.

Desirable facilitator qualities include an appreciation for people, an understanding of the role of a teacher or coach, the ability to interpret information and situations and, very importantly, the ability to remain neutral during Quality Circle operations. In very large state and local government organizations or in a highly developed and sophisticated Quality Circle process, there may be appointed an overall Quality Circle coordinator who would be a manager of the circle process and would be placed between the steering committee and one or more facilitators. This person would report to the steering committee and would be responsible for the overall total Quality Circle operation. In smaller organizations, the facilitator may act as the overall Quality Circle process coordinator. After experience has been gained, a good facilitator should be able to handle up to ten Quality Circles.

4. *Steering committee.* This committee of no more than fifteen persons is established for the purpose of providing overall policy guidance to the Quality Circle process. It may consist of the heads or representatives of major departments, divisions or functions within the organization. In smaller organizations, this committee may consist of all of the middle management in the organization. The steering committee is responsible for establishing overall Quality Circle process objectives and for providing resources to the process, the facilitator(s) and the circles themselves. This committee should meet regularly with the facilitator(s) to provide guidance and direction to the process and to keep track of circle progress. The committee should make evaluations and decisions about when and how to expand and incorporate Quality Circles throughout the organization. Representatives of the steering committee should always attend management presentations when circles are proposing solutions to work problems.

5. *Management.* This is a top manager and could include his/her assistants. This is the person or group who must commit the organization to the Quality Circle concept, who must give the concept nurturement, resources and time to grow and evolve and to whom the Quality Circles present their proposed problem solutions.

6. *Non-member employees.* These are individuals who are not presently serving as a part of the Quality Circle organization. Non-member employees may be neighboring department or division employees and/or individuals such as librarians who may perform literature searches for the circles or industrial engineers who may get quotes or other equipment, material or supply information for the circles, and so on. Non-member employees are extremely important to the success of the Quality Circle process. They need to be kept informed, receive some training in Quality Circle operations and not be allowed to be "outside critics" of the Quality Circle process.

### How Do Quality Circles Operate?

Most Quality Circles operate in a manner similar to the fifteen-step process outlined below. These steps are sequential and crucial to the logical evolution of any good Quality Circle process.

1. *Have management commitment.* This must be realistic and believable, it cannot be "lip service." It must be properly communicated throughout the organization. This does not mean that the top manager is abdicating decision making and authority to groups of people. He/she can still retain the final "say so." It means a commitment to let others participate in making decisions that affect them.

2. *Set goals.* Overall strategy goals for the Quality Circle process must be established with the involvement of all levels of management and workers up and down the organizational hierarchy. To be effective, these goals must be agreed upon at all levels within the organization. Middle management and organized labor are particularly key. If they aren't properly and systematically involved and committed to the Quality Circle philosophy, they can sabotage the process.

3. *Develop plans.* Proper planning is crucial to any managerial activity; development and implementation of an effective Quality Circle process is no exception. This should be a general plan for how the Quality Circle process will operate and will fit in with the rest of the organization. It should include enough specifics to answer most questions raised by persons within the organization. It should act as a blueprint of steps to be taken in developing the Quality Circle process, and it should include checkpoints along the way to measure progress and provide feedback to top management.

4. *Establish Quality Circle organization.* Establish a Quality Circle steering committee, select an overall process coordinator, select a facilitator(s), establish the circle(s) itself and select (or assist the circles in selecting) their leader(s). A decision should be made at this point as to whether to begin the process on a pilot basis in one department or area, or organization wide. Most experts suggest beginning with a pilot process in one division or department and gradually expanding it to other areas. In smaller organizations, a steering committee may not be necessary. Middle management can serve as the steering committee in smaller organizations.

5. *Train participants and leaders.* This may be the most important of the fifteen steps in the Quality Circle process. It is not a one-time thing. To be successful, Quality Circle training must be continuous. Considerably more on this important step in the Quality Circle process will be discussed later in this chapter. But generally all participants are taught overall concepts of the process. The steering committee, the overall process coordinator, the facilitator(s) and the circle leader(s) are rehearsed in techniques of group process (facilitation). The overall circle coordinator, facilitator(s), circle leader(s) and the circle members are all taught methods of group problem identification, prioritization, analysis and solution, as well as techniques of management presentation and solution implementation. This is not a "one-shot deal." The training must be conducted regularly and systematically to be effective.

6. *Identify problems.* Various group process techniques, such as brainstorming, may be used by the circles to identify problems for the circle to work on. After considerable experience has been developed within the Quality Circles, use of slightly more sophisticated processes such as nominal group technique, Delphi technique or interpretative structural modeling may be used.[4] These same

techniques may be used to select problems from a group and to rank priorities. Personal, personnel, grievance, wage, salary, fringe benefit and similar problems should be avoided by the Quality Circles. The problem identification process should concentrate on those significant problems affecting quality of work, cost reduction and productivity in the day-to-day work place. Management may suggest problems to the circle for its consideration, or experts from outside the circle, such as industrial engineers (within or outside the organization) may suggest problems. *It must be made clear, however, that these are only suggestions. They are not management edicts!* It must be remembered, too, that the product that will eventually be produced by the circle is a "group effort," not an individual effort. Each circle member is responsible for the overall functioning and progress of the circle. Therefore, teamwork within the circle is very important.

7. *Rank problems*. Techniques such as the nominal group technique (NGT) should be used by Quality Circles to rank the importance of problems. This should not be the leader's ranking or a ranking issued by top management but should be a product of the Quality Circle members themselves.

8. *Select the problem*. Members of the Quality Circle, not management, should select the problem that they wish to work on.

9. *Analyze the problem*. This is the major area in which the training received by the circle members really begins to pay off. Various techniques such as cause and effect[5] and Pareto analysis[6] are used to analyze the problem and clearly determine its cause(s). Outside specialists such as industrial engineers, statisticians, systems analysts, consultants and so on can be of significant value as sources of expert advice to the Quality Circle members. Literature searches can be requested from outside specialists such as librarians or data specialists.

10. *Develop a solution*. Once the problem has been thoroughly analyzed, the next step is to develop a solution, if possible. Outside resources previously discussed may be of value in this step, as well. Design of new equipment or modifications to existing equipment, layouts, systems and procedures may be necessary. Enough detail about the proposed solution to the problem needs to be developed by the circle members so that they can present the proposal to management.

11. *Make a presentation to management*. This is another step in which previous training for Quality Circle members pays off. Members or a selected member of the circle makes a presentation to top management describing the problem and its proposed solution. Various audiovisual presentation techniques such as flip charts, chalk boards, viewgraphs, 35mm slides, videos, and so on are often used during the presentation. This is the "big payoff" for circle members in that they are given an opportunity to gain recognition from top management. Management needs to listen patiently and attentively to the presentation and should not try to dominate the session. The presentations will usually consist of an identification of the problem, possible solutions and a recommended solution.

12. *Allow time for management review*. This step might normally last about two weeks but depends on local needs. It gives management a chance to review

the problem and the proposed solution, to reflect on them and to consider an alternative course of action.

13. *Decide to implement or reject.* At this point, top management reaches a decision to implement the recommended solution to the problem or reject it. The decision is communicated back to the circle via the circle leader. If the decision is to reject the recommendation of the Quality Circle, it is particularly important for top management to communicate to the circle all of the rationale for the rejection. This is particularly crucial for credibility in future work with that circle, its spin-off to other Quality Circles and the seriousness with which the circles will continue to pursue the program in the future.

14. *Implement the solution.* If top management decides to implement the solution recommended by the Quality Circle (or some modification of it), the Quality Circle that originally solved the problem has the responsibility to implement it. Management must provide appropriate resources to the circle to implement the solution, must hold the circle accountable for implementation and must get out of the way and let the circle implement it.

15. *Evaluate program.* If the plan prepared in step 3 has been developed properly, this step will be relatively easy to accomplish. The basic idea is to build check points into the plan and to evaluate actual accomplishments in accordance with planned accomplishments. Evaluation is very important to the success of a Quality Circle process as the Hawthorne Experiments of Western Electric proved several decades ago. If groups of workers know they are being evaluated, that knowledge in and of itself will place enough emphasis on the work of the group that the group's productivity will be significantly improved.

### Quality Circle Training

After management commitment, proper training of managers, particularly middle managers, employees and, when appropriate, union representatives, in some or all aspects of Quality Circles (QC) is crucial to the success of the QC process. Training cannot be just a one-time thing. To be effective, it must be regular and continuous. After initial training is completed, more advanced training will be received. Later, refresher courses will also be necessary.

Training may be both formal and informal. It may occur during classroom or seminar sessions, during circle meetings, on the job, at home, through practical participation, or more likely, through a combination of all of these methods.

Success with Quality Circle processes does not require substantial organizational changes, but it does require changes in the *culture* of the organization.[7] It is difficult, if not impossible, to purchase cultural change, but it can be learned. That is where training comes in. If training is to be done properly, however, it must be given the necessary time, resources, commitments and support from management and employees alike.

Six distinct areas of training are needed. These are top and middle management (both line and staff), first-line foremen and supervisors (both line and staff), facilitator(s), circle leader(s), circle members and staff support personnel who are not members of the circles.

Quality Circles are not systems or packages that can be purchased. Developing and evolving Quality Circles is an organizational development process. Proper QC training must be both technical and interpersonal and must address the following four skill areas: (1) group dynamics and group process, (2) information gathering and problem analysis, (3) decision making and presentations and (4) solution implementation and reinforcement of change.

The first order of business is proper training for the facilitator(s) and managers. This training should last approximately forty hours[8] and should include items such as the following:

- Experiential exercises
- Theory and practical information about Quality Circles
- Group dynamics
- Communications
- Quality Circle organization
- Teaching and coaching methods
- Quality Circle techniques
- Measurement of progress
- Volunteer group leadership
- Themes and problems

This training can be conducted in-house by an outside consultant, by sending selected personnel to seminars especially designed for this purpose, by having staff members do thorough research and preparation or by combinations of these approaches.

Once the facilitator(s) has been trained, he/she (or they) in turn often train the circle leader(s), who in turn train the circle members. The following are subjects in which circle members are instructed:

- Principles of brainstorming
- Problem-solving techniques including "cause and effect" analysis
- Statistical sampling and analysis techniques
- Knowledge of some industrial engineering and operations research approaches
- Pareto diagrams and histograms
- Management presentations
- Case study analysis and preparation

The circle leader training should encompass at least twenty-four hours. Circle member training may be conducted during the first fifteen to thirty minutes of each circle meeting, although some training prior to circle operations is recommended. Length of training varies depending on the size, needs and complexity of the implementing organization. As mentioned earlier, considerable attention should be paid to middle manager's training to ensure that this group supports the Quality Circle concept.

### Time and Cost of a Quality Circle Process

It is important to make a substantive enough management commitment to the implementation of a Quality Circle process so that it has time to grow, mature and prove its value in reducing cost, improving quality and/ or productivity to the organization. The city government of Dallas, Texas, as an example, initially made at least a three-year commitment to development and operation of Quality Circles.

A schedule of the assessment, planning and implementation of a typical Quality Circle process is shown in Exhibit 7–2. Although these phases could overlap somewhat, the assessment phase covers approximately nine weeks. This is followed by a twelve-week planning phase and a nine-week implementation phase. Most organizations that have implemented Quality Circles are of the opinion that at least six months and possibly longer are required before positive results from the circles begin to be seen. It is usually not advisable to measure Quality Circle progress too quickly. After two to three years of successful operation, cost/benefit ratios of as much as 1:5 or 1:8 have been documented by Quality Circle users, indicating very successful processes.

**Exhibit 7–2**
**Schedule for Implementation of a Typical Quality Circle Process**

| No. | Activity | Weeks |
|-----|----------|-------|
| | A. *Assessment Phase (9 weeks total)* | |
| 1. | Selected manager to Quality Circles seminar | 1 |
| 2. | Assessment by management | 2 |
| 3. | Selection of employee assessment committee | 2 |
| 4. | Visit to active circle program | 1 |
| 5. | Recommendation by committee | 3 |
| | B. *Planning Phase (12 weeks total)* | |
| 6. | Selection of facilitator(s) | 9 |
| 7. | Preparation of visual aids | 7 |
| 8. | Introduction of QCs to employees | 2 |

C. *Implementation Phase (9 + weeks)*

9.   Announcement of initial QCs                        1
10.  Selection of leaders                               1
11.  Training of leaders/facilitators                   1
12.  Selection of steering committee                    3
13.  Start-up training of circles                       7

Joseph Hanley, "Our Experience with Quality Circles," *Quality Progress*, February 1980, p. 23.

Cost of a Quality Circle process can range from a few thousand to tens of thousands of dollars. The cost depends on such things as the size of the organization, the size of the Quality Circle process, who does the training, use of in-house versus outside resources, and so on. There have been a few cases for which the cost/benefit ratio (after an appropriate period of evolution has occurred) has been other than significantly positive.

### What Do Circle Members Like about Quality Circles?

Listed below are some of the things that Quality Circle members like about their involvement in Quality Circles:

- Discussing and solving problems as a team
- Using QC techniques to solve problems and present their solutions
- Getting experts such as engineers outside their organization interested in their problems and working with them
- Having freedom to express themselves
- Influencing decisions about their work
- Meeting and working with management
- Obtaining recognition
- Reducing conflicts in their work environment

### Potential Problems in Implementing Quality Circles

Some of the potential problems[9] with Quality Circles include the following:

- Insufficient and visible management support
- Inadequate leader preparation
- Perception of management manipulation
- Process grows too fast or too slow
- Insufficient internal publicity of process (or too much)

- Failure of circles to keep management informed
- Insufficient training of all participants
- Failure to involve properly unions (as appropriate), middle management and peripheral organizations
- Starting to work on problems too soon
- Interruption or takeover by other groups
- Overexpectations by circle members or management
- Overemphasis on quick financial returns or productivity increases
- Working out details with existing employee suggestion or similar programs
- Failure of previous processes
- Poor management response to circle recommendations
- Taking on problems that are too difficult for the circle to solve
- Scheduling difficulties
- Too much or too little facilitation
- Poor recordkeeping
- Meeting too frequently or not regularly

### What Are the Advantages of Quality Circles?

Listed below are some of the advantages of utilizing Quality Circles in a typical organization:

- Improve quality and cost awareness
- Require little or no change in organizational structure
- Are educational and work-related
- Offer rewards in the work itself
- Are flexible, adaptable to any organization
- Improve communications
- Reduce conflicts
- Link all levels and functions of the organization together

### Quality Circle Implementation Checklist (√)

A checklist for implementing Quality Circles in any organization is shown below:

(√) Introduction and orientation
(√) Thorough knowledge of concept
(√) Management support and commitment
(√) Carefully developed plan

(√) Training of leaders and members

(√) Operation

(√) Monitoring progress and measuring results

The Quality Circle process is only one of several employee involvement processes that state and local governments can utilize to assist in dealing with the cost/revenue squeeze that they face. However, Quality Circles do offer an illustration of how to set up and operate an employee involvement process on a formal basis in an organization. Many state and local governments used such processes during the 1980s and many continue to do so.

### Other Forms of Employee Involvement

Other forms of employee involvement include self-managed teams, which could be a take-off on the Quality Circle approach, as could cross-functional teams. The City of Hampton, Virginia (see chapter 11 for a case study) has used the employee involvement process of self-managed teams quite effectively. Self-managed teams usually work most effectively when they focus on a specific task or issue.

Gainsharing processes include everything from the Scanlon and Rucker plans, which are basically individual suggestion programs, to Improshare, which can be an individual or group cost savings sharing process, to QUEST (Quality Utilizing Employees, Systems and Technology). QUEST combines Quality Circles and group gainsharing concepts and basically gains the pluses from both of these two approaches.

The adaptive organization, which is the employee involvement process of the 1990s and beyond, significantly flattens out the traditional hierarchical organization and uses teams of employees specifically selected to address specific tasks or strategic issues. When a task is completed, the team dissolves and another team, perhaps of different employees, is formed around another key issue. In large organizations, the computer is used to track employees and their skills and to match them to the needs of the organization. The biggest problem with the adaptive organization is determining how to evaluate and reward employees in this flattened type of organizational structure. But good managers are working on it. The 1990s will be the decade when state and local government managers make more use of the adaptive organization.

### EMPLOYEE INVOLVEMENT PROCESSES (EIPs): AN INTRODUCTION AND BRIEF HISTORY

EIPs in the form of Quality Circles stated in Japan in 1962. Around the time of World War II, Japanese products had a reputation for poor quality. A "made in Japan" label usually meant that a product was a cheaply made imitation that wasn't going to last very long but could be inexpensively purchased. After World War II, the Japanese realized that if they were going to survive and enhance their position in world markets, they would have to improve their quality reputation. They made some very basic decisions, one of which was to make improved quality their top national priority. They took several deliberate steps to support that decision.

In the years following the war and, to a degree, in cooperation with the U.S. Occupational Forces, the Japanese developed and reinforced quality standards. They also brought a number of quality experts to Japan, many from the United States. Two were particularly influential in helping the Japanese change their quality image. One was Dr. Edward Deming; the other was Dr. Joseph Juran. Dr. Deming was invited to Japan sometime in 1947 or 1948, and he essentially introduced the concept of statistical quality control to the Japanese.

During World War II, the United States had developed at least the quality control aspects of sampling and had applied these techniques to the various sampling plans that were instituted and adopted by our government at that time. People dealing with the war effort realized that there were many quality control techniques to which they hadn't conformed. All of these were based on statistics. The Japanese recognized this and became very eager students of the statistical quality control approach. Dr. Deming became a popular speaker and lecturer in Japan. In 1980, the Japanese established an award in his name recognizing achievement in quality improvement.

In 1952, Dr. Joseph Juran began lecturing in Japan. Dr. Juran—often referred to as "the Father of Quality Control"—is probably the most renowned quality control expert in the United States. His lectures espoused the philosophy that quality is everybody's business, not just the responsibility of inspectors or the quality control department. He also introduced some important techniques for managing a quality control program.

The Japanese adopted the two major components of Dr. Juran's method: (1) the statistical approach and (2) the concept that quality control is everybody's business. They developed training courses under the sponsorship of "JUSE," the Union of Japanese Scientists and Engineers. JUSE is a non-profit organization similar to many technical societies in the United States. JUSE developed statistical quality control training programs directed to all levels of management, starting with the company owner and proceeding down the line. Everyone was trained in the concept of statistical quality control and in the philosophy that "everybody is responsible for quality." Quality Circles developed from this training.

## EMPLOYEE INVOLVEMENT PROCESSES (EIPs) AT WELL-MANAGED, AMERICA: A CASE STUDY

This is a case study of the implementation of employee involvement processes at Well-Managed, America. The organization discussed in this case study is a medium-sized organization with 1,000 employees. Well-Managed started with one employee involvement process (EIP). Approximately one year later, it had fifteen EIPs operating. This is a real-life case study of the implementation and results of an on-going EIP in a large recognizable American organization. The name and actual location of the organization has been disguised at its request to protect its proprietary rights and its competitive position. This case study discusses EIPs in general and, more specifically, discusses the EIP process currently operating at Well-Managed America.

The EIP process at Well-Managed, America started in January 1980. Well-Managed built its process on Quality Circles but chose to call its approach an employee involvement process (EIP) because it thought Quality Circles had become a buzzword. After the first EIPs had firmly established themselves, four more were added. Later, four more were added and then four more. Well-Managed will expand EIPs until everybody who wants to be in one will be able to join. Well-Managed has not fixed this number precisely but believes that it is probably around forty to fifty EIPs.

### What Is an EIP?

An EIP is a group of people doing similar work who voluntarily meet on a regular basis to identify, analyze and solve quality, cost reduction and other work-related problems in their area. An EIP generally comprises five to twelve people. In some organizations, EIPs consist of three to fifteen or three to ten persons. The numbers are relatively flexible. The smallest EIP at Well-Managed has five people; the largest has fifteen.

The people in each EIP come from the same work area; in fact, most of them come from the same department. They all do the same kind of work. This is important because when the EIP members select a problem to work on, they have to understand the precise nature of that problem. They must all be able to identify with the problem and contribute to the solution. That the members do similar work is an important part of what provides cohesion to each EIP.

EIP members meet voluntarily, which also is important. Membership in EIPs is voluntary. Members meet on a regular basis. All of Well-Managed's EIPs meet once a week, for one hour, on organization time; the organization pays members for meeting in EIPs. The EIP's job is to identify, analyze and solve problems. This means investigating the problem, collecting information on it, analyzing the information and coming up with a good solution. In the past, if somebody in a given work area had a problem, his/her job was to tell a foreman or supervisor about it and hope that he/she could come up with an answer. That doesn't work in an EIP. Any worker can identify a problem. Workers also do the work of analyzing the problem and coming up with a solution. Well-Managed encourages EIPs to select quality- or cost-reduction–related problems, but they are not strictly confined to that one concern. They might work on a safety problem or a method or a paperwork problem. The problems usually concern working conditions.

Well-Managed does specify certain issues that EIPs cannot work on. This is established with EIP members from the very beginning. Organization policies, wages, fringe benefits, and personalities are unsuitable focuses for the EIP. EIPs can't negotiate or recommend pay increases or more vacation time or anything along those lines. Well-Managed will not allow EIPs to attack people or departments. The EIP must focus on problems, not personalities.

### Elements of a Successful EIP

Well-Managed has identified several elements essential to a successful EIP. First, participation by the members is voluntary. They can refuse to join the EIP initially and join at a later date; they can drop out at any time and return at any time. They can come and go as they wish. There are several reasons that the process must be voluntary. First, EIPs are learning experiences for people and normally one learns less if one is forced to learn. Second, someone who isn't interested in being in an EIP won't contribute much to the process. Such people won't derive much from the meetings and the process won't benefit from their enforced participation.

A second essential element of a successful EIP is management support. Management support is important to the success of any process. If management isn't behind a process, it isn't going to succeed. Management must be supportive. In an EIP, this support means quite a bit of commitment, more than just "O.K., you can do this if you like." At Well-Managed, for example, management provides training in EIP techniques and organization time for the EIPs to meet, define problems, gather information and recommend or implement solutions. Management makes a sizeable commitment when it starts an EIP. Once the EIP is started, it must be supported.

An EIP reflects a "people-building philosophy" rather than a "people-using philosophy." The idea is to develop people through training so that they have the opportunity to engage their work more fully and derive more satisfaction from it. The philosophy is very simple. People are going to feel prouder and do a better job if they are able to influence some of the decisions made about them. They are going to feel more important to the organization. When people take pride and interest in their work, quality improves, cost declines and other benefits evolve.

*Training* is an integral part of the EIP. People are trained in various concepts of quality control and problem solving. Also, members solve problems; they don't just identify them.

Many organizations have suggestion programs in which employees identify a problem, suggest a solution, and then somebody else does the work. EIPs don't work that way. EIP members identify the problem and, working as a team, analyze it and come up with solutions.

EIPs fit into an organization without any major change to the organizational structure. They are not separate structures or separate groups that are created. The EIP organizational structure has six levels: *members, leaders, facilitator(s), steering committee, management* and *non-members*. Non-members can be considered part of the structure because they are affected by what EIPs do. An EIP on the first shift may come up with a solution it wants to implement that will affect second shift people. The second shift, therefore, has to be considered in the solution to the problem. The EIP has to consider other people who will be affected by its solutions. So everybody, whether they're in an EIP or not, is going to be affected by EIPs.

*Management* is also a part of the structure. Management must be visibly supportive. Once the EIPs are in operation, management must continue to demonstrate support. Well-Managed is very fortunate because it has a very supportive management team. Many of Well-Managed's top managers took part in the decision to start EIPs and are committed to the success of the process. It's not unusual for a senior manager to sit in on an EIP meeting to learn how and what the EIP is doing, show interest and give encouragement.

After an EIP has defined a solution to a particular problem, its members make what is called a management presentation. This involves meeting with management and stating the problem they defined, how they solved it, what the solution is and how it can be implemented. In some instances, the solution may already have been implemented. It's important that management attend these presentations. Presentations to management are the main type of recognition EIP members receive. That management wants to hear what they have to say, acknowledges that they have done a good job and commits itself to a prompt response is very important to EIP members.

There are *support groups* to EIPs that include management in other areas—staff specialists and representatives from engineering, data processing and purchasing departments—that the EIP will occasionally need to call on for information, such as technical advice from the engineering department or from productivity improvement specialists. These people act as consultants to the EIP while it searches for information. They don't take over the problem and are not given the problem. They just provide the information.

A *steering committee* is not always required; whether one is needed depends on the size of the process. A steering committee provides guidance and direction to the EIP. A small organization generally doesn't require one. In a fairly large organization, a group of people may be needed to represent the major functions in the organization and to act as a steering committee. Well-Managed has a relatively large steering committee of sixteen people.

Before Well-Managed even started its EIP, its steering committee met almost weekly and had much work to do. This work included establishing objectives, identifying resources, designating meeting rooms, ensuring equipment availability, meeting with the facilitator and providing guidance and direction. Presently, Well-Managed's steering committee meets once every three months and attends management presentations.

A *facilitator* is responsible for the overall operation of the EIP and for training leaders and members in quality, cost-reduction, productivity improvement, and problem-solving techniques. The facilitator also coordinates activities between EIPs, acts as a liaison between the EIPs and the rest of the organization, maintains records, and works closely with the steering committee.

Once again, the size of the process dictates whether a facilitator is needed. Some organizations with very large processes say they do not have a facilitator, but someone must perform the facilitator's functions, even if under a different name. Well-Managed chose to have a facilitator take overall responsibility for the process.

Well-Managed uses department supervisors or foremen as the EIP *leaders*. The leader is responsible for the operation of the EIP and works closely with the facilitator on planning and organizing meetings, and so forth. The leader also assists the facilitator with training the members. EIP leaders use nondirective leadership techniques. The purpose of the EIP is for all its members to make decisions, analyze problems and implement solutions. The leader and the facilitator try to steer the EIP in productive directions to make sure they're working effectively.

*EIP members* basically have two jobs. The first is to learn the concepts of cost reduction, productivity, quality improvement and problem-solving techniques through the training they are given. Their second, and most important job, is to identify, analyze and solve problems and to implement solutions. When they finish with one problem, they start on another and the process continues. This creative process is the entire point of EIPs and generates the feelings of satisfaction and personal significance that EIP members experience. Organizations, likewise, enjoy the benefits of their workers' being able to use their brains to help solve problems.

*Member training* occurs during the first eight meetings. Each meeting introduces one of the following techniques:

1. The first meeting is an orientation that gives EIP members more details and information about EIPs.

2. The second meeting introduces the concept and process of brainstorming. Everybody brainstorms in one way or another, but certain rules must be followed in a true brainstorming session. These are write down all ideas, don't criticize ideas, try to get as many ideas as possible, give everyone a chance to voice ideas, don't evaluate ideas, don't encourage people to give ridiculous ideas, limit people to one idea at a time and don't allow leaders to dominate. These rules make the difference between a successful brainstorming session and a "bull session." They keep the EIP on track.

3. Next, *cost reduction techniques*, such as automation, and *quality techniques*, such as sampling, are introduced to the EIP. Informing people of the advantages and pitfalls of sampling is necessary, because many people have never previously encountered the idea. Well-Managed utilizes sampling to collect information in the process of analyzing a problem. Certain rules have to be followed if sampling data is going to be good. These rules include designating check sheets and instructions on how to record the data so that sampling can be accomplished quickly.

4. Pareto analysis involves ways to identify the most important problem, or the best solution in a group of solutions. This technique is also introduced to the EIP members.

5. Once an EIP has identified the problem, it has to try to find the cause. Well-Managed trains EIP members in three different types of cause-and-effect analysis. One is "cause classification," also known as the Ishikawa diagram or the Fishbone diagram because it looks like the skeleton of a fish when it is finished. It's a way of organizing EIP thinking to identify the cause of a problem.

6.&7. "Cause analysis" and "process analysis" are two other ways of analyzing the cause of a problem. Once an EIP has analyzed the cause, the next step is to find the best remedy for it.

8. Well-Managed does some training in presentation techniques, including how best to conduct a meeting with management. The use of charts, graphs and so on is taught so that workers learn how to convey information as quickly and accurately as possible.

These are the types of material covered in the first eight meetings of the EIP. The members, however, still aren't fully trained at this point. The techniques learned in training have to be relearned a few times in application before the EIP members really absorb them. Members have to use these techniques until they feel comfortable with them, and that takes time.

Well-Managed's *leader training* involves sixteen to twenty hours of training. In addition, leaders receive an introduction to EIPs and are trained in all the techniques and concepts. They have to be fully versed in these techniques and when and how to use them. More advanced training explores some other areas of leadership and supervisory training, motivational theories, management styles and group dynamics, leadership and group functions. Well-Managed puts a great emphasis on communication and tries to give each leader some experience in directing a meeting and conducting a training exercise.

The role of *upper management and others* is essentially to support and provide assistance to the EIPs. The main role of department managers who have EIPs in their areas is to support those EIPs and provide suggestions and assistance to them. At Well-Managed, as was mentioned, department supervisors or foremen are EIP leaders. This reduces the opportunity for criticism of the EIPs by first-line and middle management. The employees who volunteer to join an EIP identify, analyze and solve problems as a team. The facilitator coordinates this entire process.

### Operation of EIPs at Well-Managed

During an EIP's early stages, Well-Managed will contact the staff specialist and the department managers to inform them that an EIP has started in a particular area and to ask if they have anything that they would like to see this EIP work on. Anyone in the organization can suggest a problem to an EIP. The list of problems becomes long very quickly. If people ask a department if it knows of any problems, they are going to hear them in a hurry! When the time comes to select projects, the members themselves establish the order of priority. By vote, by the process of elimination or by negotiation, they will pick the problem they want to work on. At this point, the leader votes only to break a tie.

At first, the leader and the facilitator try to exercise guidance to make sure the EIP picks a problem that isn't too difficult and that will not involve a good deal of outside help to solve. Well-Managed likes for its EIPs to enjoy some quick successes to help build confidence. These early stages are typically the only time a leader or facilitator tries to influence an EIP's decision.

Beyond that point, the members themselves decide which problem they will work on. They begin the analysis, using the techniques previously discussed. They gather information. They ask "How big is the problem?" "Why is it a problem?" "What's the possible solution?" and other questions. Then they gather as much information as they can about the problem. They may ask for help from technical specialists to get information unavailable to them. This process is coordinated either by the facilitator or the EIP leader. The EIP completes its analysis and generates a solution for the problem it has selected.

If the solution does not require management approval, the EIP can simply implement it. If it's something requiring higher approval—something that overlaps another department, requires management coordination, or involves money to purchase recommended equipment, for example—the next step is to make a management presentation. The EIP then makes its case, and management reviews it and commits itself to a response within a reasonable period of time.

Well-Managed tries to conduct all EIP meetings according to a particular code of conduct: First, criticize ideas, not people. Try to focus on the problem, analyze it, and develop solutions. Avoid people considerations. Look at the process rather than the people involved in the process; this needs to be emphasized because very often the problem involves a person, an aspect the EIP cannot work on.

Second, encourage questions. The only stupid question is the one you don't ask. Create an atmosphere in which people feel free to ask questions and know they won't be criticized for doing so. Instill in everyone an understanding that each person is responsible for the group's success. Everyone is part of the EIP and has a responsibility to it.

The third step is to be open to others' ideas. Before criticizing or condemning an idea, think about it, discuss it a bit and then make a decision. Create an atmosphere in which people feel free to talk, to ask questions, to state opinions, and people will start listening to the ideas of others, accepting the ideas of others and considering what other people think. Well-Managed tries to act within this code of conduct in all its EIP meetings.

### How Well-Managed Began Its Interest in EIPs

A few years ago, Well-Managed's personnel director and general services manager first learned of Quality Circles and decided to look into them. The personnel director attended a seminar on Quality Circles in Atlanta. He brought the information he gathered back and shared it with top management, who liked what they heard and decided to look a bit further into it. At this point, Well-Managed created several teams: superintendents, general foremen, foremen, department managers, personnel managers and staff specialists were all part of these teams. They visited other organizations with Quality Circles in operation. They spent time talking with workers and management at those organizations. They observed Quality Circle meetings, watched how they were conducted, talked with the facilitator, and so forth.

These groups then came back and wrote evaluative reports. Most of these reports were sufficiently favorable that a decision was made to bring in a consultant and go ahead with an EIP. The consultant spent a week in the organization. He met with management, gave orientation sessions on

EIPs, explained the concepts, and stressed the importance of management commitment in starting an EIP.

At that point, Well-Managed created a steering committee. The facilitator was selected, and the consultant conducted the facilitator and the leader training. The consultant spent one day on the orientation meetings and four days training a facilitator and the first EIP leaders. Steering committee members were also included in the training so that they would have a good understanding of the dynamics of EIPs. Many of the steering committee members were trained as if they were going to be leaders or facilitators.

During the next few months, the steering committee developed an implementation plan, with a targeted start date. Information was distributed to personnel within the organization, letting them know that EIPs were going to begin. Introductory meetings were held with the areas selected for the first EIPs. This consisted of bringing a group of people into a meeting room with the regular work leader or meeting chairman. Basically, people were told that Well-Managed planned to start an EIP in their area. EIPs were then explained and, at the end of the meeting, workers were asked if they wanted to volunteer. These meetings lasted about one hour. The regular work leader spoke, the facilitator made a brief presentation and representatives from top management said a few words to encourage people. People were asked to let their foreman know within a day or two if they wanted to join. People volunteered and the EIPs began in three areas.

Well-Managed uses this same introductory process for every EIP it starts. Management calls a meeting, explains EIPs, asks for volunteers, gives people one or two days to think about it, and then checks to find out whether they are going to volunteer. Of course, the invitation to join remains open. Well-Managed invites people who haven't decided to come to the first few meetings to find out more about EIPs. Well-Managed's experience has been that about 98 percent of its people volunteer at the first meeting. After the first few meetings, about 10 percent may drop out. Past that point, retention in the EIPs has been exceptionally good. A few people decide "I don't need this," "EIPs aren't for me," "I don't need this kind of thing," "I'm too busy" and whatever else. EIPs are not for everyone; that's why the process is voluntary. Overall, Well-Managed has retained more than 80 percent of the people initially asked to join. Well-Managed's oldest EIPs have existed for several years.

### Why EIPs at Well-Managed?

Well-Managed initiated EIPs for four reasons:

1. To provide an atmosphere conducive to the self-development of its employees, to give its employees a chance to grow and get more enjoyment out of their

jobs. Well-Managed is trying to allow its workers to feel fulfilled by the work they do. Part of this fulfillment derives from employees being able to influence decisions made about their work and the conditions under which it is performed.

2. Well-Managed wants to improve the value, not merely the quality, of its services provided. Well-Managed is interested in the total value of the services it provides for its customers. Well-Managed didn't have a quality program when it started EIPs, but the organization's management knows that good quality now isn't going to be good enough five years from now. It needs to be much better five years from now. The more Well-Managed can interest its workers in quality now, the better off the organization will be down the road. Well-Managed wants to improve quality and value: that's the second purpose of its EIP.

3. Well-Managed wants to improve communications and teamwork between all levels of its organization. Well-Managed is a non-union organization and is working hard to stay that way. Part of that effort is making sure that workers talk to management. Well-Managed is trying to promote communications, and EIPs are a very effective way of doing it.

4. When people solve problems in their work areas, chances are that cost will be reduced, either in productivity improvement, cost savings, cost avoidance or diminished lost time. Savings do accrue and Well-Managed keeps track of them. When Well-Managed's EIPs develop a solution that involves expenditures, management tries to make it a good economic decision: Will the organization save more than it spends? So Well-Managed does monitor cost reduction ideas when savings are involved but doesn't attempt to evaluate every idea. The EIPs have come up with many good solutions whose benefits the organization hasn't tried to evaluate.

When people hear about EIPs, they usually hear several points mentioned: EIPs will improve quality, improve productivity and generate cost reductions. And EIPs can, in fact, produce all these results. Well-Managed, however, is not measuring itself in this way at this point. In the areas in which Well-Managed has EIPs, it knows that people are more conscious of quality, more aware of costs and doing a better job than in the past. Well-Managed has a difficult time trying to put a number on this. The organization is also aware that other factors influence these considerations.

Well-Managed finds it difficult to measure the success of its EIPs in quantitative terms and, fortunately, has been sufficiently quantitatively satisfied in the way its EIP functions so that it hasn't been necessary to overcome those difficulties and design quantitative measures.

## NOTES

1. William Ouchi, *Theory Z: How American Business Can Meet the Japanese Challenge* (Reading, Mass.: Addison-Wesley, 1981).

2. Paul Mali, *Improving Total Productivity: Management by Objectives Strategies for Business, Government, and Not-for-Profit Organizations* (New York: Wiley, 1978).

3. James L. Mercer, *Quality Circles: Productivity Improvement Processes*, Management Information Service Report, vol. 14, no. 3 (Washington, D.C.: International City Management Association, 1982), pp. 1–14.

4. See James L. Mercer and Susan W. Woolston, "Setting Priorities: Three Techniques for Better Decision Making," *Management Information Service Report*, vol. 12, no. 9 (Washington, D.C.: International City Management Association, 1980).

5. Cause and effect diagrams are also called "fishbone diagrams" because of their shape. In Japan, they are called Ishikawa diagrams. They are also sometimes called 4M analyses—manpower, machines, methods and materials.

6. Pareto analysis means that 80 percent of your problems come from 20 percent of your efforts or 80 percent of complaints come from 20 percent of the people served, and so on. It is basically the separation of the *important few* from the *trivial many*.

7. Scott M. Sedam, "Quality Circle Training Process Should Cover Relating, Supporting, Problem-Solving Skills," *Industrial Engineering*, vol. 14, no. 1 (January 1982), pp. 70–74.

8. In some organizations, up to eighty hours have been devoted to facilitation training.

9. J. F. Beardsley quoted in Ed Yager, "Examining the Quality Control Circle," *Personnel Journal*, October 1979, pp. 682–84, 708.

# Organizing for Improved Public Productivity Utilizing Matrix Management

About a competitor: "The gunner's command [there] was, 'Ready, Aim, Aim, Aim, Aim.' Ours was 'Ready, Aim, Fire. FIRE. FIRE. FIRE. FIRE.' "

—H. Ross Perot

How can America's state and local governments organize themselves to deal more effectively with the new and more difficult challenges for increased productivity, cost reductions and other factors they will undoubtedly face as we approach the year 2000? Traditionally, the organizational structure that has existed since people first joined to accomplish common objectives always has a boss or leader. Although this has been adequate in most instances, it is quite conceivable that new circumstances and demands may call for a different type of organizational structure. This chapter discusses some additional organizational options available to management and examines the subtleties and intricacies of personnel relationships that may exist within them.[1]

We will focus on first-, second-, and third-generation organizational structures, with particular emphasis on the latter. This third-generation structure, or mature matrix, has evolved over the past two decades to meet the more complex demands that are and will continue to be placed on certain organizations. Predecessors of this third-generation structure are by no means out of date. Most organizations, in fact, will find that their needs can best be met somewhere between the traditional organizational structure and the mature matrix.

## FIRST GENERATION

The first-generation organization is characterized as a pyramid and has been used extensively throughout history to fight battles, rule kingdoms, operate churches, manage businesses and direct governmental agencies. It embodies a unity of command from the top down. Authority to perform activities that accomplish organizational objectives is delegated downward through the organization to subordinates. Ultimately, all persons in the organization are responsible to the chief executive.

In classical management concepts, the manager's authority was based on legal rights. In most cases, the manager was the founder or owner of the business or enterprise. In this early form of organization, there were few opportunities or provisions for charismatic leadership, for horizontal lines of authority or for authority based on the expertise and interpersonal skills of the manager. It was virtually inconceivable that any manager would ever divide resources with another manager, negotiate priorities for the budget and other resources, or motivate others to act instead of simply commanding them to do his/her bidding.[2] This form of organization is quite adequate for carrying out traditional activities, but it doesn't immediately provide for emphasis of cross-functional activities or projects on a temporary or permanent basis.

## SECOND GENERATION

In the second-generation organization, the project managers or coordinators are superimposed on the traditional pyramid organization. These assignments may be temporary or permanent and usually result in a horizontal crosscutting of the vertical lines of authority characteristic in the first-generation organization. Although probably used in some form throughout history, this project-overlay type of organization was formalized and attained significant stature in the post–World War II era, primarily in the aerospace and defense industries. The new missile and aerospace systems were so intricate and complex and their timing was so critical that the pyramid style of management proved inadequate. It was difficult, if not impossible, to hold one individual responsible for such complex systems. During this period, managers were confronted with the coordination and integration of vast, resources—human, material and technical. In addition, coordination of a large number of outside contractors was crucial to the overall success of the effort. Many different activities and functions, such as research, engineering, testing, production and support, had to be intricately interwoven throughout the life of the project to produce a successful end result. The task of getting these complex and intricate systems built and delivered cut across normal organization or pyramid lines. Functional boundaries within management organizations had to be violated.

Somehow an organization had to be developed that blended the traditional structure with technical knowledge in diverse disciplines. The first-generation or pyramid organization was just not up to the test. The solution, of course, was *project management*.

Today, project management has evolved as a recognized discipline with its own terminology, tools, procedures and responsibilities. The concept basically provides a single point of responsibility for a project, exercises centralized control over information and permits contribution to the project effort from functional but decentralized organizational elements.[3]

Project management may take essentially four forms in the second-generation: (1) staff coordination, (2) project office, (3) project matrix and (4) functional matrix.

### Staff Coordination

In the first of the second-generation forms of project-management organization, one or several persons are assigned to positions as staff coordinators for specific projects. These individuals usually report to a chief executive who has authority over most or all of the functional or other resource elements that will be involved in accomplishing the project. The staff or project coordinator interacts with the various functional (contributing department) members and cuts horizontally across the pyramid organization. The second-generation project team thus consists of the coordinator or leader and various functionally assigned members. In some cases, the project coordinator works directly with the manager or a contributing functional department, which in turn delegates the required work within his/her own organization. Under this arrangement, the functionally assigned members are not wholly committed to a project; the project assignment is accomplished by virtue of the project coordinator's ability to bring together diverse functional elements and resources. The coordinator's only authority is an implied one—a reporting relationship to the chief executive. The coordinator has no direct-line authority over functional department specialists who must contribute to the project. To be successful, the project coordinator must be an unusual individual with special traits and approaches to the task. Under a project-coordination arrangement, the potentially disrupting effect on the existing line or pyramid organization is minimal.

As a case example, the city of Caution, Kansas, has been informed by its outside accountant that it needs to implement a more modern accounting system to give the city better control of all operational costs. The city manager wants to install a new system, but he wants the installation to have the least disruptive effect possible on an otherwise well-functioning organization. To carry this out, he selects and assigns a project coordinator with responsibility for the system's timely installation. The city manager announces the appointment of the project coordinator to all the managers who will be affected by the new system. The coordinator carries out his responsibilities by working through the affected department managers or other appointees. The system is installed in each department at a mutually agreed-on time. The project coordinator's only authority is that implied by his reporting relationship to the city manager. The coordinator is successful because he knows how to work with people toward the accomplishment of a task that will improve everyone's ability to do their jobs better.

### Project Office

Under this arrangement, one or more project offices are formed while the more traditional functional organization is retained. All team members report to a project manager who may hold any general management title. The project manager has considerably more actual authority than does the project coordinator previously described. No other functional departments (such as purchasing, operations or strategic planning) are involved. All contributions from within the organization (internal) are contracted for by the project office. Similarly, all contributions from outside firms or vendors (external) are on a contract basis. Contracts, both internal and external, may be selected by competitive bid. This type of project organization is almost analogous to establishing a separate function, perhaps with a limited life, to manage a major effort.

An example of developing a new service for an existing city, based on a recently completed cost/benefit analysis, is Carefree, California, which has decided to cancel its outside sanitation collection contract and, for the first time in the city's brief history, to deliver the service with city forces. Carefree's city manager wants to place considerable emphasis on the new service and to commit considerable city resources toward its success. However, he doesn't wish to disrupt the existing arrangement for the delivery of other required city services that are being handled smoothly. The city manager appoints an assistant city manager as project manager in charge of the new service delivery effort. The project manager is given authority by the city manager to create a project team whose purpose will be to develop the city's ability to deliver the new service properly. The project manager assembles a team of experts in finance, public relations, engineering, operations, purchasing, human resources and so forth, who will spend their full time developing the new sanitation collection service. Legal assistance is contracted from the city attorney's office. Sanitation collection vehicles are leased from an outside vendor. The project office operates almost like another function of the city. Once it has achieved success, the city manager wants the project manager to train a new department head and the function will eventually become another city department.

## Project Matrix

Under this organizational arrangement, team members from various functional departments are assigned to a project manager for the duration of the project. The project manager usually reports to the chief executive and is delegated strong authority for carrying out the assigned project. Under this organizational arrangement, the project manager assigns, supervises and integrates the work of the project team. Functional department heads support their project team members with technical know-how, training and provisions for staffing, hiring, promotions, salary and so forth. The project manager is responsible for project direction and controls the how, what and when of the project.

An example of the project matrix in action is the state of Hard Times. The state is facing a major squeeze between its rising costs to operate and revenues, which are not keeping pace. The state is clearly faced with the need to reduce costs in all its operations or face a deficit financial situation, which, as for most states, is prohibited by law.

At his weekly staff meeting, the governor of Hard Times instructs all state department heads to carry out a high-level, intensive cost reduction effort in their respective departments. The governor appoints a key staff member as a project manager and instructs each functional department manager to assign a key person full-time to the project manager for the duration of the project. The project manager specifies what efforts are to be undertaken to reduce costs and how and when those efforts occur. The project's team members support the project manager with technical expertise and carry out his/her directions. After the project is completed and ongoing cost reduction is achieved, the project team is disbanded, and the team members return to their respective functional departments.

## Functional Matrix

Under this form of project organization, a project manager is appointed by a chief executive. The project manager interacts directly with the contributing functional department members who have been assigned to the project. The project manager cuts horizontally across the lines of authority of the functional department managers. The project team consists of a leader—the project manager—and team members representing functional departments. The team, however, is not wholly committed to the project, as in the last two examples. In this case, the team must work within an organizational matrix of project versus line authority.

The individual project team members retain their primary reporting relationships to their functional department supervisors, who are responsible for their technical performance and support, training, professional growth, salary and so forth. The functional department supervisors control the *how*, and the project manager controls the *what* and *when*. In this framework, the major effort of the project manager is to integrate the team members' performance into the overall project objective. Some of the tools that the project manager uses to accomplish this task are his/her own defined position, persuasion, broad knowledge and, occasionally, if conflicts arise, a compromise agreement with the functional department head and the chief executive. The project manager has responsibility for project direction.[4]

As an example, the state of Progressive wants to develop an improved program budgeting system that will allow the state legislature to gain a broader perspective of state operations during budget review. Progressive's governor appoints a key staff member as project director for the new project and directs each of the functional department heads to assign one key individual to the project. The project manager specifies the timing and details of the new program-budgeting development effort. Each functional project team member makes contributions to the effort based on experience, departmental specialty and need. The project manager must integrate all team efforts and develop the new program-budgeting system within time and budget constraints. The project team members never sever their reporting relationships to their functional departments.

## THIRD GENERATION

This third-generation organization may be characterized as a *mature matrix* and is one of the project-oriented organizational structures that is expected to command the largest amount of management attention during the 1990s and beyond. The mature matrix may be defined as an organizational structure that employs a multiple-command system and associated management, support systems, organizational culture and behavior pattern. This type of organization has evolved over the past two decades primarily through the project-management stages previously described. The mature matrix is not just another minor management technique or buzzword, and the move to a mature-matrix organization is truly a significant step.

The mature-matrix organization should be considered when all three of the following conditions exist:

1. Intensive managerial attention must be focused on two or more key issues simultaneously, for example, complex technical issues and unique service requirements. An example might be the development of a resource recovery system for solid waste at the city landfill while simultaneously operating the landfill in the normal manner for the city, the county and private haulers.
2. The need for human information processing and complex problem solving is overwhelming because of changing and relatively unpredictable demands, the

complexity of the organization and the interdependence among people on organizational issues. An example might be the same resource recovery system that is about ready to reach the critical decision-making stage in a large and highly diverse and complex local government setting. Suddenly, a competitive approach to resource recovery is announced that significantly reduces the cost of the process and significantly advances the state of the art of the technology involved. The local government needs to know how to reach a possible alternative decision quickly.

3. The organization is under considerable pressure to achieve economies of scale in human terms while simultaneously achieving high performance in terms of outputs, such as rapid redeployment of human resources. In the example of the resource recovery system, a cost/benefit analysis must be quickly developed to determine whether the new approach would allow for the best use of finances, technology and people; would be the most efficient; and, at the same time, would provide maximum flexibility in the use of the city's resources.

The mature matrix violates all the rules of one person, one boss. In a third-generation organization, the project manager clearly has at least two bosses. Success requires a particularly effective chief executive and unusual people in project and functional roles within the matrix organization.

Under the mature matrix, a dual-authority relationship exists over the project manager, who may sometimes be referred to as a "two-boss" manager. (The project manager could have more than two bosses, but for ease of discussion, two will be used here.) Power is balanced and shared equally between the two bosses, each representing a different dimension of the organization—operations and staff development, for example. Both managers create an environment in which the project manager can be successful. Their success, measured by the chief executive, is based on how well they work together in achieving common, positive results. The three key roles in the mature matrix are the top leadership, the matrix managers who share subordinates in common and the two-boss project manager. Although the mature matrix places contradictory demands on the project manager, it is the best approach known for accommodating simultaneous, competing demands within an organization. As an illustration, the border town of Big Gun, Texas, is facing a "cutback management" situation because of increasing costs and declining revenues. As one of several approaches to the problem, the town manager wants to develop an appreciation for and a utilization of labor and cost-saving technology in the Big Gun Public Works Department. Given the present state of the art in the department, however, it will be necessary to develop an intense and continuous training program for employees of the department so that they can begin to appreciate the benefits that new technology can bring to the department.

Therefore, conditions seem right to establish a mature-matrix organization to focus on a continuous training effort in the public works department. The chief executive informs the department managers at public works and staff development that a mature-matrix organization is being established with both of them as key elements. The department managers, in turn, are instructed to select and appoint a "two-boss" project manager to be responsible for the training effort now and in the future.

At this point, the chief executive, who sits atop the mature matrix and is really outside of it, has three key aspects to his role. He must (1) carefully balance power between the matrix managers (in this case, the manager of public works and the manager of staff development), (2) manage the context within which key decisions relative to the project manager are made and conflicts are resolved and (3) establish performance standards for the project and the project team.[6] In other words, the chief executive sets the stage, and the two matrix bosses (the public works manager and the manager of staff development) carry out the continuous training program through joint assignment of the task to a project manager. The matrix bosses are evaluated equally by the chief executive on how effectively and timely the effort is executed. Therefore, each manager shares in the desire to create a climate in which their joint subordinate, the project manager, can be successful.

In this case, an individual outside the public works function is needed to ensure that the necessary expertise, attention, time and effort are devoted to the development of the new training program. The public works manager does not have the time or overall perspective to develop the program. The manager of staff development has the time, the expertise and the resources. However, he can't conduct a successful training development effort without the full functional support and enabling authority of the public works manager. The project manager has the necessary authority to carry out his assignment, but he must satisfy the two bosses in the process.

Under this mature-matrix form of organization, the project manager meets jointly with his/her two bosses to establish a plan of action for the project. The plan sets forth goals, objectives, a schedule and specific checkpoints along the way. The project manager obtains general agreement to the plan from both bosses. Both also inform their other subordinates of the plan and direct appropriate cooperation within the organization.

Using any or all of the tools of project management deemed appropriate to the situation, the project manager carries out the assignment and develops and conducts the training program. If conflicts arise during the course of the assignment, the project manager makes every effort to work them out alone or with the two bosses. If resolutions cannot be obtained, the project manager and the two bosses take the problem to the chief executive for resolution. The major advantage to the town of Big Gun of using a mature-matrix form of organization for this project is that the required training can be started more quickly and with less stress on the organizational elements than it could have been by other methods. Also the organizational shift to the mature matrix provides for ongoing emphasis on the program to keep it relevant to the training needs over the longer term.

The mature matrix is the most flexible of all organizational forms. With it, new programs, services, thrusts and so forth can be regularly phased in or out without making major changes in the basic form of the organization. A mature-matrix organization is being used by a few public sector organizations where a need clearly exists. The mature matrix offers many positive features to those organizations undergoing significant changes in their services, constituencies and approaches.

## WHICH STRUCTURE TO USE?

Several types of project-management and matrix organizations have been described. Which works best? The answer quite obviously depends on what is to be accomplished. In many cases, the traditional functional organization is best—that's why it has lasted so long. In others, a special need may be met by the mature matrix. In most situations, somewhere in between is probably best.

The staff or project coordinator may be effective in certain circumstances, but this individual lacks authority to direct activities within the project environment. This manager must be effective by sheer force of personality and by getting others to work together toward a common objective, based on the "reasonableness" of the effort. This is, at best, an impotent form of project organization. However, in a delicately balanced functional organization, it could be the least threatening to the line functional manager.

The project office can be effective, but it basically establishes another functional entity that is concerned with completing a major project. Because it is the type of organization that lends itself to large complex projects, such as the construction of a major new facility, it is not widely applicable.

Some form of matrix-management organization may be the best bet. Although the various forms of matrix violate the one-boss rule of conventional management, the matrix is being increasingly used in both the public and private sectors. This form of organization offers a method of integrating today's complex requirements so that the traditional organization can be maintained while proper and appropriate emphasis is placed on activities and items of special need.

One of the biggest problems in the introduction of any new organizational scheme is overcoming resistance to change. Most people within the organization fail to recognize the new and increasing demands being placed on managers. Managers and subordinates alike feel uncomfortable in a new, loosely defined matrix organization. However, as more experience has been gained over time by individuals and organizations working with various forms of matrix, myths have been exploded and the barriers to change have begun to erode. The positive results that a matrix type of project organization can produce in the development of managers, in increased organizational cooperation and in bottom-line performance are being seen.

The project matrix can be very effective in producing results, but it has a jolting effect on the traditional organization. Many of the technical and managerial portions of the project work are transferred from the line functional departments to the control of the project manager. Functional team members have to be uprooted from their present organizations and placed under the direction of a new boss. Even if this doesn't involve a physical move on their part, traditional relationships are disturbed. The project matrix also raises questions about the team member's niche in the functional department once the project is completed.[7] Many career-path questions are raised by this form of matrix organization.

The functional matrix has less of a collision impact on the existing functional organization. The responsibilities and duties of line departments don't basically change. Functional departments continue to provide technical expertise related to the project, while the project manager provides the management. This is in direct contrast to the project matrix previously mentioned and is usually more palatable to line functional managers.

Even though the functional matrix provides for less centralized control by the project manager, it does offer a practical framework for integrating intricate and complex projects. In most cases, the project manager and the team stay together for the duration of the project. If the project doesn't place full-time demands on team members, they have time to work on other projects or on functional efforts in their line departments. Their career paths are clearer and not disrupted as much as they are by the project-matrix or the project-office forms of organization.

Even though each team member, in effect, has two bosses, the functional matrix is not as formalized and often not as long-lived as is the mature matrix. In a large project, functional team members can be assigned full-time over long periods, thus lessening the opportunity for conflict between the project and functional line managers. When team members are assigned to several projects at the same time or when functional duties in their home departments keep them occupied part of the time, conflicts may arise. Three rules have been suggested to minimize such conflicts:

1. When possible, plan work on a full-time basis for a short period of time rather than shared work over a longer period of time
2. When time-sharing is required, plan for a fixed schedule over a fixed period of time (e.g., twenty hours a week)
3. Establish at the outset that conflicts should be resolved by the chief executive[8]

The mature matrix represents a total splitting of the project manager's relationships with two bosses. As long as the pendulum swings rather evenly between the two, very few conflicts are apt to arise. Problems occur when one boss starts making more use of the project manager than the other, or when one boss is strong. Clearly, the chief executive to whom the two bosses of the project manager report must be an unusual individual and must create a climate for success in this kind of relationship. This is a most sophisticated type of organizational arrangement. Care should be exercised in its use unless the flexibility exists to do a bit of experimenting.

Exhibits 8–1 through 8–3 provide comparisons of organizational characteristics and potential problems versus structural forms.

## CHARACTERISTICS OF A MATRIX MANAGER

As has been discussed, it takes a special kind of individual to perform well in a matrix- or project-management environment. What are some of the important characteristics of such an individual? Exhibits 8–1 and 8–2 indicate the management characteristics that a good project or matrix manager must possess when working in the various forms of project-management organizations.

All forms of matrix or project management are potential areas for conflict (Exhibit 8–3). Line or functional team members have a primary loyalty to their own manager and department. The project manager is in direct competition for each line manager's resources, budgets and prerogatives. Since the project manager generally has no formal authority over the functional managers, the biggest problem is gaining the support of these other managers for the project goal. This is accomplished largely by knowledge and persuasion. The project manager's basis of authority is very fragile and must be supported by top management's presence and participation. It must be made known that cooperation at all levels is expected for the good of the total organization. The project manager's authority will be facilitated when he/she is accorded the same status as other managers, as evidenced by office space, involvement in policy decisions and participation in key staff meetings.[9]

## FUTURE OF MATRIX MANAGEMENT

The use of project or matrix management is expected to increase dramatically during the next decade as managerial requirements increase in complexity. The key to success in applying matrix management is to select a diplomatic, but forceful, individual who can gain the respect of line and staff managers alike.

If any word is descriptive of state and local government bodies during the 1990s and beyond, it is "change." Not only is change itself inevitable,

**Exhibit 8–1**
**Organizational Characteristics versus Structural Forms**

| Organizational Characteristics | Traditional Pyramid | Staff Coordin. | Project Office | Project Matrix | Functional Matrix | Mature Matrix |
|---|:---:|:---:|:---:|:---:|:---:|:---:|
| Large Organization | * | | | * | | * |
| Small Organization | * | * | | | | * |
| Complex Technology | | | * | * | | * |
| High-volume Services | * | * | | | * | * |
| Manufacturing Organization | * | * | * | * | * | * |
| Service Organization | | | * | | * | * |
| Geographically Dispersed | | | * | * | * | * |
| Multiple Service Lines | * | * | | | * | * |
| 3-4 Major Service Lines | | | * | * | | * |
| Long-Duration Projects | | | * | * | | * |
| Short-Term Projects | * | | | | * | |

NOTE: * indicates favorable structural form for organizations having that characteristic.

but the rate of change is constantly increasing. For government to deal with significant change, its organizational structures must remain flexible. This chapter has presented several forms of matrix management that, when correctly used, can bring needed flexibility to governmental agencies and effectively manage systematic change.

## DESIGNING A CAPITAL IMPROVEMENTS PROJECT CONTROL SYSTEM: A CASE STUDY

### The Problem

As city manager of a medium-sized city, you are under increasing pressure to cut costs and improve management. The city's capital improvements program (CIP) involving construction of streets, sewers, buildings, bridges, parks and so on is a major consumer of revenues. Because of the non-repetitive or "once-through" nature of many of the projects, the interre-

**Exhibit 8–2**
**Management Characteristics versus Structural Forms**

| Management Characteristics | Traditional Pyramid | Staff Coordin. | Project Office | Project Matrix | Structural Forms Functional Matrix | Mature Matrix |
|---|---|---|---|---|---|---|
| Persuasiveness | | * | | | * | * |
| Technical Knowledge | | * | | | * | * |
| Leadership | * | | * | * | * | * |
| Ability to Integrate | | * | | | * | * |
| Knowledge of Organization | | * | | | * | * |
| Proven Record | | | * | * | | |
| Ability to Motivate | | * | | | * | * |
| Ability to Allocate Resources | * | | * | * | | |
| Flexibility | | * | | | * | * |
| Good Judgment | * | * | * | * | * | * |
| Ability to Act As Planner | | * | | | * | * |
| Knowledge of Project-Management Tools | | * | | | * | * |
| Effectiveness With People | | * | | * | * | * |
| Good Communications Ability | | * | | * | * | * |
| Skill at Resolving Conflicts | | * | | | * | * |

NOTE: * indicates management characteristic is particularly necessary.

lationships between various projects within the entire CIP and the difficulties in coordinating the activities of numerous contractors and local government agencies throughout program development, the capital improvements program poses a series of management problems. The number of projects, the amount of money (millions) involved and the variable time schedules associated with various projects combine to make managing this city activity in a systematic manner very difficult.

There is a need for a system that will enable you and your staff to obtain

**Exhibit 8–3**
**Potential Problems versus Structural Forms**

| Management Characteristics | Traditional Pyramid | Staff Coordin. | Project Office | Project Matrix | Structural Forms Functional Matrix | Mature Matrix |
|---|---|---|---|---|---|---|
| Divided Authority | | | | | | * |
| Inadequate Project Authority | | * | | | | |
| Inflexibility | * | | | | | |
| Duplicate Functions | | | * | | | |
| Divided Loyalties | | | | | * | |
| Confusing | | | | | | * |
| Conflict | | | * | * | * | * |
| Diffused Accountability | | * | | | | |

NOTE: * indicates potential problem exists for that structure.

timely, accurate information on the status of projects. This will help keep track of the projects themselves so they are kept on schedule, and the improved overall management coordination can save the city money. For example, projects that are delayed will no longer be inadvertently overlooked and assumed to be on schedule.

### The Task

You are to design a step-by-step implementation model for such a capital improvements program monitoring system. Use the city manager perspective and include consideration of the questions listed below:

1. *Implementation team.* What city personnel should participate? Who should have overall responsibility? How large should the team be? What support skills are desirable?
2. *Project control system coverage.* What projects should be included (e.g., should there be a minimum cost level before inclusion of a project into the system)?
3. *When should the system begin tracking a project?* What are the relative merits of including projects for which construction has not started?
4. *Where should the system be physically headquartered? How often should the program team meet?* How best can they keep others in the city administration informed of the system?

6. *How can comprehensive information for setting up the system best be acquired?*

7. *What should a master program schedule and tracking forms look like?*

8. *How could you modify the system to allow for tracking of project expenditures?*

9. *In what ways might the system improve productivity and save the city money?*

### Project Control System Implementation: The Solution

The following description of suggested steps for implementing a project control system assumes that a jurisdiction has selected a system appropriate to its needs, that a person within the jurisdiction has been identified as having overall responsibility for the implementation of the system and that sufficient funds, time and resource commitments for implementation have been made by appropriate officials.

*Review System*

The person charged with overall responsibility for implementation of the selected project control system should become thoroughly familiar with the system. Project control, in its broadest sense, involves the following:

• Establishing a set of plans for a program
• Generating standards against which to judge progress
• Scheduling work activities
• Designing an information system that can track expected versus actual progress

The essence of the project control system is to generate a master control schedule for the entire program based on (1) "raw" or "unconstrained" schedules submitted by those in charge of individual projects and (2) reports from individual agencies involved in the program concerning their projected resources available for work on the program. Once these reports have been meshed into a master schedule, a monitoring system is established to check actual versus planned progress. The following subsections describe these basic system elements in more detail.

1. *Unconstrained schedules.* Raw or unconstrained schedules are simply schedules of normal or expected project duration that are developed without regard to other projects or workloads. The distinguishing characteristic of unconstrained schedules is that they concern the expected duration of work activities but *do not refer to actual dates.* These schedules reflect, when appropriate, the interrelationships between subtasks for each project. Most important, these schedules indicate when a task must be started so it will be completed in time to coordinate with other tasks. This makes it possible for the different groups involved in the program to anticipate when they must begin their work responsibilities.

Exhibit 8–4 illustrates a simple unconstrained schedule for a single proj-

**Exhibit 8–4**
**An Example of a Project Unconstrained Schedule**

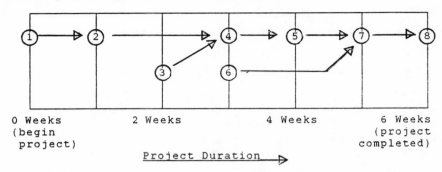

| 0 Weeks | 2 Weeks | 4 Weeks | 6 Weeks |
| (begin | | | (project |
| project) | | | completed) |

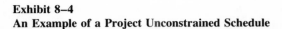

Project Duration ▷

ect. In this diagram, the arrows indicate work activity duration; the circles indicate the beginning or completion of a work activity (referred to as an event). In this case, event 1 is the beginning event and event 2 is the ending event of work activity 1–2. According to this notation, activity 4–5 cannot begin until event 4, which in turn depends on the completion of activities 2–4 (planned to require two weeks) and 3–4 (planned to require 1 week). Likewise, activity 7–8 cannot begin until event 7, which in turn depends on the completion of activity 6–7 (which requires two weeks) and activity 5–7 (1 week). The following points are important to understanding of this example:

- Activities 1–2, 3–4 and 6–7 can be started at any time, but no other activities can begin until previous activities have been completed
- The entire project is planned to take six weeks, although no dates have been assigned as yet
- For activity 4–5 to begin as scheduled at the end of the third week, activity 2–4 must begin after one week and activity 3–4 must begin after two weeks

Obviously, this is a very simple generalized example. Even so, it illustrates the basic method of coordinating and scheduling work activities for a simple project. A similar, more complex network could be established for any real problem by breaking the project into its basic steps and organizing these steps into a logical plan that recognizes the interrelationships between different work activities.

2. *Resource reports*. In addition to these unconstrained schedules, all departments involved in the program should submit reports on their projected resources available for work on the program. These resource reports are used to ensure that participating agencies are not assigned overloads

during any period of time in the master schedule. Obviously, if most of the work in the program is awarded to contractors, this resource constraint is not a very serious consideration.

### Determine Application

Decide whether the system is to be applied jurisdiction wide or to one department or division as a pilot test.

### Identify a Program Team Leader

Whereas the person with overall responsibility for the implementation process has been previously identified, a program team leader should also be selected. This person should be assigned responsibility for the actual implementation details and the day-to-day management of the project control system.

In some instances, the staff member with overall responsibility for system implementation might want to assume the role of program team leader. In other situations, the person with overall responsibility for the system might want to delegate this authority. In any case, the staff member selected to act as program team leader should already have an overall perspective on the program to which the control system is applied. The advantages of the system might not be appreciated by someone who has had responsibility for only part of the program.

### Select a Program Team

In addition to the staff person responsible for implementation of the project control system, a program team should be selected. Those individuals in charge of capital improvement projects within specific departments are obvious candidates. These people must assume responsibility for gathering the unconstrained schedules for each of the projects within their departments (either generated in-house or provided by contractors), and reporting on the status of these projects throughout the life of the program.

In addition to these various department heads, the chief purchasing officer, the head of the planning department, and the head of the engineering department might also be included. The most important consideration in selecting program team participants is that the team include a representative from every organization or agency that has a significant responsibility in the overall program. These people will either be able to contribute important information to the monitoring process or benefit in terms of meeting their own responsibilities by being involved in the project monitoring process.

As a technical aide to the program team, a person with network scheduling skills and familiarity with Gantt charts, PERT and CPM techniques should also be included, if possible. This person should have responsibility for the actual development of the master schedule. Finally, a program secretary should be assigned to handle all system paperwork.

### Establish an Information Network

In addition to selecting the program team, it is also important to establish a program information network. Although there are those who need to be included in the program team because of the project status information they can supply, there is likely a vast group of people with no project status information to contribute but who would benefit by receiving the system reports. As such, a distribution list for progress reports should be established.

### Decide on a System Format

It will also be necessary to decide on a format for the system. The following issues must be considered:

1. *What projects should be included in the system?* Some local governments with project control systems include all projects within their capital improvements program as well as any other local construction projects. Alternatively, some local governments include only projects involving a specified minimum total cost. Other local governments use different criteria for selecting the subset of local projects that should be included in the system. Those local governments that do not include all projects in their control systems argue that many projects are of low priority, involve small dollar amounts and are not interrelated with other projects. As such, it is believed that including these projects would only overburden the system with details and detract from its true advantages.

At any rate, the system should at least include all projects that are interrelated with other projects as well as those projects that involve a significant commitment of time, labor and dollar resources. The final decision concerning criteria for selecting projects to include in the system should rest with the system team leader.

2. *When should the system begin tracking a project?* For the most part, the project control system yields the greatest benefits of coordination during the actual construction phase. However, there are very positive benefits of tracking a project as soon as it is authorized. By following a project through design, planning, land acquisition, opening to bidders, and so on, those involved in the actual construction phase receive advance notification of when they have to begin a project and can make preparations accordingly. Obviously, managers cannot ensure that a project will stay on schedule as it passes through the city or county council (or other levels of government if the project involves intergovernmental grants) and the legal/legislative phases. However, having an initial "best guess" schedule of these phases once the project is authorized (and regularly updating this

schedule) makes it possible for those involved in the actual construction phase to anticipate workloads and make contingency plans.

As such, it is suggested that the system be organized to monitor projects as soon as they are authorized. The most complex construction scheduling networks can be introduced into the system as soon as it appears that the projects will be funded. However, if system users see no value in tracking projects before the construction phase, they can design the system accordingly.

3. *Where should the system be headquartered?* Some state and local governments with project control systems have designed elaborate system control rooms where all projects are charted on the walls. Other state and local governments have found less sophisticated systems perfectly adequate. Although it is essential that a single location be found for charting project progress, the program team leader should decide on the appropriate degree of sophistication. If all project control benefits can be realized by displaying program stats on a single bulletin board, there is no reason to make the system more complex.

4. *How often should the program team meet?* Some systems feature regularly scheduled meetings every two weeks. Other systems have regular reporting schedules but have meetings only when scheduled by the program leader. Although the frequency of meetings and reporting are best determined by the needs of the administration as seen by the program team leaders, some regular meeting or reporting is strongly advised.

*Gathering Project Networks*

The next major step in implementing the project control system is to gather the unconstrained schedules for all projects. It is important that program team members fully understand the importance of the system so that they can help their departments develop a set of fairly detailed project schedules. It is also important that each schedule have enough milestones, or checkpoints, built in so that regular monitoring of project status is possible. The more frequent the milestones, the sooner schedule slippages can be detected and master schedule adjustments can be made.

Appropriate milestones can be set up either on a standardized basis or uniquely for each project. Alternatively, certain types of projects can be assigned a standard set of milestones while other projects can have a unique set of milestones. Because of the varied nature, most projects do not follow a similar sequence of steps through any of the different project phases. For those projects that do follow a similar set of procedures, a standardized set of milestones can be used. In other cases, a unique set of milestones can be used at the discretion of the program team leader or the team members most closely associated with the project. The important thing is that enough milestones be used so that schedule slippages can be detected early. However, these checkpoints will largely be influenced by the official procedures of the state or local government (especially in the legal/legislative phase).

In many cases, individual projects involve work from several agencies and/or contractors. In these cases, the program team member from the department with greatest overall responsibility for the project must take the lead in seeing that the schedule is produced. This person must see that all involved departments or contractors submit raw schedules for their parts in the project and from these develop a complete project schedule for introduction into the master schedule. Obviously, when a project involves several agencies and/or contractors, a great deal of cooperation is required.

### Developing the Master Program Schedule

The most important problem in developing the master schedule is recognizing the interdependence of different projects. Although many projects are virtually free standing, some projects are definitely interdependent. In addition, some projects, although not being absolutely dependent on each other, might best be worked on in a logical sequence. Taken together, these projects must form the core of the master schedule and should be scheduled in an appropriate sequence recognizing interrelationships and the local progression of work activities.

Taking weather considerations into account, the master schedule should start with the beginning of the funding period. Obviously, to the extent possible, projects should be organized so that outside work is scheduled during the construction season and indoor work scheduled during the winter and during uncertain months on either end of the construction season.

Once the core schedule has been developed, the remaining freestanding projects can be added. If these projects are truly freestanding, there will be a great deal of flexibility in the way the schedule can be developed. The only essential consideration in scheduling the freestanding projects is preventing any participating agency from being assigned an overload. If the core projects are scheduled first and an overload is avoided, the freestanding projects can be scheduled according to other efficiency criteria or state or local government priorities at the discretion of the program team participants.

Once the master schedule has been agreed upon, it must be distributed to all appropriate individuals. This will give these individuals an advance picture of their workloads over the coming months. When the need for schedule adjustments occur (which it likely will), these individuals will know their scheduled slack periods and can adjust themselves accordingly.

### Monitoring Project Status

Once the master schedule has been developed, the system must be monitored to check actual versus planned progress. This is simply a matter of seeing whether milestones are being reached according to schedule. Actual progress should be continually mapped on the system chart using any graphic technique desired. This makes it possible for any individual involved in the program to check the progress of any project at a glance. Updating the status of projects should take place at the scheduled meetings of the program team. At these meetings, individual members of the team should each be given an opportunity to report on the status of those projects for which they are responsible.

Prior to these meetings, each member of the program team should submit individual exception reports to the program secretary. These reports should list those projects that have fallen behind schedule, the reasons for the slippage and an estimate of the new milestone dates. These reports should be collected and summarized into one master exception report to be distributed to the program team members for discussion at the scheduled meetings. At this time, the master schedule can be adjusted to reflect these changes. By making these schedule changes at the program meeting, all members of the team will be aware of changes in their individual schedules and workloads in advance and can adjust accordingly.

### Tracking Project Expenditures

In addition to tracking physical project progress, the system can easily be modified to track expenditures. For financial tracking to be possible, the planned events that should signify progress payments to contractors must be included as project milestones. This implies that progress inspection work activities must be incorporated in the project schedules to coincide with these progress payments. As such, those people with inspection responsibilities will have advance knowledge of their inspection workload and when they must authorize payments.

In addition to progress payment milestones, financial milestones should be set at the end of each department's involvement with a project. For example, once the planning department finishes with a project, that department's costs should be identified and noted. More detailed financial milestones can be added as desired.

If these procedures are followed, the amount of money spent on a project can be charted alongside the chart of physical project progress. There are three major advantages of including cost information in the project control system. First, costs can be kept by project. The primary cost accounting system of most state or local governments typically follows department or organizational lines. Tracking costs on a project basis, however, satisfies the logical notion that the responsibility for expenditures on a project should rest with those who have responsibility for managing it. Second, actual versus budgeted expenditures can be monitored. This is especially useful in detecting cost overruns and identifying the appropriate corrective action. Third, the true support costs of a project can be clearly identified. Oftentimes these costs are included in a large overhead cost and are never properly allocated among the efforts they actually supported. Although some indirect and overhead costs cannot be allocated without an inordinate amount of additional effort, tracking costs in this manner represents an important first step in identifying true project costs.

## NOTES

1. James L. Mercer, "Organizing for the 80's—What About Matrix Management?" *Business*, July–August 1981, pp. 25–33.

2. "Project Management: Past, Present and Future: An Editorial Summary," *IEEE Transactions in Management*, August 1979, p. 49.

3. Charles H. Marks, "Managing Industrial Projects," *Automation*, February 1979, p. 70.

4. Ibid., pp. 70–71.

5. Stanley M. Davis and Paul R. Lawrence, *Matrix* (Reading, Mass.: Addison-Wesley, 1977).

6. Ibid., p. 77.

7. Marks, "Managing Industrial Projects."

8. Ibid., p. 72.

9. "Project Management," p. 50.

# 9

# Contingency Planning for Changed Circumstances

"You really never lose 'til you stop trying!"

—Mike Ditka

Contingency planning provides a state or local government administrator with a course of action for events not planned. Public sector organizations are almost always the targets of changing political attitudes and economic shifts. This often causes "crisis planning" or "knee-jerk reactions" that can cripple or render ineffective even the best-managed organizations. Such factors produce an acute need for contingency plans to be available to react more quickly to changes in the environment. A Civil Defense emergency plan is an example of a contingency plan currently possessed by most state and local governments.

## WHAT ARE CONTINGENCY PLANS?

Contingency plans are preparations to take specific action(s) when an event not planned for in the formal planning process takes place.[1] As the definition states, events in the governmental, political, or even personal worlds of employees and decisionmakers can have an effect upon strategic direction and organizational operations.

## NEED FOR CONTINGENCY PLANNING IN STATE AND LOCAL GOVERNMENTS

Although contingency planning may not be a new concept to for-profit organizations, state and local governments often have historically been viewed as self-perpetuating entities that can adapt to any shifts in internal or external factors. The science of "muddling through" often became the standard for many years. Recently, enlightened state and local government leaders have seen the need for contingency planning as a part of strategic planning and as a part of their ever-gloomy revenue picture. Some factors contributing to this change are noted below.

### Professionalism

The growth and expansion of professionalism in all levels of government has brought about the need for contingency planning. Professional state agency heads and city and county managers have replaced the old political crony of the governor, mayor or county chairman as the person responsible for daily operations. These professional managers are expected by elected officials to have contingency plans in the event of unforeseen circumstances that arise in all governmental organizations. As Sun Zi said: "Weak leadership can wreck the soundest strategy; forceful execution of even a poor plan can often bring victory."

### Technology and Communications

With advances in technology and communications, state and local government managers are able to use historical precedent from other areas to react in the most advantageous manner when unforeseen events occur.

### Economic Change

Like all organizations, state and local governments are altered by economic shifts. Although economists are able to predict shifts in national, state and local economic trends, managers must also be able to plan for increased or decreased tax revenues, and increased or decreased need for government services. For example, a resort community town administrator underestimated revenue from tourism activities one year by $600,000 (in a $5 million budget). The town council was very upset because it had no plans to utilize the additional funds.

### Legal Changes

Court decisions affecting all areas of government constantly change policy. Areas most affected in state and local governments are bidding and contract awards. Managers should always have alternative plans available for conditions/events affecting areas of government operations and management.

## WHAT IS CONTINGENCY PLANNING?

Contingency planning is viewed as an integral part of good overall strategic planning. As discussed in chapter 3, strategic planning is a system of decisions based upon occurrences that are likely to happen. Before implementation of a truly effective strategic planning process, selected contingency plans should be devised for those conditions less likely to happen but are possible and if they did occur, could cause difficulty. An important fact to remember, however, is that contingency planning is not limited to those factors that could cause harm to the organization. Factors presenting windows of opportunity to expand or improve service should be a part of any organization's contingency planning process, as well.

## STEPS IN CONTINGENCY PLANNING

Like strategic planning, there are some basic steps to effective contingency planning. First, state and local government organizations should identify specific contingencies for which plans are to be made. Second, probability of occurrence should be developed for each event. "What if ..." questions should be asked for a wide range of possible occurrences, both advantageous and disadvantageous for the organization. Since no one organization can expect to plan for all occurrences, the most serious or wide-ranging problems or opportunities should be discussed by the strategic planning team and have a probability of occurrence attached to each. Some additional events with no probability must be addressed because of the crucial nature of the circumstances. For example, a court order disallowing a tax relied upon for a large proportion of revenue could have a low probability of occurrence, but very serious consequences, if such an event should occur.[2] The succession to the U.S. presidency by the vice president, speaker of the house, and so on, is another form of contingency planning. For example, the president and vice president will rarely be seen together in public and never fly in the same airplane. This is a contingency plan based upon the likelihood of a plane crash or other negative event. The possibility of the occurrence of the event is low, but the circumstances resulting if it occurred would be disastrous.

The next step is to neutralize or offset as much as possible the effects of the event when and if it occurs. Contingent strategies should be identified and evaluated in the light of the organization's capabilities and constraints in dealing with the event. Organizations can decide from this information whether it is better to simply plan for the occurrence happening, or whether to take precautionary action to further lessen the likely occurrence of the event. Contingent strategies should be as specific as possible. If a tax base drops in a certain jurisdiction, simply stating "raise revenue" or "cut expenses" will not suffice. The more serious a change such as this, the more specific the contingency plan should be. Specific, factual steps to implement the contingency plans are necessary, as well.[3]

Trigger mechanisms, points or warning signs of a change from the organization's original strategic plan should also be an integral part of the overall contingency plan. When a trigger point is reached is when a good manager begins to look at his/her contingency plan for assistance with proceeding. This trigger point can range from a bad economic forecast to the sudden death or resignation of a key official or line manager to changed politics. Two levels of response to such a situation that could possibly be generated are as follows.

1. *Higher-level monitoring.* No precipitant action should be taken: in fact, no action plan may be required. However, the *possibility* of a need for a change in main-line assumptions should be noted and indicators should be watched.
2. *Action.* At this level, the decision is made that conditions are different, and a contingency plan is implemented or some aspect of a strategy is modified.[4]

With good contingency planning, effective state and local government managers will be able to seek procedures and structures in the wake of an unforeseen deviation from the original strategic plan. Sufficient detail in the contingency plan should allow the decisionmaker flexibility but have information enough for an informed decision to be made.[5]

Contingency planning is an integral part of effective strategic planning and should not be done as a second thought. Some managers do not believe in contingency planning, preferring to allow unplanned circumstances to occur and to react at that time. This almost always leads to "crisis management."

## ELEMENTS OF CONTINGENCY PLANNING

Like all aspects of strategic planning, the contingency planning process in state and local government has specific elements that, when used in proper order and context, will produce an effective contingency plan. The five key concepts of contingency planning are as follows:

1. The contingency planning matrix, which helps an organization to recognize organizational vulnerabilities and opportunities from both internal and external perspectives
2. The operational status indicator, which allows an organization to determine a single indicator that is most descriptive of the fiscal and operational viability of the organization
3. The economic indicators, which are available from the environment and are determined to be most significant to the organization

**Exhibit 9–1**
**State and Local Government Contingency Planning Matrix**

Focus

|  | Internal | External |
|---|---|---|
| Vulnerability | Quadrant A | Quadrant B |
| Opportunity | Quadrant C | Quadrant D |

Emphasis

4. Strategic planning-environmental indices, which are to be monitored by the various departments

5. Budget-variation indicators, which provide indications as to the accuracy of the current year's budget, with a variance indicator that can be keyed to both opportunity and vulnerability triggers for contingency plans[6]

Examples of these five key concepts are presented below.

### Starting Point for Contingency Planning

The starting point for state and local government contingency planning should be the development of a contingency planning matrix (Exhibit 9–1). This matrix divides contingency planning into two major categories for monitoring purposes: internal vulnerabilities/opportunities and external vulnerabilities/opportunities. Most state and local government organizations are very adept at planning for Quadrant A, organizational vulnerability from internal threats. Managers are easily able to see attitudes, work ethics, turnover and office demeanor as indicators of strategic planning failure or oversights. Internal threats such as these are common to all organizations regardless of sector, public or private, or to the nature of the organizations, manufacturing, service or governmental. Trigger mechanisms can be tangible either through perception of attitude or through statistical evidence that can be gathered and evaluated.

Quadrant B has more intangible trigger mechanisms. These may include an increased public attitude of dissatisfaction with the organization or its delivery of a service. This is much harder to detect due to the difficulty of a state or local government organization to measure its success. Private-for-profit organizations can use a drop in sales or profits as a measurement, whereas in government, the public must still support the organization by paying taxes. Complaints will usually increase, however, as we all know.

Quadrant C is where opportunity to improve the internal organization comes from within. Increasing the efficiency or effectiveness of service delivery to the public with the same budget could be an example. This could be suggested by a self-managed team and triggered by it as well.

Quadrant D is where an opportunity arises for the state or local government as a result of an external occurrence. An example is a new corporation relocating to a state or city and creating new jobs. Trigger mechanisms for this can be tangible, such as increased revenue.[7]

### Who Focuses on Contingency Planning?

In state and local governments, those who control budgets and regulate organizations are the ones most capable of focusing upon the forces of opportunity and vulnerability, internally and externally. Strategic planning as a whole and contingency planning in particular should be practiced by political decisionmakers as well as line managers.

A complete state or local government's strategic plan should include key issues to be monitored from all four quadrants. Top-level managers should be the ones charged with monitoring the internal and external vulnerabilities and opportunities. They should also be responsible for formulating contingency plans, along with the strategic planning team. It is acceptable to delegate preplanned actions to middle or first-line managers, but the monitoring of the indices and trigger mechanisms in each quadrant should stay, at all times, with the chief executive officer or be delegated to the strategic planning team.

### Operational Status of the Organization

The next key concept is that of identification of the operational status of the state or local government organization. In all organizations, there should be a single indicator to describe viability of an organization. This indicator reflects organizational health and is derived from a consensus of top management and elected officials. The concept here is for top managers and officials of the organization to devise an operational status scale. This scale, usually numbered 0 to 10 (10 = best), shows the different stages of viability. The level of current operations can include such factors as the number of citizens served, the amount of increase ordered in workload, the increases or decreases in funding and/or citizen and employee satisfaction. Whatever is selected should receive an action level of monitoring. Once this scale is established, any change should be a trigger mechanism for the organization as a whole to shift to a contingency plan. All managers should be updated constantly on this key indicator. An example of an operational status scale is shown in Exhibit 9–2.

**Exhibit 9-2**
**State and Local Government Contingency Planning Operational Status Scale**

| Level | Definition |
|-------|------------|
| 10 | Exceptional situation -- Viable/diverse revenue base, no debt, high economic activity, highly optimistic future, outstanding commitment from competent/key staff, new infrastructure, cash rich. |
| 9 | Exceptional situation -- Viable revenue base, high economic activity, some debt, optimistic future, excellent infrastructure, excellent staff, good cash position. |
| 8 | Exceptional situation -- solid revenue base, good economic activity, reasonably optimistic future, some debt, good staff, some cash. |
| 7 | Transitioning Down -- level eight moving to level five. |
| 6 | Transitioning Up -- level five moving to level eight. |
| 5 | Good Situation -- good revenue base, viable economic activity, future is satisfactory, good staff, debt somewhat high, cash satisfactory. |
| 4 | Transitioning Down -- level five moving to level two. |
| 3 | Transitioning Up -- level two moving to level five. |
| 2 | Survival Needs -- revenue base declining, economic activity flat, moderate commitment and enthusiasm from staff, very high debt, cash poor. |
| 1 | Survival Mode -- insolvent, operating on guts and credit, waning enthusiasm and commitment from staff, at debt capacity. |
| 0 | Survival Mode -- insolvent, can operate less than three months without case infusion, staff bailing out, notes being called. |

J. William Pfeiffer, Leonard Goodstein and Timothy Nolan, *Applied Strategic Planning: A How to Do It Guide* (San Diego: University Associates, 1986), p. 139.

### Indices

Economic indices are the next key concept to be addressed. Although state and local governments are often not initially tied directly to business fluctuations, business market fluctuations will have the same effect on the buying and spending power of the government as they will on that of the business. Planning for revenue from taxes and fees for services will be affected by a swing in the economy. Local governments are hit first by localized business fluctuations and state governments second.

Often communities in the Midwest and South can be devastated by the loss of one plant or factory. State and local leaders should always be wary of downward trends but should also be able to see upward trends in the economy, or technological changes that could benefit an area. Attracting new industry to an area or expanding existing industry can increase the tax bases of local governments and allow expansion of economic opportunity.

Expanded strategic planning environmental indices include changes in population, demographics, legislation, politics, international affairs, values, and so on. Budget variation indicators are those that show how projections of the current year budget compare to actual spending. If needs for financial shifts dominate budget meetings, contingency plans should be triggered to shift funds or priorities. Alert levels indicate the need for action if percentages of budget allocations over a three-month period fall into certain categories:

*Alert level 3*: 10–15 percent over or under budget—some action required

*Alert level 2*: 15–20 percent over or under budget—immediate action required

*Alert level 1*: 20 percent or more over or under budget—emergency action required

These key concepts are vital to all state and local government managers in successful contingency planning and, in the broader scope, in strategic planning. It is the duty of all chief executives to watch a trigger mechanism to indicate the need or possible need for implementation of contingency plans.

## A CONTINGENCY PLANNING CASE STUDY

As has been discussed, an effective state or local government organization must be able to react to unforeseen or unplanned circumstances. Contingency plans should be seen as ways to avoid organizational destruction and take advantage of opportunities for expansion. The following case study and reaction to circumstances surrounding a strategic plan will provide an opportunity to see where contingency planning can save a public sector organization from internal or external forces of vulnerability or opportunity.

A midsize intergovernmental organization (regional council) is charged with regional planning, aging and local community technical assistance. Funding comes from four counties, two major cities and several small communities. Staffing consists of twenty-one professional administrators in the areas of planning, aging and community assistance. Funding for all except aging is controlled by the board of directors, a group consisting of seventeen local elected and appointed officials who set internal and external policy and pay scales. Although no member community is bound to pay into the council, all have paid in full for twenty years. The council budget consists of state, federal and local contracts, mostly local. The bulk of state and federal money covers specifically the aging program. Since the communities are all in one area of the state, regional economic forecasts are a good index of economic activity. For the past two years, all indices have shown strong growth in most professional and service areas; however, agriculture has shown a decline in strength relative to other indices.

The council has in place a strategic plan, but no contingency plans exist. The board has asked the professional staff of the council to prepare selective contingency plans for the council. As it begins the contingency planning process, the council staff decides that developing a contingency planning matrix is an item necessary to begin. The team finds that Quadrant A, internal vulnerability, is easily defined. The planning team can see through employee attitudes, turnover and the work ethic how the organization is working. One of the most significant items for this review is the rate of employee turnover in the last year as compared to the regional average. What should be the trigger mechanism for a contingency plan? What is the plan? Of twenty-two professional positions, eight have had a turnover in the past twelve months. If a trigger mechanism is set at 5 percent, should a contingency plan be set in motion? These figures indicate that more than 36 percent of the staff has turned over in the last year.

What has caused the high turnover and what should the planning team do? A short-range contingency plan is to conduct a salary survey of other similar organizations in the area and to bring those findings to the board of directors. Another contingency plan is to shift some workers who may be able to help those areas hurt by higher turnover. The planning team, however, believes that it must look for a long-term, permanent solution, such as pay increases or better benefits. As discussed before, one person, in this case the council executive director, should be responsible for monitoring this data.

The planning team finds that Quadrant B, external vulnerability, is more difficult to pinpoint. Business and industry can use sales figures. An intergovernmental organization such as this one could use the satisfaction/dissatisfaction with services provided. This can be measured in two ways, the first and most important being the attitude of members as expressed to the directors in monthly meetings and through daily contact. Since the organization is so heavily reliant upon funds from many different sources, it should treat any type of communication from members as a trigger mechanism. The planning team decides that a system of procedures to follow up on these communications is a good contingency plan reaction. It is decided that the plan should include a reporting system back to the originator of the complaints.

The planning team also decides that a more active system may be the monthly distribution of a questionnaire to all members. With a standardized scale, a statistical figure can be obtained to indicate dissatisfaction. A scale allows an indicator to be set, possibly at ± 5 percent, to trigger investigation of problems or possibilities for expanded services (Quadrant D).

Quadrant C, internal opportunities, is one about which many managers are myopic. Few managers see needs for contingency planning based on internal opportunities because such plans often focus on negatives or on external opportunities. Quadrant A was where we saw that pessimistic employee attitudes and high turnover can necessitate contingency planning. If a director sees turnover rates drop and employee attitudes improve, he/she should then look for the sources. If turnover rates drop 5 percent (the trigger mechanism for Quadrant A), this should be viewed as an opportunity for internal improvement. This 5 percent drop should trigger the same level of reaction as a 5 percent increase should. If a policy or program is changing attitudes toward the positive, it should be expanded. Quadrant C should have the same trigger mechanisms as Quadrant A, and the contingency plans should be as important as Quadrant A results would be.

Quadrant D, external opportunities, are as closely related to Quadrant B as are Quadrants A and C to each other. As previously described, one of the best measures would be attitudes expressed by member representatives. When one is praised rather than criticized, one should take notice. Most public organizations usually hear only critical information, so when praise is passed on, it is a trigger mechanism. The active system of questionnaire distribution as described in Quadrant B should include the opportunity-type questions to help in Quadrant D.

These are only examples of how a contingency planning matrix would help a regional council of governments. There are far more possibilities, however. By linking procedures in Quadrants A, C, B and D, one can complete the matrix with little description or duplication of effort. This would also create the circumstances to remember opportunities, as well as vulnerabilities, in a matrix.

The next key element is the construction of an operational status indicator. As described earlier, this scale shows the level of organizational operations as described by management at a level of 0–10. All organizations should reach for the top (usually a 10); however, it is not always possible to maintain such a high rating. For example, a state government organization is now at level 5. Since the organization is in a constant state of flux, it is agreed that a monthly review is necessary to determine a current level for that period. What should be the trigger mechanism? A drop of one level takes the organization to level 4 (transitioning down), and an increase in one level goes to level 6 (transitioning up). Both of these are trigger mechanisms to determine where success or failure has changed the level. Determinants could include such factors as employment levels, employee turnover, workload, member satisfaction, new projects, additional members, response to job advertisement and pay levels as compared to other state government organizations.

Contingency plans for this type of organization should include reassignment of employees, reevaluation of priorities in departments, establishment of new departments, further studies or a combination of all. Since this key element is an indicator of the vitality of the entire organization, any change should become the priority of all managers and employees.

The next key concepts are economic indicators and strategic planning environmental indices. An organization such as the intergovernmental council discussed earlier must pay close attention due to the close association, but typical lagging, of government finances with economic trends. Key trends that should be monitored by this council are unemployment rates, housing and building permits, new business licenses and tax increases or decreases.

Combining all factors reflects local or regional economic trends. A change in any one of the factors may not change overall economic forecasts, but a trigger mechanism could be set if there is a change of three points in any indicator. This should trigger the contingency plan of shifting resources away from one particular area to another.

The more diverse the area, the more possibility for fluctuation in economic trends. As we have seen, this fluctuation presents opportunities as well as vulnerabilities. If agriculture prices drop, one may expect some backlogging of payments from members who rely heavily upon farming areas. The converse is true in the case of a boom in one industry or a good crop, because more money can be brought into or invested in an area that may be undergoing an economic downturn at the same time. A contingency trigger may be set up from a percentage of money collected from more stable, non-seasonal, professional or technical service areas. These key indices should be monitored monthly, if not weekly.

Finally, budget variation indicators can be used to show where money may be "hard" or "soft." For example, in the regional council example, the budget is divided by the following elements:

- Local member government assistance—50 percent
- Federal and state aging program money—25 percent
- Interests and investments—20 percent
- Miscellaneous—5 percent

Looking at these figures, one can see how heavily the council relies on government assistance. Federal and state money is specifically needed for the aging program. Since money is received daily from different sources, one should use a monthly review of budget variation indicators. Since the percentages of money are so great, a trigger mechanism should be set at ± 10 percent of levels for the local government assistance and ± 10 percent for federal and state money and interests and investments. What if the money for local government assistance drops to 37 percent? The only contingency to use without affecting services would be money from interest and investments. Aging money is in federal grants; therefore, it is untouchable and typically cannot be used for any other program. Another contingency plan would be to find where the deficit is coming from and cut back on services to those communities that are not paying their share into the fund. A cut in the same percentage of the deficit would be a solution. If money for the aging program is cut, a priority list of programs should be drawn up to see which ones should be kept. If funding is cut out completely and given to another agency, a plan of employee attrition into other areas of the organization or layoff should also be part of a contingency plan.

### Summary

This is by no means meant to be a complete evaluation of a contingency plan for an organization such as the regional council. It is, however, meant to be an example of how every state and local government organization is able to make contingency planning a part of strategic planning. One can see from the limited examples how many different factors must be considered when making decisions regarding contingency plans.

## PROS AND CONS OF CONTINGENCY PLANNING

Contingency planning, like all aspects of state and local government strategic planning, has detractors who believe the negatives in the process make it more trouble than it is worth. A basic problem is the fact that contingency planning is time-consuming, especially for events that may not take place. Managers who say "I'll cross that bridge when I come to it!" don't want to spend time and money on this aspect of strategic planning.

There also are some negative aspects of contingency planning. First, it sometimes places too many negatives in the hands of managers. These pessimistic possibilities generate fears, negative thinking and general pessimism that many organizational leaders do not want to generate. Second, overly optimistic plans may also have a negative effect on managers if predicted objectives are not met. Finally, negative contingency plans, such as cutbacks and layoffs, can be devastating to employee morale and those outside the organization when revealed.

Conversely, the advantages of contingency planning are simple. It is a vital aspect of strategic planning. The world is not perfect, and circumstances do arise that are unforeseen or unplanned, and it may be more convenient to plan for them before they happen rather than expend precious resources in a crisis mode if/when they do occur. The effect can be lessened if an organization is properly prepared through contingency planning. Managers and organization leaders are more prepared to deal with events that may be potentially beneficial or devastating. If their solutions are rationally thought out before they occur, emotional elements associated with a death or other devastating personnel failure can be dealt with quickly and effectively. A state and local government manager who does not take contingency planning seriously probably can't be considered a complete executive.

As one advances in a career, he/she will face unplanned situations and occurrences. This is where the major benefit of contingency planning lies. If a manager and organization can react to those unforeseen and usually unwanted events in a professional, rational manner, the organization can survive. One must remember that contingency planning also includes opportunity planning. The manager who wants to include ways to improve an organization or move up the operational status indicator will most likely be effective and successful.

## CONTINGENCY PLANNING PROBLEMS

The following four situations are problems that might be faced by state or local government managers as they try to be successful in carrying out their strategic plan. How would you develop contingency plans to deal with these situations?

### Situation A: A State Government

The current State House is seventy-five years old. Conditions are bad: the roof leaks, the building is drafty in the winter and there is no privacy for employees due to overcrowding. The state was forced to rent offices for 15 percent of its employees in nearby buildings. Citizens are outraged because when they come to the State House to visit legislators or experience the history, they can never find a place to park. There is a severe need for meeting spaces for the committees and interest groups who use the State House on a regular basis. A $125,000 space needs study prepared by the governor's brother-in-law was completely useless, except that it mentioned a potential asbestos problem. Three alternatives have been discussed: rehabilitate the existing facility, add a 40,000-square-foot addition or construct a new facility. A statewide citizens task force has been created by the governor. It is chaired by a local developer owning the single largest vacant parcel in the state capital downtown area where the new building would most likely be placed.

Construction trade leaders are pressing for a new building. Downtown state capital merchant groups insist that the new facility remain in the downtown area. Statewide citizens groups stridently request that the facility be located away from downtown, perhaps as an anchor for the new lakefront redevelopment property. They cite less expensive land and construction costs, along with the opportunity to provide ample convenient surface parking. The capital city's property tax rate is at the maximum allowed. Property assessments have increased by double-digit figures for the last five years. The state legislature is apathetic about the proposed project. Members anticipate receiving a substantial unfavorable ruling from a pending labor arbitration. Little enthusiasm and no clear consensus for the project exist at the legislative or key committee levels. The governor and the state legislature are severely split on almost every issue, and the situation is worsening. In this particular situation, the legislature expects the governor to take a leadership role.

What would you do? Who would you involve? What would be the contingency plan(s) and associated triggers for this situation?

### Situation B: A Municipality

The city of Parched is suffering a major drought situation. The rainfall this summer has been 15 to 18 inches below normal. The level of Lake Paradise, which is the city's major water supply, has dropped from 624 feet to 611.7 feet. The city has two major industrial water users that are crucial for the economic livelihood of the community. One of two water treatment plant intake valves is close to being above the lake surface due to the drop in the level of the lake.

The city water fund is extremely healthy with a large surplus of several million dollars. A pilot dredging program for the lake is in place. The city is currently selling water to three surrounding communities. Water usage has been peaking at 46 million gallons per day.

The city has been suffering from both a tremendous summer heat as well as a tremendous dry spell. The lake level is dropping at about one foot per month. The weather forecast calls for a very dry period for the next thirty days. This weekend, the city is expecting 100,000 people to be involved in a major softball tournament. The ball fields are dry and the teams and organizers of the tournament are very concerned.

The park district, which is a separate entity from the city, has three 18-hole golf courses that require considerable water to keep greens in prime condition. Without golf fees, the park district will be in a serious financial condition.

What would you do? What contingency plans would you develop?

### Situation C: A Resort Community

It is June 30 in a resort community.[8] A story breaks in the local media about fire code violations at beach hotels. Simultaneously, there is a hepatitis outbreak at resort strip restaurants. The city manager has just been informed by the director of parks and recreation that 100 dolphins have washed up on the beach. The civil defense director has also just informed the city manager that a hurricane is four days south of the city, and the computer says the hurricane will hit the city with force 5 winds (about 140 mph). The state transportation department has also just informed the city manager that a light rail line has been approved to connect with the beach at 19th Street. The state department of economic development has also just informed the city manager that a new state plan indicates that no more investments should be made in oceanfront property. A promoter has scheduled a major music concert for the fourth of July weekend. The last time this occurred, 30,000 students attended and the National Guard was called in.

If you were the city manager of this community, what issues would you deal with and in what order of priority? What is the approach that you would use to deal with these issues? What contingency plans would you have?

### Situation D: Various State and Local Governments

What contingency plans would you develop for the following situations?

### Situation A: Municipal Public Works Department

Strategy                 Privatize collection of municipal solid waste

Situation                Contractor arrested for felony

What would be your contingency plan?

### Situation B: State Government Buildings and Grounds Department

Strategy                 Use volunteers to cut grass in parks and public rights of way

Situation                Volunteers demand comparable worth dollars

What would be your contingency plan to deal with this situation?

### Situation C: State Government Department of Transportation Fleet Maintenance Operation

Strategy                 Contract out major overhauls

Situation                New revenue source provides 25 percent more funds annually

What would be your contingency plan to handle this situation?

### Situation D: Local Public Housing Authority

Strategy                 Do repairs with own forces

Situation                Plumber's wages triple to $200 per hour

What would be your contingency plan to handle this situation?

**Situation E: County Building Maintenance Department**

Strategy          Doing 50 percent maintenance with own crews, 50 percent with private contractor

Situation         Technology breakthrough allows for in-house crews to do same work in 40 percent less time

What would be your contingency plan to handle this situation?

## NOTES

1. J. William Pfeiffer, Leonard Goodstein, and Timothy M. Nolan, *Applied Strategic Planning: A How to Do It Guide* (San Diego: University Associates, 1986), p. 135.

2. George A. Steiner, *Strategic Planning* (New York: Free Press, 1979), p. 231.

3. Ibid., p. 232.

4. Leonard Goodstein, J. William Pfeiffer, and Timothy N. Nolan, "Applied Strategic Planning: A New Model for Organizational Growth and Vitality," *Strategic Planning Selected Readings*, ed. J. William Pfeiffer (San Diego: University Associates, 1986), pp. 20–21.

5. Steiner, *Strategic Planning*, pp. 233–234.

6. Pfeiffer, Goodstein and Nolan, *Applied Strategic Planning*, p. 135.

7. Ibid., p. 138.

8. E. T. "Joe" Buchanan, dean, Campus and Community Services, Tidewater Community College, Virginia Beach Campus, Virginia Beach, Va., 1988.

# *10*

# Strategic Management for the Future

"The future belongs to those who believe in the beauty of their dreams."

—Eleanor Roosevelt

The only constants that will face state and local government organizations as they move into the 1990s and beyond will be change and the need to continue to manage in a constrained revenue environment. One of the most effective tools that can be used in this setting is strategic management.

Because the need for change management methods is, and is expected to be, so acute at the state and local government levels, public administrators need to break some new ground in the use of heretofore mainly private sector techniques. Strategic management is one such technique. Such new approaches are not without risks, but those risks can be effectively reduced through a good understanding of the strategic management process. As a wise sage once stated: "The pioneers are the persons with the arrows in their chests."

The purpose of this chapter is to define strategic management as it applies to state and local governments.[1] The chapter includes such a definition and a discussion of the components of strategic management and how these may differ from more conventional planning and management practices and of characteristics that should be present in successful strategic management processes in state and local governments. This chapter is designed to enhance understanding about the principles of strategic management and to understand how to use it to manage effectively in a state or local government cutback management situation in the future.

## WHAT IS STRATEGIC MANAGEMENT?

Strategic management can be defined as the effective management of change influencing an organization. Other definitions include the steps one takes to carry out a strategic plan or, conversely, the overall response to one's environment of which strategic planning is only one part. Strategic management is the implementation of strategies and tactics developed to determine a new direction for the organization as it proceeds through transition, so it may fulfill its responsibilities in a dynamic and rapidly changing environment.

For purposes of this book, it is suggested that strategic management be defined as the process of articulating a future mission/vision for the state or local government and planning, directing and controlling its complete activities to meet the desired mission/vision. It is clear in both the private sector and in state and local government that the definitions and practices of strategic management vary widely. There is no single, widely accepted or commonly understood description of the strategic management process. Each organization typically develops its own version of strategic management. It does so in light of its own environments, organizational culture, styles of leadership, frequency of crises and executive interests and acceptance.

### The Need for Strategic Management

Few state or local government agencies operate in a stable environment and few, if any, have experienced stable demands, funding and service levels over a long period of time. Whether up or down, state and local government organizations have been required to adjust to reflect these changes. This often has had to be accomplished in a crisis mode without proper preplanning for a smooth transition. Strategic management cannot prevent change; however, it can affect change, influence it, anticipate it and help prepare for it and adapt to it. Strategic management focuses on the changing environment within which a state or local government operates. It considers the way the organization is impacted by change and develops strategies and tactics for the organization to effect desired change. It accomplishes this by influencing the organization, by providing leadership in shaping the organization's future and by managing the organization in such a manner that when change does occur, the organization can address it quickly, efficiently and effectively. To be effective, such a strategic management process involves the following:

- Understanding the organization's internal and external environments
- Actively monitoring these environments

- Collecting data on program/service delivery management, demand, supply and performance
- Sending the necessary message to decisionmakers (knowing its content, to whom it should be sent, and how it should be communicated)
- Allocating resources on the basis of the organization's mission/vision, strategies, tactics and reallocating resources when necessary

By using strategic management, state and local governments can gain control over their own activities and their own destinies. All organizations are impacted by external and internal forces. Frequently, these are very important for public sector organizations because of the nature of political decisions and civil service systems affecting staff. A state or local government doesn't have to be powerless to decide its direction and to move in that direction. Strategic management encompasses issues of what a state or local government wants for itself, what it will have to do to achieve the desired goal, and how it can facilitate achieving it. Success involves scanning the internal and external situations facing the state or local government, listing opportunities and threats presented by the situation and developing strategies and tactical plans that meet those challenges.

## A Description of Strategic Management

If you grasp the bigger picture of strategic management defined above, you understand that strategic planning is the beginning step in strategic management. Described in chapter 3, strategic planning identifies and analyzes the trends and events likely to be encountered in the future that could have a significant impact on the organization, on its direction and on the way it operates. Strategic management is an effective tool to implement the approaches necessary within a state or local government organization to position it to meet its future responsibilities in the face of the impacts of change. Although the benefits of strategic planning are well documented, some state and local government officials have criticized the lack of a close relationship between strategic planning and the implementation of the strategies and tactics derived from the process. Because of this void, strategic management has evolved to provide the necessary system.

Strategic management has been used in the private sector for a number of years; however, its use by the state and local government sectors has been fairly sparse until recent times. Previously, it was believed that state and local governments were constrained from the use of certain management practices because of the political process and the statutes and regulations governing their duties and responsibilities. Therefore, strategic management in a state or local government organization was not thought to be feasible. Many of the strategies for state and local governments were thought to be generated by factors outside of the organization itself.

Recent changes resulting principally from tight revenues and increased costs have brought about a recognition that considerable flexibility does exist in the administration of state and local governments. It has been seen that the political process itself develops policy but does not develop strategies or tactics for carrying it out. Such strategies and tactics usually result from decisions of professional managers within the state or local government organization.

Strategic management could be described as a guiding star (i.e., vision/ mission) indicating a direction that the state or local government should take. The direction is shrouded with an environment external and internal to the organization that consists of political, social, demographic, economic, technological and related factors that have to be considered or dealt with as the organization follows its directed course. As it tries to be successful, most of management's attention will be focused on a forward view so as to identify opportunities and challenges for the future. Attention should also be paid to the past and what can be learned from it (i.e., what tactics and strategies of the past have worked, which haven't worked and so forth).

The mission/vision of an organization sets its direction and influences the development of strategies and tactics. The development of the mission/ vision statement is a part of the state or local government's strategic planning process. Mission/vision and the subsequent strategic management process are heavily influenced by the organization's "stakeholders," that is, the concern and interest of citizens or others who have an interest and "stake" in the outcome of the organization's efforts. In the case of CALTRANS, the California State Transportation Department, such stakeholders include the administration; Departmental Transportation Advisory Committee; the California Transportation Commission; state, regional and local agencies; special interest groups; and highway user groups.

Beyond addressing the external forces impacting a state or local government, strategies are needed to address its internal forces (i.e., its strengths and weaknesses) and to identify the resources it currently possesses and will need in the future. Strategic management of internal forces requires their thorough identification and evaluation. This analysis should lead the state or local government to develop strategies to enhance the areas of organizational strength and to reduce organizational weaknesses (in reality and in perception).

### Successful Strategic Management

The experiences of several state and local governments in implementing successful strategic management have identified five key features to success:

1. The strategic management process should be custom designed to a particular state or local government

2. The process should influence the annual budgeting process and all other internal management systems

3. The process should be flexible

4. The process should foster a sense of vision and "strategic thinking" throughout all levels of the organization

5. The process should be utilized to convey both within and outside the organization a specific direction and purpose for several years into the future

The strategic management process that has been adopted by CAL-TRANS addresses each of these key factors. Further, it has been implemented in such a way that

- It has been built on existing functions; thus, it was relatively easy to implement because many of the components were already in place

- It was not necessary to create an elaborate new organizational structure, but only to redirect what was already available; thus, it required few new resources

- It has already led to improved internal and external understanding of the department's long-term direction, primarily through distribution of the annual policy direction statement

### The Focus of Strategic Management

The "strategic" portion of strategic management derives from the fact that it is characterized as follows:

1. Is comprehensive in involving and affecting the essential elements of an organization (i.e., the top and the bottom)

2. Is purposeful in attempting to progress from the present state of being to another (often improved) state of being

3. Encourages an organization's members to view the present and future with detachment and perspective

4. Recognizes that changes to the organization usually must occur over long periods (two to four years) of time

Strategic management is visionary in terms of describing a direction and methods to achieve it.

The "management" portion of strategic management derives from the sense that the accepted elements of good management practices are present in the process (i.e., allocating resources, providing for accountability, monitoring results, adjusting plans and so forth). To put it another way, by using strategic management, the state or local government focuses on these aspects:

1. Defining precisely the mission/vision, goals and strategies of the organization
2. Developing tactical plans to achieve the goals and strategies as efficiently and effectively as possible
3. Providing resources necessary to implement the plan
4. Establishing responsibility and accountability for implementing the plan
5. Instituting performance measurement systems to monitor and report progress
6. Making provision for incentives (recognition and rewards) to fulfill individual and departmental/divisional responsibilities

Further, the strategic management process is dynamic and cyclical. In fact, the measurement system provides for reviewing and evaluating plans and progress and for revising plans as needed.

Although a major purpose of strategic management is to manage change successfully, the process also results in certain interim deliverables. For example, the strategic planning element produces key strategic issues, organizational goals, directions and program strategies. Implementation produces tactical and operating plans and achievements, and feedback produces performance measures. These results (deliverables) should be, and usually are, documented and sometimes published.

### Components of the Strategic Management Process

The basic components of the strategic management process are interactive and ongoing; that is, an organization is never completely finished with any step, only with one iteration of it. The components of the process feed each other. They also involve continuous monitoring and modification so that each organizational component is working toward the same desired ends (within a constantly changing environment), both external and internal.

Basically, the components of strategic management do not vary significantly from the conventional planning processes of the private sector and state and local government. One key difference, however, is that strategic management is focused on an overall vision of where the organization should be heading and how it can get there. Conventional planning processes, on the other hand, are typically program or project oriented or they are extrapolations of the present. That is, they focus on individual program or project plans, or on doing more of the same in the future. Other key characteristics that differentiate strategic management, especially in state and local government environments, include the following:

• Strategic management provides for greater consideration of external environmental influences

- It provides an orientation toward shaping an organization's own future and questioning its issues and opportunities
- It provides for integration and involvement of the entire organization (across levels and functions, top down and bottom up) in managing the organization toward successful accomplishment of its mission/vision
- It is oriented toward its mission/vision and service/product outputs, which, in turn, guide its inputs or resources needed
- It is based on continuous (or at least periodic) modifications, enhanced by ongoing monitoring of internal and external environments and the organization's accomplishments
- It requires solicitation and institutionalization of feedback from all levels of the organization concerning all aspects of its environments, plans and operations

With these points in mind, strategic management can be described as containing the following fundamental and essential components:

- Mission/vision statement (planning)
- Environmental scan (planning)
- Strategy development (planning)
- Tactical (action) plan development (planning, organizing, directing)
- Resource allocation (staffing, etc.)
- Performance measurement (controlling)

These components are described briefly in the following sections.

### Mission/Vision Statement

The development of the mission/vision is a part of the strategic planning process (chapter 3). The mission statement specifies the state or local government organization's basic function and responsibility: why it exists and what it is striving to achieve. Vision is a description of what things will look like when the mission has been accomplished. The mission relates more to an organization; vision more to a state or community. You could have both a vision statement and one or more mission statements in a strategic management process.

As a state or local government initiates the strategic management process, it normally has a sense of its mission or vision—at least historically, or as established by charter or statute. The further development and careful expression of the organization's mission/vision statement takes place at the initiation of the strategic management process. It should reflect traditional understanding of the organization's purpose, as well as any current modifications. As the organization examines its internal and external environments and decides what its future should be, the mission/vision statement (and supporting goals and strategies) may be modified, if necessary, to reflect accurately this new future mission/vision of the organization.

### Environmental Scan (Analysis of Strengths, Weaknesses, Opportunities and Threats—SWOT)

The environmental scanning process is also part of the strategic planning process (chapter 3). This process identifies the strengths and weaknesses of the state or local government's internal environment and the opportunities and threats presented by the external environment in which the organization operates. This step in the process is often referred to as strengths, weaknesses, opportunities and threats (SWOT analysis). To develop effective strategies to accomplish the mission or achieve the vision, the external environment must be considered. This includes the organization's customers/users/clients, its competitors, its funding sources, the community at large and the opportunities and threats associated with them. These external factors must be constantly monitored, updated and explored, checked for reasonableness and, as changes in the external environment are identified, evaluated as to their implications for the organization. Strategies are then developed in light of the external environment.

Similarly, strategic management requires sensitivity to the characteristics of the internal environment—the state or local government organization itself. This internal analysis should focus on the strengths and weaknesses of the organization—who actually does what, how and how well. The organization should be honest in viewing its own operations, and it must be willing to identify and address problem areas and limitations. It also should assess the capabilities of the organization to meet its mission/achieve its vision and to accommodate change. The strategic management process should include an evaluation of the new or improved resources necessary to support the evolving strategy. It could be that a proposed strategy may require more resource than the organization is capable of mustering. This could call for a variation of the suggested strategy. This process, like all those of strategic management, is ongoing (i.e., the organization must be sensitive to and respond to its own situation and changes to operate and progress effectively).

### Strategy Development

Again, strategy development is a part of the state and local government strategic planning process (chapter 3). Strategies are statements of what the state or local government organization will do to work toward achieving its mission/vision in terms of its processes, products, personnel, resources and organizational structure. Given an improved understanding of the organization's internal and external environments (from the above process), options for achieving the organization's mission/vision can often be developed.

Such options involve considering current realities and limitations, and also exploring ways to modify or adjust to them when considering possible future scenarios. The set of options should reflect various perspectives in terms of the organization's ability to change itself and to influence its externalities. This is the organization's opportunity to examine its desired future and its commitment to it, as well as its perceived limitations and to decide what it is willing to commit in order to accomplish its mission/vision. In particular, through the development of meaningful strategies, the organization should articulate the policies it endorses, the processes and procedures it uses, the products and services it provides, the personnel it employs, the resources it commits, and the way it is organized to fulfill its mission/vision. This is also a time for great creativity in deciding which strategies are possible for the future.

### Tactical (Action) Plan Development

Tactical planning is a part of the strategic planning process (chapter 3), but it also involves elements of strategic management in relation to organizing and directing the organization toward plan accomplishment. The tactical (action) plan consists of a set of specific, measurable, accomplishable, assignable, realistic, detailed objectives or steps that upon successful implementation, lead to the realization of a particular strategy. For each strategy, the tactical plan includes a time frame or schedule of work elements, completion dates and delineation of responsibility to specific organizational components for each step of the plan. Scheduled reviews of progress are also included so that actions are implemented as planned, or implementation problems are identified and addressed as they arise.

This thorough specification and implementation of the tactical (action) plan drives the state or local government toward its goal. Tactical (action) plans represent the translation of mission/vision statements and strategies into day-to-day activities. The successful accomplishment of these tactical objectives provides the incremental progress necessary to realize the strategic mission/vision for the organization.

The tactical (action) plan, like all other components of strategic management, will change in response to changes in the state or local government's internal and external environments. Without ongoing review and revision, an action plan becomes ineffectual as inevitable changes in the environments occur.

### Resource Allocation

Resource management involves deciding on the necessary staffing and other resources. This is a strategic management step. All resources (i.e., human, financial and material) should be allocated in accordance with the state or local government's mission/vision, strategies and tactical (action) plans. Resources should be readily available at the required levels for timely and successful implementation of the tactical (action) plans. Contingencies should be provided to address changes that occur (see chapter 9). This involves basing allocation decisions on strategies, objectives and organizational priorities; understanding and addressing each department's/division's resource requirements; and planning contingencies to address changes that will most likely occur.

The strategic management process should also be integrated with the state or local government budgeting process. Resource allocation should reflect the focus exhibited by the strategic plan and its tactical planning actions. Clearly, tactical (action) plans can't be accomplished without adequate resources, assigned according to priority and expended in an efficient and effective manner.

### Performance Measurement

Performance measurement is a strategic management step. It is the process of tracking implementation of the tactical (action) plans, the current tracking of progress toward mission/vision accomplishment of the strategic plan and indicating changes needed. Performance monitoring clearly delineates what each department/division in the state or local government is expected to contribute to the organization's mission/vision and how they are progressing. This includes specific performance measures that are consistently reported on and reviewed, incentives and disincentives linked to performance, and clearly delineated accountability for their accomplishment.

Performance measurement at both the organizational component and individual manager levels is critical because it reveals whether and how well various department/divisions of the organization are fulfilling their specified responsibilities. It also reveals how effective the tactical (action) plans are in realizing mission/vision accomplishment. In addition, it reports what activities or processes require change or refinement.

### Key Characteristics for Success

Successful strategic management processes may be characterized by the following:

- Active commitment to and leadership of the process by the chief executive officer
- Continuous commitment to the process by senior and middle managers
- The "businesses" of the state or local government must be defined properly so that focused strategies can be developed for each one

- The process is rigorous in its execution but flexible in its response to changing environments and situations

- The process is planned and accomplished by line components and supported by staff resources

- There exists a sincere effort to influence the organization's future, not just accept it as a result

- The implementation (tactical) plans address a time horizon of two to four years (it is recognized that longer horizons are too uncertain)

- There is true integration of the several components, including performance measurement, into a "closed loop" system, with active feedback to respond to strategy modifications

- Strategic planning, as an element of strategic management, is continuous and regularly yields products that are implemented

- There is substantial evaluation and analysis of the external environment on a continuous basis

- The process is based on reality, with a realistic vision of the future that is articulated and understood

- Appropriate recognition and reward systems are in place that cause people to "do the right thing"

- Agency managers exhibit patience and perseverance with the process

Those state and local government organizations that report successes and concomitant benefits of their strategic management process have realized these key characteristics. These are not always attained initially but are always reached ultimately if true success is to be achieved.

**SUMMARY**

This chapter has provided a working set of definitions and components about the strategic management process. Again, we recognize that there exists substantial diversity of opinion and judgment within the theory and practice of this process. Further research will undoubtedly address these diversities, confirm the realities of the process and lead to comprehensive guidelines for all organizations. Inasmuch as each state or local government organization is different from all others and its culture is unique, applications of the strategic management process will differ. A general checklist for strategic management in a state or local government organization is provided in Appendix A to this chapter, and an outline of the steps to take in implementing a strategic management process is shown in Appendix B.

## CUTBACK MANAGEMENT FROM THE BOTTOM UP

As has been discussed in this chapter, strategic management can be an effective tool for state and local governments to utilize to manage from the bottom up in a cutback management environment.

This book has discussed the trends that state and local governments will most likely face in the 1990s and beyond, not the least of which is the continuation of the need to manage in a restrained resource environment. It has also discussed some tools and techniques that may be of value to state and local government administrators and managers as they try to be successful in carrying out their responsibilities in light of the environment they will most likely face. These tools and techniques include strategic planning, organizing around critical success factors, ways of improving employee productivity through shared values, employee involvement processes, organizing for improved public productivity utilizing matrix management, contingency planning for changed circumstances, and strategic management for the future. The last chapter in the book will also include a number of case studies of specific actions that have been taken by a number of state and local governments across the United States in order to manage from the bottom up in a restrained resource environment.

The challenge is certainly a large one, but all managers who have been successful in either the public or private sectors have met large challenges many times during their evolutionary processes. It won't be easy, but there are certainly some tools and techniques that can be of assistance in achieving success. Perhaps the challenges and opportunities ahead are best characterized by the following poem:

It's cutback, reduced
revenues and telecommuting.
It's downsizing, GIS'ing
and productivity improvin'.

It's diversity, less water
and privatization.
It's drug problems, increased demand
and homelessization.

It's employee involvement,
and strategically managing.
Providing transportation
without environmentally damaging.

It's energy efficiency and
city/county consolidating.
It's user fees and
internationally relating.

It's professionally managing
our states and locals.
And outdistancing the
loud doubting of vocals.

It's onward and upward
and rising to Eagles.
'Stead of being whimpering
puppies and Beagles.

There isn't any question that managing our state and local governments in a reduced revenue environment in the 1990s and beyond will be difficult. However, the old adage that "when the going gets tough, the tough gets going" is true. Experimentation and risk taking, which are not the main fare of state and local government administrators, will be needed, and it will be uncomfortable. But this track may be the only way to success. Risk taking in the state and local government public sector is always difficult, but if successful, the rewards are enormous.

## Appendix A
## A State or Local Government Strategic
## Management Checklist

This checklist is divided into two components: a process checklist and a participant checklist.

A. Process Checklist

    1. Examination of the mission/vision of your organization:

- What are you trying to accomplish?
- Where are you now? How successful are you in achieving your mission/vision?
- Where do you want to be organizationally in five years? Do you need to change your mission/vision?
- How do you define success?
- Does the organization have a written statement of its mission/vision that has been clearly communicated to all members of the organization (top down and bottom up)?
- If so, does the mission/vision statement succinctly establish a direction for the organization?
- Has the mission/vision statement been reviewed in the last two years to determine if it is still appropriate?
- Is the mission/vision statement used as the basis for establishing organizationwide strategy?

    2. Environmental scanning

- What are the economic, social, technological, demographic and public policy trends and how will they affect your mission/vision and organization?
- How will these trends affect the demand for your services?
- Who else can provide the services or alternatives to your customers/clients/citizens?
- What are the competing demands for the same resources?
- What will happen to the cost structure in providing future services? Will there be major changes in technology or service delivery methods?
- Where will future financing come from?
- Who are your customers/clients/citizens and how are their needs changing?
- Does the organization engage in environmental scanning?
- If so, is it done on a continual basis rather than cyclically?
- Is responsibility for scanning shared by staff and line functions of the organization?

- Does the scanning conducted by the organization include
    - —The internal environment?
    - —The intragovernmental environment?
    - —The intergovernmental environment?
    - —The external environment?
    - —Strengths and weaknesses of the organization?
    - —Opportunities and threats facing the organization?
- Is the data used in the scan dependable?
- Is the time frame of the scan five years or less?
- Is the scope of the scan directly relevant to the activities and programs of the organization?
- Does the scope of the scan cover every operational and program area of the organization?
- Can specific scans be requested by organizational elements?
- Is the data from the organization's scan routinely compared with other externally available information?
- Is the information from past scans checked periodically to judge the accuracy of the methodologies being used?
- Are methodologies established for each type of scan conducted by the organization?
- Are the analyses performed during the scan reviewed by upper management before they are used as the basis of plans and strategies?
- Are all scan results shared with all senior managers?
- Are the results of the environmental scan provided in sufficient time to be incorporated in the annual planning cycle?
- Are new technologies available to assist in scanning being utilized?
- Are there new needs or special needs that you should serve?
- What alternatives exist for those who use your services and facilities?
- What are your customers'/clients'/citizens' goals? How do they define success? How do you provide services to help them achieve their goals?
- Strengths and limitations of your organization
    - —What are the key factors that have made your organization successful? Will these key factors lead to success in the future?
    - —What are the weaknesses and strengths of your organization and of other agencies serving the same clientele? What factors keep you from being more responsive to your customers'/clients'/citizens' needs?
    - —What are the cultural and institutional constraints on your organization?
- Stakeholder analysis (constituency analysis)

—How will changing your services, your goals and the structure of your organization affect those who share with you in the current support of your agency and its activities?

—Do your stakeholders have multiple, diverse, and sometimes conflicting goals and objectives? How can you best provide services to such diverse groups?

- Analysis of threats and opportunities (scenario building):

—How should you act or react to changes that may occur in the demand for your services, in the cost of your services and to changes in technology? What are your strategic alternatives?

—What are current trends that need to be exploited now?

—What dangers exist if you delay making changes?

—Are there activities that you should drop, combine or add? What will be the impact on your support, the customers/clients/citizens you serve and your employees?

- Critical issues and strategies

—What are the top critical issues that have surfaced as a result of your strategic management process?

—What strategies and options do you have to respond to these critical issues?

—What are the risks and benefits of the proposed scenarios to the organization and to the stakeholders?

—What losses can the agency sustain?

—Where are there substantial problems within the organization that warrant making changes?

—How do you coordinate the strategic plan with the budget process?

—How do you coordinate changes in your activities with continuing demands for ongoing services?

—How do you cope with limited resources?

- Does the organization prepare written results of its environmental scan?
- Who decides how these results are measured?

3. Identification and development of strategies

- Does the organization develop overall strategies to achieve the mission/vision it has established for itself?
- If so, are these strategies communicated to all managers in the organization before strategic objectives are set and tactical action plans developed?
- Can a direct relationship be shown between the organization's mission/vision and the strategies it develops?
- Does each component of the organization develop substrategies that are consistent with the organization's overall strategies?

- If so, are these substrategies reviewed by senior managers prior to their implementation?
- Does the organization have a formal strategy development process?
- Are strategies reviewed on at least an annual basis?
- Are strategies set for each major category of the organization's activities?
- Do all strategies tie directly to the organization's mission/vision statement?
- Are the overall strategies general in nature?
- Are goals/strategies without any time parameters?
- Are there five or fewer strategies for each element of the organization?
- Do all strategies have a real possibility of being carried out without the occurrence of extraordinary, unpredicted events?
- Are all levels of the organization's management involved in the strategic development process?
- Are clear priorities established among the strategies for each planning category?
- Are overall priorities established among all the strategies of the organization?
- Are the strategic objectives for the achievement of each strategy developed before specific tactical objectives are determined?
- If so, are these strategic objectives shared with all managers involved in setting program objectives and in implementing the action plans for meeting those objectives?
- Is there an analysis of the gap between a strategy and the current situation before strategic objectives are set in particular areas?
- Do strategic objectives attempt to close only a portion of the existing gap, if it is considerable?
- Do all strategic objectives tie directly to one or more strategy?
- Are all strategic objectives stated in measurable terms?
- Do all strategic objectives have a time frame of two years or less?
- Is there a real possibility that all strategic objectives can be achieved in the proposed time frame without the occurrence of extraordinary, unpredicted events?
- Are all levels of the organization's management involved in the setting of strategic objectives?
- Are there fewer than five to seven strategic objectives for each element of the organization?
- Are priorities established among the strategic objectives in each planning area?
- Are overall priorities established among all the strategic objectives of the organization?

- Are the strategic objectives used as the basis for the development of operating objectives?
- Are the strategic objectives reviewed prior to each planning cycle to determine the extent to which they have been met and the extent to which they are still relevant?
- Have at least 80 percent of the strategic objectives changed over the last two years?

4. Tactical (action) planning

- Do written tactical (action) plans exist for the achievement of each strategic objective?
- If so, do these action plans include
  - —All of the specific actions to be taken in sequence to meet each strategic objective?
  - —The function or individual responsible for each action?
  - —The start and end dates for each action?
  - —The resources that will be devoted to each action?
  - —Realistic and measurable action plans?
- Are action plans reviewed by superiors before they are implemented?
- Does each component of the organization develop action plans for the achievement of the strategic objectives for which it has responsibility?
- If so, are these action plans reviewed for internal consistency within the components?
- Are the action plans written?
- Are the action plans accessible to all managers in the components?
- Does a methodology exist for coordinating action among two or more departments/divisions?
- Does a methodology exist for coordinating actions that impact two or more strategic objectives?

5. Budgeting

- Does the organization budget by program?
- Is the budget cycle annual?
- Is a budget process initiated at the beginning of the planning process?
- Is the final budget developed to accommodate program plans—as opposed to program plans being developed to meet predetermined budget marks for each program area?
- Are funds freely transferred among program areas depending on their priority?
- Is the budget routinely adjusted during the course of the budget year on the basis of performance or shifting program priorities?
- Are all program decisions made external to the budget office?
- Is the organization's budget based on actual revenues expected?

- Are funding decisions to resolve conflicts among competing priorities made at the highest levels of the organization?
- Are the program budgets used as the basis for regular financial reports to managers?

6. Performance measures

- Does the organization have written program performance measures for each of its programs?
- If so, are these performance measures clearly understood by each of the affected program managers?
- Do the management reports received by program managers reflect progress against these measures?
- Does the organization have written performance measures for each manager that are directly related to their responsibility regarding meeting specific strategic or tactical objectives?
- If so, are these measures clearly understood by each manager?
- Does a superior review performance with the manager against these measures on at least a quarterly basis?
- Do the performance reports of individual managers reflect the regular management reports on their programs and activities?

7. Performance monitoring

- Are regular management reports provided to all managers in the organization?
- If so, are the reports
  —Timely?
  —Accurate?
  —Directly related to the operational and financial performance against established plans?
- Are managers at all levels responsible for providing raw data to serve as the basis for management reports?
- Are the organization's management reports void of information extraneous to performance/effectiveness?
- Do managers use the reports provided in discussions with subordinate managers about their performance and that of their units and programs?
- Does a mechanism exist to adjust plans and budgets if management reports indicate that such is necessary?
- Are the results indicated by management reports at year-end used as an integral component of the annual strategic and tactical review and direction-setting process?
- Are the organization's information systems
  —Up-to-date?
  —Capable of producing accurate information in a timely manner?

—Free of non-essential information?

• Is essential information collected on a regularly scheduled basis?

• Do all managers receive the quantity and quality of information they need to make management decisions?

• Is the information collected designed to serve as the basis for management decisions?

• Is the information disseminated to managers in a format that facilitates the execution of their decision-making responsibilities?

B. Participant Checklist

  1. Manager/Administrator/Executive

    • Is the chief executive actively and visibly involved with the major planning and control activities of the organization, for example

      —Developing the mission/vision?

      —Deciding organizationwide priorities?

      —Developing organizationwide strategies?

      —Setting primary policies?

      —Reviewing program plans?

      —Reviewing budgets?

      —Monitoring program operations?

      —Reviewing the performance of senior managers?

    • Does the chief executive seek the advice of the senior managers on critical decisions?

    • Does the chief executive meet regularly—that is, at least once a month—with senior managers, individually and collectively, to assess their performance and that of the department/divisions in relation to established plans?

    • Does the chief executive willingly make the "tough calls" in a timely manner, for example

      —Deciding among competing priorities?

      —Acting on poor manager performance?

      —Adjusting plans on the basis of new information?

  2. Senior managers

    • Do senior managers actively provide advice to the chief executive on critical decisions affecting the organization?

    • Are senior managers actively and visibly involved in the planning and control activities of the organization, particularly with regard to the functions for which they are responsible?

    • Do senior managers closely monitor the performance of the managers reporting to them?

    • Do senior managers make decisions within their scope of authority in a timely manner—as opposed to delaying decisions or passing them up to the chief executive?

- Do senior managers work together to address problems confronting one or more of them?

- Do senior managers meet regularly with their subordinate managers to assess their performance and that of their departments/divisions in relation to established plans?

- Do senior managers willingly adjust plans and programs on the basis of performance or new information, even if it is out of the normal planning and budgeting cycle?

- Do senior managers surface issues for resolution when they occur?

3. Staff Managers

- Do managers of staff departments/divisions function in a support rather than control role?

- Do staff departments/divisions provide line managers with sufficient information and assistance to facilitate the efficient and effective execution of line programs, for example

   —Internal and external environmental information?

   —Program performance reports?

   —Current and accurate budget/financial information?

   —Quick turnaround on personnel requests?

   —Timely procurement of needed supplies and services?

   —Timely action on systems requests?

- Are all staff managers knowledgeable about the scope of activities for which the line departments/divisions are responsible?

- Have staff managers thoroughly informed their personnel that their purpose is to support, not control, other departments/divisions of the organization?

- Is the budget staff precluded from making decisions on the availability of specific legal plans for line functions or programs?

- Is the planning staff precluded from developing plans for line functions or programs?

4. Line managers

- Are line managers actively involved in setting the strategic objectives and priorities for the programs/activities for which they are responsible?

- Do line managers have the authority to make decisions in their areas of responsibility as long as they are consistent with established plans and budgets?

- Do line managers readily make these decisions rather than pass them along to their supervisors?

- Do line managers have input into the organization's administrative and management process?
- Do line managers meet regularly with their superiors to discuss performance and emerging issues?
- Are line managers reluctant to surface issues and problems with their supervisors?
- Are most operational decisions in the organization made by line managers?[2]

# Appendix B
# An Outline of Steps to Take to Implement a State or Local Government Strategic Management Process

Strategic Planning
• Preparing to plan
     —Commitment and resources
     —Training
     —Development of planning team
        Who?
        When?
        Where?
        Five to twelve members (can vary)
     —Time frame of individual
     —Planning horizon
     —Top-down versus bottom-up
     —Statewide, organizationwide, functional, programmatic, single issue (e.g., human resources, economic development)
     —Establish feedback loop
     —Establish evaluation criteria
     —Schedule planning activities
     —Decide on information and education effort
     —Decide on strategic management rituals

Mission/Vision Statement (First Cut)
• Frame scanning activity

Environmental Scanning
• External trends
     —Economic changes
     —Population/demographic shifts
     —Changing federalism
     —Technological changes
     —Employment shifts
     —Climate changes
     —Others
• Opportunities created by these external trends (e.g., increased economic activity produces additional revenue)

- —Assessment of data gaps
- —Research on issues
- —Assignments for monitoring
- —Constant monitoring and updates
- Threats created by these external trends (e.g., reduced program funds due to federal cutbacks)
  - —Assignment of data gaps
  - —Research on issues
  - —Assignments for monitoring
  - —Constant monitoring and updates
- Internal environment
  - —Review external trends
  - —Assess internal organizational strengths to respond
  - —Assess internal organizational weaknesses to respond
  - —Identify and rank strategic issues and goals
  - —Possibly identify strategic objectives and rank
- Mission/vision
  - —Develop and finalize organizational mission/vision statement (overall)
  - —Develop functional/program missions/visions
  - —Embody driving force
  - —Focus on direction of the organization
- Critical Success Factors (five to seven)
  - —Related to carrying out mission/achieving vision
  - —Identify critical success indicators (one or two for each factor)
- Strategic Objectives
  - —Planning scenario
    - Leader?
    - Responder?
    - Follower?
    - Other?
  - —What to do to carry out mission/achieve vision or to respond to a strategic issue or to a strategic objective
  - —Overall (e.g., economic development)
  - —Specific
  - —Risk/benefit of each strategy
  - —Alternate possibilities that never get considered
  - —Implementation considerations
  - —Make sure strategic controls are in place

- Critical success factors (alternate)
    —As related to ability to achieve strategic objectives
- GAP analysis
    —Present state versus desired future state of organization's ability to carry out mission or achieve vision
    —How to close the gap?
    —Straight line or incrementalize?
- Internal assessment
    —Ability to carry out mission/achieve vision
    —Sequence of events
    —Ability to achieve strategic objectives
    —What to do?
- Contingency planning
    —Unforeseen occurrences
    —+
    ——
    —Triggers, if any, when contingency plan supplants base strategic plan
- Integrate functional/program plans
    —Pull together at top/cohesive plan
- Feedback/reiteration as necessary
    —Fine tuning of major changes
- Kickoff/launch plan
    —Stage major event
    —Begin bottom-up process

Tactical Planning
- Establish tactical objectives
    —Key result areas (KRAs)
    —Put in operational terms
    —Make sure tactical controls are in place
- Tie to operating/capital budgets (if possible)
- Incrementalize if annual budget and multiyear strategic plan
- Develop parallel action plans if unable to tie to budget
- Tie to performance measures of accountability on functional/program basis
- Tie to individual performance appraisal/reward system
- Operate
- Feedback to tactical plan and strategic plan
- Reiterate as necessary

Evaluate process
- Strategic plan
- Tactical plan
- Total strategic management system
- Feedback/further steps
- Do bottom-up
- Reevaluate

## NOTES

1. *Strategic Planning for State and Local Transportation Agencies*, Outline of Videotape Presentation (Washington, D.C.: Transportation Research Board, 1988), pp. 1–35.

2. *Areas of Inquiry for Strategic Management Process* (Washington, D.C.: Ernst & Young, 1988), pp. 1–15.

# 11

# Case Studies in Cutback Management and Employee Involvement

> "Make no little plans;
> They have no magic to stir men's blood
> And probably themselves will not be realized.
> Make big plans; aim high
> in hope and work.
> Remembering that a noble, logical diagram
> Once recorded will not die."
> —Daniel H. Burnham

State and local governments throughout the United States are abundantly aware of the reduced revenue environment brought about by decreased economic activity. Some are harder hit than others, depending on the diversity and basis of the local economy. Several of the harder-hit state and local governments are now involved in the second, or even third, rounds of expenditure reduction decisions as they prepare their annual budgets. Because of this, many of the obvious approaches have already been implemented, and a need now exists for new and more innovative ways to reduce budgetary costs or find new sources of revenue.

The purpose of this chapter is to share the experiences with cutback management and employee involvement from a variety of state and local governments. Hampton, Virginia, has been cited a number of times because it has been a highly innovative city government. Although some of the Quality Circle case studies date from the 1980s, they offer good examples of how employee involvement processes can work effectively to address a broad range of cutback management issues.

## CUTBACK MANAGEMENT IN LAREDO, TEXAS

In Laredo (population 117,000), former City Manager Marvin Townsend was forced by the oil bust to reduce $4 million from a total general fund budget of $16 million. In approaching this, he developed the motto "Know what the enemy is, and hit it head on." He took total control of the situation and, among other things cut sick leave in half, consolidated the retirement system, reduced vacation accumulations and challenged well-established things.

## CUTBACK MANAGEMENT IN ODESSA, TEXAS

John D. Harrison, former city manager of Odessa (population 101,000), was faced with a boom and bust situation. In the summer of 1982, there was an incredible oil boom. By December 1982, "The bloom was off the rose!" There were 600 fewer oil rigs; sales tax revenues declined from $10.7 million in 1982 to $7 million in 1986 to $6.2 million in 1987; and there had been $370 million more of corporate business in the community than is now the case. Mr. Harrison and his key managers took actions to generate a projected general fund surplus of $9 million. These included reducing expenditures and reducing the base cost of government across the board. Specific actions included the following:

- Reduced people costs more than 50 percent by eliminating thirty positions
- Froze vacancies
- Developed an evaluation process to restructure and prioritize things
- Stopped step increases (went strictly to merit)
- Made other changes in salary administration
- Addressed supervisory reorganization
- Established stronger position controls
- Considered "Z-time" (giving days off without pay four to five times per year in order to avoid salary cuts)
- Conducted strategic planning sessions to force managers to "think"
- Converted street lights to sodium vapor and reduced cost by several hundred thousand dollars per year
- Installed dimmers on traffic signals
- Built an extra loading dock at the solid waste shredder and thereby eliminated the second shift
- Substituted capital for labor by upgrading technology (e.g., electronic meter reading)
- Contracted out some things (considered custodial services, mental health/mental retardation to run cafeterias, possibly sanitation)
- Went to self-funded health, liability and workers' compensation insurance

Overall, the "cutback process" became an important management tool to increase efficiency and productivity.

## CUTBACK MANAGEMENT IN KILGORE, TEXAS

Former City Manager Ronald E. Cox says that Kilgore (population 12,000), functions like a city of 25,000 from the standpoint of its budget for services. In 1982, the city had sales tax income of $2.5 million. In 1987, it dropped to $1.4 million. The situation was serious, but the budget kept escalating. The city went from 177 employees in 1982 to 205 in 1984. In 1985, serious problems occurred. The budget was 22 percent less than the one for the previous year. To accommodate this change, the city had to take the following actions:

- Reduce payroll by 30 percent
- Eliminate forty positions (including fourteen in the fire department)
- Contract out solid waste collection (this eliminated fifteen people)
- Reduce the number of people in every department
- Automate numbers of processes
- Cut meter readers in half
- Stagger billing cycle
- Review rates and income fees
- Allocate money from perpetual care funds to operate cemeteries
- Write letters to major suppliers to request them to roll back or hold the line on prices
- Save $200,000 by privatizing the water system
- Use foundations some and begin to use them more, particularly to pay for capital needs
- Change and turn out every other street light
- Develop a litter cleanup program
- Eliminate fire marshall's office
- Combine police/fire dispatchers into one unit
- Work on productivity and morale mindsets

As a result, the city is now down to 135 employees.

## CUTBACKS IN TYLER, TEXAS

City Manager Gary Gwyn took action to combat a similar situation. Specific options considered by Tyler (population 73,000) city management included:

- Raising all user fees/added new fees
- Selling surplus city property
- Combining fire/police dispatch
- Reviewing liability insurance cost
- Stopping utilities to Caldwell Zoo
- Decreasing contributions to outside agencies
- Eliminating transit system
- Reviewing Workers' Compensation insurance
- Reviewing telephone costs
- Increasing county participation in fire, health, library and parks
- Reducing overtime paid to workers to take place of people sick or on vacation
- Implementing user fees in parks
- Increasing franchise/contract fees and charges
- Contracting tax collection
- Cutting off street lights on major arteries
- Reviewing street light costs
- Implementing no salary increase (trade-off was other benefit reduction)
- Conducting cash flow analysis to improve interest income
- Suggesting that city and county split the airport costs
- Running equipment an extra year via good maintenance
- Reducing travel
- Conducting energy audits (reduced power costs, possible expenditures, repairs)
- Reducing personnel, including public safety
- Doing no work for free, contracted for services
- Providing early retirement incentives
- Hiring as much contract labor as possible
- Utilizing interest in perpetual maintenance fund

## CUTBACK MANAGEMENT IN OTHER COMMUNITIES

Many other local governments are now facing, or have faced, cutback management demands. These areas include the farm and rust belts and selected other regions such as Virginia and Florida. Some of the methods that these local governments have utilized include the following:

- Using volunteers
- Implementing privatization
- Developing realistic franchising

- Developing internal operations analysis teams (e.g., Corpus Christi, Texas; Hampton, Virginia; Dade County, Florida; several California cities)
- Selling excess property
- Abandoning the jail to the county (if a city)
- Conducting strategic planning
- Marketing the local government to increase activity, development and so on
- Implementing self-managed teams
- Paying attention to the suggestions of staff members

## SELF-MANAGING TEAMS IN THE HUMAN RESOURCES DEPARTMENT

The Hampton, Virginia (population 130,000), Department of Human Resources,[1] with a staff of eleven employees, was structured in branches, each consisting of a branch chief, one or two professionals, and a clerical employee. Levels of expertise within branches was high, but little information was shared across branch lines, turf issues had developed over the years, response to problems was slow and employees had expertise in only one functional area. A new city manager was placing strong emphasis on organizational development and employee involvement, two areas in which the staff had virtually no experience.

The Human Resources Department, with employee participation, reorganized into two self-managing teams—one professional and one technical. Modeled after the overall city structure, the department is flat, with all staff members reporting directly to the department head. Through their teams, employees are expected to meet daily and decide on work assignments and priorities that may be accomplished by one or more team members. Formal and on-the-job training in all human resource disciplines is ongoing; initially, employees worked in teams of two or more to gain on-the-job training in each functional area. There are several levels of positions within each team; performance standards have been developed for each position. The department performance appraisal system has been redesigned to incorporate peer review. The director serves as liaison between the department and upper management, markets human resources programs inside and outside the organization, acts as team leader at weekly staff meetings, encourages innovation within the department, evaluates progress and functions as cheerleader.

The department is down to nine full-time employees from eleven prior to the reorganization. Day-to-day work continues to be accomplished, and significant strides have been made in the organization development area. In FY 1988, more than 800 registrations were received for all types of employee training and more than 900 memberships on task forces, problem-solving groups, Quality Circles and other employee involvement activities were identified (the city's full-time work force is about 1,200 employees). A recent survey of city department heads indicated high levels of satisfaction with human resource services. Skill levels within the department have increased dramatically along with innovation and risk taking. Peer pressure supports high standards of performance, personal and professional development and commitment to organization and department goals.

## HAMPTON'S ELECTRONIC REAL ESTATE SYSTEM

Every day businesspersons and individuals come to City Hall for information. Providing the data that a community wants is time-consuming and expensive. The cost of accessing information is also expensive and time-consuming for businesses and citizens. Considerable community efficiencies could be realized if information could be reviewed without the assistance of public employees and without the need for a trip to City Hall.

Cities are exploring new ways to improve communications with their communities. Using the power of the computer, homes and offices can be electronically linked to City Hall, providing twenty-four-hour information on community programs and technical data.

The city of Hampton, Virginia, has developed an on-line data base that provides information on all real estate in the city.[2] The system can be accessed by personal computers via telephone lines. The Assessors Department in Hampton receives an average of 175 telephone requests for information each day. Additionally, it handles a large number of persons who visit the office to research property files. Three full-time positions are dedicated to servicing citizens' calls and visits. Other staff members also regularly answer questions and perform research. The majority of requests are received from businesses (i.e., real estate, mortgage, titling and insurance companies; banks; commercial appraisers; and attorneys). Most of these organizations have computers in their offices.

Hampton's appraisal system has been automated for several years. Its design, however, was tailored to the needs of the internal staff. Although most of the information requested was available in the computerized appraisal system, it could not be extracted in an easy-to-use format.

A meeting was held with twelve representatives of businesses normally using Hampton's files. The purpose was to determine their interest in a computer system that they could access from their offices. Their reaction was enthusiastic. The group reviewed the computer files then available and recommended additional information that they needed on a regular basis. The result was a file that integrated assessor information with information from the building, zoning and planning department files.

Development of the software to combine the files in a simple-to-use manner presented some difficulty. Developing the computer program was easy, but paying for the work was a problem. Data-processing staff were unable to add this to their work load. If it was to be developed in-house, it would have to be done after normal work hours. If it was contracted out, the cost estimate was $20,000. The answer was to use the city's "achievement award program" to pay for in-house development of the software.

The "achievement plan" is a gainsharing approach to motivating and rewarding employee problem solving. In this case, a programmer willing to develop the program and provide continuing maintenance of the system (for two years) would share in the revenues. All work would be conducted after normal hours. The person who was selected was loaned a computer to work with at home. His share of the profits will be 20 percent for the first two years, not to exceed $20,000 (the cost of outside development). The advantages of this approach are that (1) the employee gets a challenging and interesting project, (2) the city gets to defer its development costs for two years, (3) the cost of development is incurred only if it is an economic success, (4) it caps the cost of development and (5) it provides an opportunity for an employee to share monetarily in the project's accomplishments.

The product development is simple to use. It is totally menu driven. Users need only to be able to punch a menu number or enter a street name or owner's name to use the system. Users do not have to learn any commands. The product allows the user to look at many types of information about real property in Hampton. Examples of types of information follow:

- Appraised value
- Type of real estate—commercial or residential
- Sales history
- Present and past owners
- Building permits issued to property
- School zones associated with property
- Zoning, census tract and school zone information
- Projections of future land development through 2010

Information can be accessed by (1) property owner's name, (2) property address, (3) subdivision and (4) school zone.

A user who finds an error can report it using the on-line program. The appropriate department reviews the error reports and investigates. Users will receive a credit for correctly identifying errors in the data base. This feature allows the users to become extensions of the city staff. The accuracy of Hampton's information should improve as a result.

The system has been put into effect with excellent results. Subscription fees paid by private users of the system have provided discretionary income for the city. The system has become so successful that it is now being shared with six other municipalities in the Hampton area. Developers can now obtain development information in any of the seven cities by using one telephone number.

## QUALITY CIRCLES IN LAGUNA BEACH

Laguna Beach, California,[3] Assistant City Manager Municipal Services Terry Brandt examined the Japanese and American industrial use of Quality Circles and decided to implement the concept in the mechanical maintenance division of his city. The division consists of a shop foreman, three mechanics and one maintenance worker. The division was chosen because of its small number of personnel and the team efforts required in repairing public works vehicles. In addition to the shop foreman, the public works superintendent was considered to be the key middle management support person for the program.

After obtaining the support of the shop foreman and public works superintendent, the next step was to explain Quality Circles (QCs) to the mechanics and maintenance workers. During the introductory meeting, various techniques for improving organizational effectiveness were described. These included team building, job enrichment, career planning, and QCs. The QC presentation covered the following facets of the program: (1) steps to implementation and (2) assumptions on which the process is based, including (a) employees are experts at their jobs, (b) employees want to contribute, (c) QC participation is voluntary, (d) management is not automatically obligated to accept QC recommendations, (e) the QC process would have a general goal to improve shop organization and effectiveness and (f) the QC process would involve volunteers for one hour a week in problem-solving activities. The group agreed to proceed.

During the second meeting, it was made clear that those problems that should or could be resolved by the shop foreman should not be addressed by the QC. At this meeting, six problems were identified and isolated and their causes and possible solutions were discussed. These were (1) the lack of priorities for vehicle repair, (2) the lack of parts inventory, (3) insufficient information available regarding required repairs, (4) working hours, (5) the necessity to repair shop equipment and (6) poor maintenance of vehicles by drivers. During subsequent meetings, these problems were analyzed and potential solutions were developed. In addition, new problems were brainstormed.

Workers appear to be in favor of the QC program in Laguna Beach because it gives them a real opportunity to express an opinion and have it heard. One disadvantage cited was that the employees did not feel that they could be totally frank at the meetings.

From Mr. Brandt's perspective, the initial beginnings of the QC program in Laguna Beach established the process and justified the time spent in meetings. The positive feeling achieved, however, is tempered slightly by the preliminary nature of the results.

## QUALITY CIRCLES AT RAMSEY COUNTY COMMUNITY HUMAN SERVICES DEPARTMENT

A few years ago, the Ramsey County, Minnesota, Community Human Services Department[4] began a pilot program of five Quality Circles. Prior to the actual start up of these Quality Circles, division directors participated in a series of management meetings to discuss their implementation. These discussions were facilitated by a consultant provided via the Local Government Productivity Improvement Project of the Minnesota Association of Counties. These discussions resulted in the establishment of the Quality Circle Coordinating Committee composed of the division directors and two representatives from the union. The facilitator for the Quality Circles project was selected and the goals and objectives of the project were established. Information meetings were then held with the supervisory personnel and employees to describe the Quality Circle process and to encourage participation. As a result of these information meetings, the work groups and team leaders were selected. The selection was based on those supervisors who expressed interest in the project.

The team leaders participated in a special two-day training program sponsored by the Local Government Productivity Improvement Project. As a result of this training experience, the team leaders and facilitator designed a one-day training program for the people who volunteered for the Quality Circle teams. Upon completion of this day of training, all Quality Circles began regular weekly, one-hour meetings.

The five Quality Circles are operating in three different divisions within the department and involve various classifications of personnel. Three of the Quality Circles are located in the Income Maintenance Division: two in the AFDC Case Management section and one in the Medical Assistance Intake section. The people participating are classified as financial workers and clerk/typists. One Quality Circle is located in the Child Protection section of the Social Services Division and one is composed of the secretaries of the mental health clinic. Altogether there are forty-five people participating in the five Quality Circles with the size of the circles ranging from five to eleven members. With the exception of the mental health clinic Quality Circle, the other QCs are composed of individuals from various work units within the same section. This cross-section facilitates the exchange of information and practices within the different work units.

After six months of operation, all of the QCs had either completed one or two projects or were at the proposal presentation phase of their first project. One circle, however, chose a more complex project and, as a result, is just now preparing to present its recommendations. All project proposals were accepted by management for implementation. In general, the first projects focused on procedural improvements in areas close to the workers' day-to-day job responsibilities and, thus, did not require extensive changes outside the scope of the workers. Currently, the Quality Circles are selecting their next projects and appear to be interested in tackling more complex issues.

The two most critical aspects of the Quality Circle process are the support given by all levels of management to the QCs and specific training in problem-solving techniques. The ability to get information and technical assistance to Quality Circles requires open communication between Quality Circles, management and other work sections so that efforts can be co-ordinated and duplication of previous work can be avoided.

Quality Circles have not been a magical cure for all that ails work groups. The experience of trying to solve problems has helped workers become familiar with the dilemmas of trying to improve existing procedures and practices. The sense of accomplishment experienced by the workers has given them greater commitment to making the improvements work. It is obvious that Quality Circles are a long-term process that demonstrate to workers the commitment management has to making use of the talents, skills and perceptions of the employees. There is now a vehicle for the employees to find solutions to the problems they experience on their jobs. On the other hand, there is a heightened awareness on the part of the employees of the fact that, at times, it seems easier to identify problems and expect someone else to work out the solutions.

## QUALITY CIRCLES IN DALLAS, TEXAS

The management plan prepared by the Dallas, Texas, city manager[5] described four objectives for providing efficient and quality services at a low cost and for utilizing the creativity and resourcefulness of the city's employees. These were (1) to improve productivity, effectiveness and re-sponsiveness in the delivery of city services; (2) to improve the affirmative action and equal employment opportunities for minorities and women in recruitment and employment; (3) to improve the long-range planning pro-cess; and (4) to increase employee participation in the development and achievement of organizational goals.

One of the methods that the city of Dallas has used to accomplish these objectives is the development of a comprehensive Quality Circle program. According to productivity/management analysis supervisor, Bob Winslow, and Quality Circle facilitator James Mongaras, "quality circles, a method of utilizing worker brainpower," are prospering in the city of Dallas.

Dallas began investigating the Quality Circle concept and hired an out-side consultant to assist the city in the development of a Quality Circle program. Initially, ten team leaders received training in Quality Circle techniques and Quality Circle teams began meeting throughout the city. The program has now expanded and there are plans to open the program to all city departments. The initial departments in Dallas having Quality Circles were the convention center, data services, equipment services, housing and urban rehabilitation, management services, parks and recreation, police and water.

The Quality Circle teams in the city of Dallas meet once a week for one hour. With one exception, the circles meet during regular working hours. For the exception, the participants receive one hour of overtime pay. Quality Circles provide an avenue of communication from the people who have actually performed the job to management of the city. The employees have the opportunity to describe those obstacles that get in the way of their performing their jobs and that make their jobs more difficult. The next step is to analyze those problems, find out their cause and make recommendations to management about how best to solve them. If management approves, the employees actually implement and monitor their recommended solutions.

Some of the problems that have been identified and solved by the Quality Circle teams in Dallas include the following:

- *Housing and urban rehabilitation.* This Quality Circle decided to tackle the procedural problem of rewriting notices of violation for each individual unit in apartment complexes. The team recommended that a cover letter be developed that eliminates the rewriting of the notices. The new procedure costs far less and accomplishes the same goal.

- *Convention center operations.* This Quality Circle decided to work on the problem of misplaced or lost supplies. When supplies such as mops, brooms, dustpans, and so on were issued to contract laborers from the storerooms, there were no procedures established to keep track of these items once they were checked out. This resulted in an inadequate supply of necessary supplies and high replacement costs. The Quality Circle decided to develop a check-out and follow-up procedure for these supplies. To date, the system has worked flawlessly.

- *Police: Southwest Patrol.* Police officers at Southwest Patrol realized that when they had to cover another officer's beat, they were not familiar with the beat and didn't know who the at-large criminals were, the buildings and alarm systems and so on. To aid the officers, the Southwest Patrol developed a comprehensive crime and information book that is used to identify the criminals on the particular beat and describe buildings, alarms, hot-spots and so forth. The officers see this as a tremendous aid in the prevention of crime and the apprehension of criminals.

The city of Dallas' Quality Circle program has proved that Quality Circles can and do work in a municipal government environment. Not only is the cost of producing city services being reduced by operating in a more efficient manner, but other aspects of job functions are being analyzed as well.

Factors such as machine downtime, absenteeism, tardiness and sick leave are beginning to be reduced as a result of the action of the Quality Circle teams. Quality Circles also increase morale of the work group because people now know that they do participate in the decisions being made about how their jobs are done and that they are responsible for making their solutions work. In addition, communications between workers and management have been enhanced and strengthened through the use of Quality Circles. Employees are given access to more information, thereby allowing them to learn more about the total operation of the department. Management has the opportunity to learn from the employees exactly what is occurring on a day-to-day basis, which can and does influence their managerial decisions.

## QUALITY CIRCLES IN FORT COLLINS

The Fort Collins, Colorado, city manager and his staff formed their first Quality Circle[6] with the city's automotive mechanics. At the beginning of the project, the equipment superintendent and service manager identified several concerns as follows:

- Mechanics were not accounting for eight hours on their daily time cards
- When one job was complete, mechanics would not always ask for the next job
- Mechanics were wary of management attempts to discuss their productivity
- The shop workload was difficult to predict and was uneven
- Mechanics were not held immediately accountable for "unfixed problems"
- Mechanic position classifications no longer reflected actual work responsibility

In addition, other city departments had been expressing concerns about the seemingly poor service and high cost of the equipment operation.

The mechanics also listed a number of factors they would require to be more productive:

- Faster parts delivery and better work scheduling
- Better explanations of mechanical problems by user departments
- More information sharing with management and better relations with other departments
- Better and more specialized tools and better training
- Monetary and non-monetary incentives

The advantages and disadvantages of utilizing Quality Circles were believed to be the following:

**Advantages**

• Mechanics would have a commitment to any changes

• The incentive program would be meaningful to the mechanics

• Mechanics would have a better understanding of the equipment operation

• Productivity potential and willingness on the part of mechanics to implement measurement systems would be enhanced

• A system for researching future problems would be established

• A more cohesive work group would be formed

**Disadvantages**

• Commitment of two hours per week for all mechanics and parts employees for a period of three to six months was required

In addition, management was required to assist mechanics by providing direction and sharing information. Management was also reminded that it would need to commit to listening to and giving serious consideration to group suggestions.

The initial Quality Circle was formed and began operations with training on problem solving, group dynamics and data analysis, plus additional information and division goals and objectives. This training lasted for a period of four weeks. The mechanics were then ready to apply their training to solving the previously identified problems. To ensure that they had accurately identified the problems, they collected data from work request and repair records, and surveyed user departments. Improvements were then made in various equipment repair and maintenance operations. As a result of the Quality Circle's efforts, savings documented were in excess of $33,000, half of which became available in monetary incentives for the members of the Quality Circle. Other efficiency improvements were also made, including these:

**Internal Changes**

• Mechanics have been assigned to perform mechanical work for specific departments

• A new service request form is being used to improve communications and to track specific repairs

• Departments are receiving copies of work orders with related costs identified

• The service writer position has been formally identified as a contact for mechanics to receive work assignments

• Needed tools for equipment have been ordered

• One auto service worker and one mechanic position have been eliminated through attrition

**External Changes**

- Some departments have begun to assign operators to specific pieces of equipment, thereby increasing the operators' sense of ownership and reducing repair time
- Departments now know who to contact for scheduling work, emergency repairs, complaints or praise
- Departments can now decide on repair priorities for their equipment when they have multiple pieces of equipment in the shop
- Mechanics make recommendations to departments on ways to reduce fuel consumption, maintenance, overall equipment conditions, minor repairs that operators could make and so on

**Work Environment Changes**

- Mechanics' morale has improved and they now feel free to make suggestions and provide backup data
- Management support is perceived by the mechanics
- Mechanics now have a better understanding of equipment fund revenues and expenditures and how their work affects both
- Communication with other city departments has improved
- A methodology for measuring productivity and effectiveness has been implemented
- An incentive pay plan for the mechanics was developed, approved by management and implemented

When the Quality Circle operation began, one mechanic said that this was the first time he had been asked to "use his brain" instead of being "just two hands on the end of a wrench." At this point, all members of the Quality Circle are using analytical skills and making sound recommendations regarding improving the shop operations. As a result of the success achieved in the mechanics Quality Circle, the city has now begun Quality Circles in parks, streets and traffic maintenance departments and with clerical support groups.

## PRODUCTIVITY IMPROVEMENT TEAMS IN HENNEPIN COUNTY

For many years, Hennepin County, Minnesota,[7] has sought to be innovative and forward looking in its approaches to internal organization and service delivery. As a part of this effort, the Board of County Commissioners created a productivity improvement program. The program is formed around a nucleus of four professional staff members with diverse educational and experience backgrounds. This group functions as a productivity improvement team and is housed in the office of planning and development. The program is largely voluntary in that members of the productivity team function as internal consultants based on various county department heads' voluntary requests for assistance. In addition, the team receives occasional assignments from top management.

The productivity improvement (PI) team offers assistance in three basic areas: direct analysis, process consulting, and development of participative systems. *Direct analysis* involves (1) examining operating methods, procedures and policies to recommend changes for optimizing efficiency and effectiveness; (2) applying statistical analysis and industrial engineering techniques to reduce cost and more effectively allocate resources; and (3) using various work measurement techniques to arrive at appropriate staffing levels. *Process consulting* involves training and guiding managers to accomplish systematic or planned change in their respective units.

Hennepin County utilizes two vehicles for involvement of personnel at all organizational levels in *participative systems* (PS). These are *Project Teams* and *Quality Circles*. The Project Team is formed by a manager using his/her people to address a specific problem. The team's activities are usually guided by a member of the PS team, but the analysis and recommendations are products of the team members. When its task is complete, the team usually dissolves.

Quality Circles, as used in Hennepin County, differ somewhat from the Project Team. The QC is formed from persons in a natural work group in which identical, similar or closely related work tasks are performed. In addition, a QC is intended to exist into perpetuity for the purpose of seeking out challenges and opportunities for improvement and identifying and solving problems associated with the work place. Further, QC members receive training in analytical techniques provided by PI team members.

QCs meet regularly, usually once a week for approximately one hour. QC members cooperatively research and analyze their issues and their results, and recommendations are presented to management for approval and eventual implementation.

One of the specific improvements developed and implemented by a Quality Circle in Hennepin County was in processes used in preparing documents for microfilm. As a result, errors were reduced by 80 percent.

Gordon Prentice, head of Hennepin County's program, indicates that the success of the program is owed largely to its participative, non-threatening character. He states that "it is the orderly application of our own common sense that allows Hennepin County to work smarter, not harder."

## PARTICIPATION METHODS IMPROVEMENT TECHNIQUES (QUALITY CIRCLES) IN NORTH CAROLINA

North Carolina State University's Productivity Research and Extension Program (PREP)[8] worked with a consortium consisting of two North Carolina state government agencies and Wake County government in a pilot study involving Quality Circles. The primary objectives of the study, which was made possible by a grant through the Intergovernmental Personnel Act of the Office of Personnel Management, were to (1) improve productivity in both local government and state departments and (2) study the appropriateness of the participative Quality Circle approach in government agencies.

The need for the study was obvious. With most state and local governments operating in a period of fixed or declining resources, most managers were having to make difficult decisions about the use of scarce funds. Therefore, the maintenance of a high productivity level was and is imperative. The participating managers also agreed that those who perform day-to-day jobs are the best source of ideas as to how to improve those jobs. Since personnel costs are such a high percentage of governments' total budgets, it follows that an employee participation team approach would be both effective and comprehensive. Therefore, a Quality Circle approach was selected as a way of involving employees and increasing productivity.

One hundred eighty-five city, county and state employees participated in twelve-hour training sessions where the concept of Quality Circles was introduced. The participants then went back to their home jurisdictions and applied the tools and techniques to their actual work area problems and projects. In the aggregate, more than $150,000 in net first-year savings were identified with an implementation rate for recommended improvements of more than 70 percent. These improvement ideas came from thirty-nine Quality Circles that were developed subsequent to the training sessions. A sampling of typical projects undertaken by the participating state agencies and Wake County government and their respective Quality Circles included the following:

- Lost production time as a result of lengthy trips to the reproduction machine was a project addressed by the Wake County Tax Supervisor's Quality Circle. The circle determined that an expenditure of twelve minutes per copy could be reduced to two minutes per copy with the lease and installation of a reproduction machine assigned to the Tax Supervisor's office. This resulted in a *net* first year savings of $2,700.

- The Quality Circle in the State Department of Commerce recommended that the North Carolina Industrial Commission Information Bulletin be revised to include a question-and-answer-section comprising questions most frequently called into the department by telephone. This reduced telephone inquiries by 20 percent and provided a net first year savings of $5,300.

- The State Division of Community Assistance's Quality Circle (which includes in its membership three town managers) recommended an improved method for handling citizen complaints about such items as signs being down, manhole covers being off, potholes and so on. A consolidation of three different work orders into one, plus an improved follow-up system, provides better public relations benefits and a modest annual savings in printing costs per town.

Feedback from the participants indicates an overall enthusiasm for the project because it gave them the following opportunities:

- To perform together as a team in solving problems
- To get to know their fellow employees better
- To have a say in the way their work is to be accomplished
- To have an opportunity to be involved with management in work simplification and problem solving
- To obtain recognition for their ideas

A follow-up evaluation of the project indicates that 50 percent of those persons attending the workshops intend to continue utilizing the Quality Circle approach.

## TEAM MANAGEMENT COMMITTEES IN CHAMPLIN, MINNESOTA

The city administrator of Champlin, Minnesota[9] (population 9,006), and his staff began to use a form of team management to formulate administrative policy and to recommend legislative policy to the city council. In Champlin, team management meant a commitment by the city staff to meet together on a routine basis to discuss issues affecting all city departments. The results have been that day-to-day departmental issues have been handled better, new perspectives have been gained, the city staff has felt more involved in decision making and the staff has been able to work more effectively on many issues that were previously beyond their individual purviews.

The concept is for staff committees to work on specific issues that require greater effort than just a general review by the city administrator and the city council. When a city staff team has identified a specific issue, a committee made up of line and staff personnel is formed. This committee researches the issue in detail and develops conclusions for the staff team. The staff team can then present the conclusions to the city council for review and action.

The committee approach has proven quite successful for Champlin. It is an attempt at applying Quality Circles in a small city setting. A cross-section of individuals forms each committee. Each individual has his/her own viewpoint equal to other members of the committee. The committees in Champlin are not standing committees but do review the operations of the city relative to the tasks of the committee. This is done to present conclusions that could change or modify the way a city department delivers its services.

The first committee established in Champlin was for the purpose of surveying and evaluating replacement policies on police vehicles. The committee reviewed in detail the type of police vehicles used by the city, the length of time the vehicles were in service and maintenance records on the vehicles. The committee consisted of police personnel, maintenance personnel and non-related city staff. Once the committee fully understood the way in which police vehicles were purchased, utilized and maintained by the city, they met with police personnel in the area to gather data about police vehicles from other cities. The data compiled allowed the committee to draw conclusions that could be utilized by the city. The conclusions were presented with all of the supporting data to the staff team for its review. The data, in turn, was presented to the city administration and city council. The council reviewed it and drafted a policy.

Involvement by all levels in the decision-making process increases productivity in the city operation. Champlin's team management approach is a commitment on the part of the city employees to the most efficient and effective service. It also gives the city the flexibility to adjust to the needs of the city's residents.

## TEAM MANAGEMENT IN COUNCIL BLUFFS

The Council Bluffs, Iowa,[10] city manager, Michael Miller, has developed participation management team-building approaches within two of the cities that he has managed, Council Bluffs and Maplewood, Minnesota. Although Miller has not utilized Quality Circles as such, he believes they would fit very well in Council Bluffs because of the susceptibility of management/supervisory personnel toward group consensus and input and because most of the city staff is already trained in group facilitation techniques.

Miller had seen no reason to change the traditional management style that had worked so well for him in other cities until changes began to occur within the Maplewood organization that made the approach of listening to top advisors, asking pertinent and penetrating questions, and then unilaterally making decisions ineffective. Finally, in near desperation, he attended a retreat on managing change where he was shown the value and quality of group decisions as opposed to individual decisions and where he discovered that team management is not decision by committee but rather a free flow of information within the established chain of command. He also learned that authority and responsibility must remain intact if an organization is to retain its viability and responsiveness. Miller was also trained in team management skills, including group facilitation, consensus-building, active listening, action research and training techniques.

Upon his return to Maplewood, Miller applied what he had learned and developed an effective team approach to managing the city, with excellent results. When he was appointed city manager of Council Bluffs, he immediately began the team management training there. Training and participation are voluntary. The training was completed in eighteen months with 86 percent of city employees taking part in formal management teams. All city department heads are actively participating in teams. Sixteen formal teams are presently active in such areas as employee orientation, budget, energy conservation, development of an administrative manual, community relations, transit records and city permits. Ad hoc teams are also established on minor problems and issues. The teams work in this way:

- Teams meet every two to three weeks for approximately one and one-half hours
- Team recommendations are made in writing to the city management and, if applicable, the city manager passes them on to the city council
- Team recommendations have had a very high acceptance rate by the city council
- The city manager periodically attends team meetings
- To be effective, team recommendations must have a visible and positive impact on decisions
- One member of the team (usually on a rotating basis) acts as a facilitator of team meetings

The level of excitement by city employees about the team-building concept in Council Bluffs is very high. One side effect of the program is that department heads use "informal teams" in arriving at important decisions.

As an example of the effectiveness of the team-management program in Council Bluffs, Miller writes:

We have also had an administrative team negotiating the extension of an animal control service contract with our local humane society. The humane society requested much more money than the council was willing to spend. About three weeks prior to the termination of the existing contract, the humane society expressed its desire to terminate its relationships with the city and the council asked the staff to assume the duties for animal control at that time. The humane service refused to extend the contract. This left the city with the need to purchase all new equipment and hire new personnel within three weeks. The team which had been negotiating the contract understood the job of instituting the new service. After one month's operation under city control, the city council actually complimented the staff on its "miraculous" takeover of the animal control service in such a short time. A few years ago, such a compliment would have been unheard of. If the takeover of the animal control service had been the responsibility of only one department (in this case, the Health Department was the prime provider of the new service) then we never could have provided such a smooth transition to a city operation. As it was, the Purchasing Department helped in speeding up the purchase of necessary equipment and the Personnel Department aided in speeding up the hiring of necessary personnel. A feeling of ownership of the new system so pervaded the team that the members spent a Saturday at the animal shelter (which was already owned by the city) for a clean-up day.

I have not utilized quality circles as such; however, I feel that this type of technique will fit very well into our organization considering the attitude of management/supervisory personnel toward group consensus and impact. In addition, many of our people are already trained in group facilitation techniques. We will be looking with interest toward utilization of the quality circle technique within our organization in the future.[11]

## QUALITY OF WORK LIFE IN GARDEN CITY

Garden City, Michigan, City Manager Cam Caldwell has developed an effective quality of work life program[12] that he considers to be an alternative approach to self-defeating labor management problems. The quality of work life (QWL) concept is a process of management that has been applied for several years in the private sector. It is usually implemented through the establishment of labor management committees, which meet on a monthly basis to discuss ways to improve the working environment and employee productivity. The primary goal of these monthly meetings is to improve communications and increase the understanding of labor and management regarding problems in the workplace and to identify steps that can be taken to resolve those problems. The concept reflects the management philosophy that employees are capable and intelligent and that management can work with employees to maximize organization and individual goals. But management must be willing to respect and trust employees and must manage the organization in a manner that merits that same respect and trust in return.

In Garden City, four labor management committees are in operation throughout the city. In addition to resolving intradepartmental problems through QWL, Garden City employees have served on an employee budget advisory committee and developed a list of 101 ideas that they presented to the city manager and elected officials to help the city balance the budget. Many of those ideas were adopted and the budget presented to council. Employee input helped the city council to reduce the city budget below the level of the previous year without reducing city services.

Garden City has determined that organizational change will be resisted by those who are affected by it unless those persons (1) understand why the change is needed; (2) are given the opportunity to contribute to decisions that affect their work, the workplace, and themselves personally; and (3) are given respect and consideration when changes are ultimately implemented.

## QUALITY OF WORKING LIFE IN PIMA COUNTY, ARIZONA

The Pima County manager and his staff have developed a quality of working life program[13] at the Pima County Department of Transportation and Flood Control District. The program has been so successful that attempts are currently being made to expand the program to other county departments. In its basic form, the concept of quality of working life suggests that if workplace conditions are improved, employee morale will increase, which in turn will increase productivity. Through the implementation and conduct of a quality of working life program, management maintains responsibility and authority for control of the organization. These functions of management are not given up to employees.

In Pima County, the QWL structure consists of three elements: (1) the QWL committee structure, (2) the QWL representative system and (3) the QWL proposal process. Most divisions within the county have set up their committees according to existing division and section organizational charts. Committees operate very informally. The goal was to set up an environment in which all participants feel free to participate and communicate openly. Most of the committees have a chairperson whose role is to generate participation instead of restricting involvement by sticking to strict agendas or imposing rules of order. The goal of the committee structure is to reach a consensus about how best to solve a particular problem.

In Pima County, the employees of each division are responsible for electing QWL representatives. This is referred to as the QWL representative system. Because of its democratic process, it ensures theoretical representation of peer concerns and ideas within the program.

The life blood of the QWL system is the proposal process. A proposal is a comprehensive written document used to request that something be done or that some specific problem be resolved. Proposals can be generated at any level of the QWL committee structure. Some proposals can be acted upon within the committee of origin; others require the input and the consideration of upper-level committees. In all instances, the object is to reach a consensus based on the merits of the proposal. In Pima County, the maintenance division has been participating in the QWL activities for over a year. Although there have been many statements of support by employees and supervisors, introducing and maintaining support for the program has not been easy. QWL requires organizational change, and change is never easily accepted by all people. At various times, misunderstandings have occurred that have caused employees to question the value of the program. But so far, reason has prevailed and detractors soon find themselves back in the midst of QWL activities.

In the area of short-term results, an immediate benefit has been an increasing willingness to communicate among employees, supervisors and managers. In addition, supervisors and employees are beginning to feel better about job satisfaction, job autonomy and fairness in job assignments. Performance indicators also indicate that positive changes are occurring.

## FLORIDA LAUNCHES QC

Selected Florida state agencies are currently trying Quality Circles.[14] Under the direction of the state productivity coordinator, the Quality Circle concept was researched for potential inclusion in Florida's productivity improvement effort. An airline company cooperated with the state of Florida by giving state agencies their first training and assistance in the Quality Circle concept.

Initially, six state agencies implemented Quality Circles on a pilot basis. These agencies were the Department of Business Regulation, the Department of Health and Rehabilitative Services, the Department of Labor and Employment Security, the Department of Law Enforcement, the Department of Natural Resources and the Department of Revenue. The Florida Center for Productivity at Florida State University provided leadership training and a subsequent Quality Circle facilitator workshop.

The Florida Center for Productivity offers several prerequisites for a successful Quality Circle program. These include the following:

- Management must support the Quality Circle program
- A limited number of successful circles will lead to expansion through word of mouth
- The program should be voluntary
- Facilitators must be selected carefully
- Quality Circle meeting times must be sacred

In the state of Florida, the Quality Circle program is not to be confused with suggestion systems or human relations. The objectives of the Quality Circle program in Florida are improved communications, quality, productivity and motivation. The key is participative management based on a belief in the ability and integrity of the worker.

## QUALITY CIRCLES IN PENSACOLA

A plan for the development and implementation of a pilot Quality Circle program in the city of Pensacola[15] was developed by the Personnel Department. The Quality Circle concept is a way of involving people at all levels of the organization in decision-making and problem-solving activities in their normal workplace. Participants are all volunteers.

Quality Circles were initially implemented in Japan on a wide-scale basis. Their initial acceptance in American organizations took place in 1974. Some organizations that have successfully implemented Quality Circles include Ford Motor Company, Xerox, Westinghouse, General Motors, Lockheed, Monsanto and the United States Navy.

The objectives of the Quality Circle program in Pensacola were to accomplish the following:

1. Improve productivity
2. Improve employee participation
3. Improve employee understanding of the managerial process
4. Improve employee concepts of budgetary needs
5. Get more employees involved in their work situation
6. Improve employee self-concept and self-worth
7. Increase understanding of the city's role in the community and employee functions that support that role
8. Teach employees the methods for bringing about positive organized change
9. Increase communications among employees, supervisors and management about the work being performed
10. Improve the quality of service delivery

Quality Circles are structured with six basic elements: circle members, circle leader, facilitator/coordinator, steering committee, management and non-member employees/resource people.

A typical Quality Circle consists of a small group of employee volunteers, ideally seven to eight persons, who perform similar work. Each circle has a leader who is responsible for the operation of the circle. Leaders are trained in Quality Circle techniques, group process and management skills. Additionally, each circle has a recorder who is responsible for maintaining documentation of the circle's process.

The steering committee, facilitator/coordinator from the Personnel Department, management and non-member employees/resource people all play a supportive role in the Quality Circle process. The steering committee, consisting of managers and top-level staff, provides policy guidance to circles within the department. The Personnel facilitator/coordinator acts as a liaison between the steering committee and the QC, trains circle leaders, and maintains records of the group's progress. The coordinator may also serve as a member of the steering committee. Non-member employees or persons outside the organization function in a resource capacity to circles by providing technical expertise. Management remains involved by providing resources to circles and listening to presentations on proposed situations to problems.

The Quality Circle process includes regular meetings to identify and analyze work-related problems and develop solutions using a problem-solving process. These problems may be suggested by circle members, other employees or management. They must be problems that affect the circle members' work process and/or workplace. *Circles may not address*

*problems involving employee complaints, hiring or firing policies, pay pol-
icies or personalities.*

Once problems are identified by circle members, the members select the
problems they will work on. With the help of resource people, the members
then analyze the problem using a variety of Quality Circle techniques:
check sheets, sampling, graphing, charts, brainstorming, cause-and-effect
diagramming and other analysis/data-gathering techniques. From the data
gathered and analyzed, members develop a solution and present it to management in a formal presentation, sharing all documentation used to analyze the problem, including cost comparisons and benefit analysis when
applicable.

After a management review period, usually about two weeks, a decision
on the recommended solution is given to the circle. If the decision is to
accept the recommended solution, the *circle members are responsible for
implementation.* Management may also request further research on the
problem, or reject the proposed solution, providing a detailed explanation
for this request or decision.

Several departments volunteered to participate in Pensacola's pilot program: the Public Service Department and Police Departments were chosen.
In these two departments, there are currently four active circles: sanitation,
police services, police departmental and inspections. The circles have been
meeting on a regular basis.

Two circles have completed their first project. The problems addressed
were gun registration safety and inadequate police jackets. The police
service circle has developed an improved procedure for handling gun registration within the department. This involves a training component for
non-sworn personnel and a community relations/citizen awareness component for citizens registering guns. Both will provide increased safety at
no additional cost to the city and will eliminate potential public financial
liability from accidental firing of weapons in the police department.

The police departmental circle has recommended the purchase of a
warmer, more useable service jacket, at less cost than the current service
jacket. The current service jacket was identified as being deficient in du-
rability, appearance, warmth and fit. A survey of all officers in the department was conducted by the circle to get the opinion of all those who
are issued jackets. Three different jackets were passed around the department to look at, try on, or wear on duty. The 107 voting members
were also allowed to suggest any alternative jackets. The results of the
survey by collected vote were fifty-eight votes for the flight jacket, ten
votes for a three-quarter length jacket with side zippers and inserts, no
votes for the current jacket, thirty-one votes for a suggested alternate jacket
purchased by traffic officers and eight no preference votes. The results
indicated that the majority of officers wished to replace the current jacket
with the flight jacket. In addition to the survey, a cost analysis of the

jackets proved to be a good choice. With the cost of the current jacket of $40, the $24 bulk rate for the flight jacket will be a welcomed savings for the department and the city. Management has accepted both circles' proposals for changes in policy and materials purchasing.

The other two circles are working on problems consisting of more durable rain suits for sanitation workers, improved radio communications in public service, and the need for enforcement of the Southern Building Code requiring an approved job copy at the work site. If the pilot program continues its success, Quality Circles will be expanded to other departments that have indicated an interest.

## LEADERSHIP CHALLENGES IN HAMPTON, VIRGINIA

Leadership challenges is a three-track training and development program for city of Hampton, Virginia,[16] supervisors, midmanagers and executives. The program builds on a foundation of core courses designed to provide basic knowledge needed for first-line supervision (Track 1), adding courses oriented toward the broader management skills (Track 2) and culminating in a variety of development experiences at the executive level that provide opportunities for creative thinking, strategic planning, and problem solving in a variety of settings (Track 3).

The city of Hampton is committed to supporting the development of all employees who hold leadership positions within the organization. Therefore, all supervisors, managers and executives are expected to participate in the wide array of training and development opportunities offered by the city. The leadership challenges program has been carefully designed to assist Hampton's supervisors and managers in developing the kinds of skills that make them effective leaders within the context of the Hampton organization. Courses are tailored to Hampton's participative management and work styles and, in most cases, will emphasize teamwork, experiential learning and problem solving. Completion of the leadership challenges program provides an understanding and experience of the latest in management and leadership theory and, in addition, gives the manager direction in the application of his/her new knowledge and skills.

Track 1 is offered as a three-day seminar, and program participants are required to register, with management approval, for the entire three days. Track 2 is offered as a two and one-half–day seminar, and participants are also expected to register for the entire track. Certain basic criteria must be met at each level of the program. In some cases, work experience, outside courses and/or successful demonstration of course knowledge may be applied for advanced standing in the program. Specific dates and times of course offerings are contained in the training brochure published annually by the department of human resources.

Each leadership challenges class will be asked to participate voluntarily in the design of an innovative approach to an organizational problem or opportunity. At the end of each fiscal year, all completed projects will compete for a City Manager's Award of Excellence, which may be monetary or non-monetary, depending on the potential impact of the winning project on organizational effectiveness.

The content of the leadership challenges training is as follows.

## TRACK 1—"A FOUNDATION"

**Criteria**

- Must currently be on the "M" scale or PO2 and above
- Must be able to read and write
- Must have supervisor's approval

| Course Title | Length |
|---|---|
| Active Listening | ½ day |
| Motivating People | ½ day |
| Performance Appraisal | 1 day |
| Workstyles and Teamwork | ½ day |
| Dealing with Problems | ½ day |

## TRACK 2—"TRANSITIONS"

**Criteria**

- Must complete all core courses of Track 1 (education and/or experience may substitute for some courses)
- Must currently be on the "M" scale or PO3 and above
- Must have supervisor's approval

| Course Title | Length |
|---|---|
| Effective Meetings | ½ day |
| Facilitating Groups | ½ day |
| Team Problem Solving | ½ day |
| Decision-Making Options | ½ day |
| Planning and Goal Setting | ½ day |

**Electives**

| | |
|---|---|
| Analytical Skills | Speed Reading |
| Communication Skills | Train the Trainer |
| Ethics | Roles and Initiatives |

Effective Presentations

Elements of Teamwork

Computer Skills

Effective Writing Skills

## TRACK 3—"LEADERSHIP IN ACTION"

**Executive Development Opportunities**

- Tape library
- Serve as in-house trainer
- Management innovation groups
- Graduate program in public administration
- Leadership development institutes/seminars

- Roundtable discussions
- Executive think tanks
- Management retreats
- Focus group facilitator
- Leadership assessment

## ORGANIZATION DEVELOPMENT IN THE CITY OF HAMPTON

A way of approaching work that supports employee ownership and positive results is the basis of the organization development effort of Hampton, Virginia.[17] The process of restructuring the way work was being done began in 1984 when the operating departments were aligned into task forces that take responsibility for day-to-day operation of the city.

Facilitated by one of the member department heads, each task force generates its own annual priorities, works on shared performance goals and solves problems within its functional area. The task forces are also free to address any issue they see as important to the organization's success. Departments may belong to one or more task forces as they deem appropriate. The current operational task forces function in the areas of infrastructure, public safety, management resources and community services. Although department heads report directly to the city manager, through their task forces they are able to solve most problems with the cooperation and assistance of their peers. The same task force approach to work is used throughout the organization in an effort to take the concept to the lowest level possible.

Hampton has a full-time organization development professional in the department of human resources who is responsible for assisting departments and employees in the design and implementation of human resource systems that encourage a high level of productivity and esprit de corps and the accomplishment of the organization's goals.

Following is an organization development model, a listing of activities and programs ongoing or under development in each functional area depicted on the model and a series of program highlights describing some of those activities that may be of particular interest. The organization development effort in Hampton is focused on *how* work is done rather than on *programs*. The programs listed were created to support the organization's participative management and work style.

### Hampton's Organization Development Model

The model for organization development (OD) consists of the following key elements:

1. Council and top management support for OD
2. Funding for OD
3. Organization values affirmed
4. Commitment from Department heads and supervisors
5. Vision and policy from the human resources task force
6. Participative management and work styles

The model has been implemented by a series of management processes:

1. Training and development
2. Employee-management handbook
3. Employee involvement
4. Rewards and recognition
5. Performance measurement
6. Career development

Results have been that organization goals have been accomplished and a high level of employee satisfaction and ownership has been achieved.

Programs and activities within functional areas have included the following:

| Career Development | Employee Involvement |
| --- | --- |
| Recruitment | Task forces |
| In-house promotions | Venture groups |
| Career ladders | Focus groups |
| Cross-training | Quality Circles |
| Affirmative action | Women's network |
| Career counseling | Administrative support group |
| Interest and aptitude assessment | Supervisor's Club |
| Temporary assignments and promotions | Personnel policies review committee |
| | Employee council |
| Executive exchange | Hampton challenge |

Self-managing work teams

Problem-solving groups

City hall beautification committee

Investment club

**Rewards and Recognition**

Salary

Benefits

Achievement program—monetary and non-monetary awards

Citizen satisfaction bonuses

Executive compensation program

Service pins and certificates

Employee newsletter

City manager's memo

Letter of congratulations

**Training and Development**

On-the-job training

Supervisory program

Management training

Clerical training

Public relations training

Education loan program

Apprenticeship program

Literacy program

Safety program

**Performance Measurement**

Productivity analysis

Department head performance contracts/executive compensation program

Performance appraisal tools unique to departments

Citizen satisfaction surveys

**Employee/Management Relations**

Attitude surveys

Standards of conduct

Disciplinary system

Grievance procedure

Employee assistance program

Posters and bulletin boards

City manager's open house

Employee/city manager lunches

Selected OD Program highlights are discussed below.

*Task Forces*

The task force concept is fundamental to Hampton's organization development effort because it reflects a shared belief in employees' willingness to take personal responsibility for the organization's success and to work with others in the accomplishment of that goal. Chairmanship of the operational task forces is rotated among the member department heads on an annual basis. The chairperson acts as a team leader and facilitator but has no actual supervisory authority over the members, and decisions are reached by consensus. The task force chairpersons meet with the city manager several times a month, both to share information about what is going on in their respective task forces and to be briefed on ongoing work in the city manager's office. The task force chairpersons then report to their task forces any relevant information gained in these meetings. The meetings also allow the task force chairpersons to keep each other informed relative to what their task forces are doing. In some cases, several task forces are working together on one issue. The four assistant city managers also chair task forces that focus on broad issues of particular concern to the city council and top management. These task forces are policy and future oriented rather than concerned with day-to-day operations. The human resources, quality of life, financial management, and economic development task forces are currently functional. The uniqueness of the task force concept as it exists in Hampton is that the task forces develop their own agendas. They are expected to think about the needs of the organization and find ways to satisfy these needs by working together. It has taken approximately three years for the task force concept to come to fruition in the way it was originally conceived. This particular way of working seems to be a real success, judging from the results of a citizen satisfaction survey recently conducted in which more than 93 percent of Hampton's citizens polled rated the performance of city employees as satisfactory or very good.

*Venture Groups*

These groups are made up of employees from all levels of the work force whose task is to research and investigate successful and innovative programs in other organizations and communities. One of the unique features of this program is that the employees involved do not necessarily have expertise in the areas under discussion and are, therefore, viewing each issue with a new perspective. Two recently formed venture groups are looking into the fiscal impact of economic development and physical appearance in the community.

*Focus Groups*

Groups consisting of employees from all levels throughout the organization have been used to address specific areas of concern, such as tobacco use in the workforce and the impact of health care costs. The Tobacco Use Focus Group, for example, surveyed the workforce to ascertain the feelings of employees on the issue of tobacco use in the workplace and subsequently made recommendations for a tobacco use policy in the city of Hampton.

*Administrative Support Group*

This organization is composed of clerical employees who meet on a regular basis for the purposes of enhancing their professional development and image in the workplace, networking, mutual support and the implementation of various projects. One of the projects the group has undertaken has been the publication of a "how-to-manual" that is a compilation of all the city's administrative procedures. This manual is oriented toward the clerical employee who actually uses these procedures and will be provided to all current and new clerical employees. The value of the work for the handbook, which was one and one-half years in the making, was approximately $10,000. This group also initiated a bosses day brunch in which the members invite their bosses and announce a boss of the year.

mentation of various projects. One of the projects the group has under-taken has been the publication of a "how-to-manual" that is a compilation of all the city's administrative procedures. This manual is oriented toward the clerical employee who actually uses these procedures and will be pro-vided to all current and new clerical employees. The value of the work for the handbook, which was one and one-half years in the making, was ap-proximately $10,000. This group also initiated a bosses day brunch in which the members invite their bosses and announce a boss of the year.

### Hampton Challenge

Hampton employees have formed this unique organization to encourage employee participation in projects outside of their normal work assign-ments. For example, Hampton challenge recently undertook several fund-raising projects to benefit the new Virginia Air and Space Center and Hampton Roads History Center soon to be built in Hampton. The group, as a part of one of the city's festival organizations, raffled off a luxury condominium, the proceeds of which will benefit the new museum. "Out of This World Holiday Fashions," which included local media celebrities as models and narrators, was recently held at a luxury hotel on the down-town Hampton waterfront, also to benefit the new museum. These two efforts combined raised almost $40,000 for the new museum and were managed entirely by employees who donated their time on nights and weekends to make these projects a success.

### Self-Managing Workteams

(See previous case study, chapter 4.)

### Achievement Award Program

(See previous case study, chapter 4.)

### Citizen Satisfaction Surveys and Bonuses

This program provides for cash bonuses for all full-time and part-time city employees based on the results of a citizens' satisfaction survey. A rating by citizens of at least 80 percent "satisfied" or "very satisfied" was required for the granting of a bonus, with $200 established as the maximum bonus in the first year. The first survey was completed and resulted in a 93.2 percent citizen satisfaction rating for Hampton city employees. Per-manent full-time employees received 93.2 percent of the $200 ($186.40), and part-time employees received half that amount ($93.20). The bonuses were paid prior to the Christmas holidays.

### Executive Compensation Program

(See previous case study.)

## Performance Appraisal Tools Unique to Departments

The department of human resources provides assistance to city departments in developing performance appraisal systems that are unique to their particular departments. The police department completed a job-specific system that meets national accreditation standards. Basic information about performance appraisal—its benefits and pitfalls—is provided by human resources staff members to departments that are interested in developing their own systems. Human resources also assists the department in defining the areas critical to successful job performance and establishing performance standards for those areas.

## Productivity Analysis

The department of productivity programs functions differently than those typically found in other organizations in that studies are done by invitation only. The department head makes the final decision as to whether the study results are implemented. Results of these productivity studies are also shared with the city manager, and discussions take place between the city manager and department heads, with implementation sometimes being a part of the department head's performance contract. The thrust of the program is essentially one of service and assistance to departments in the improvement of their operations. Productivity programs staff are not seen as "spies" from the manager's office but rather as fellow employees with specific kinds of expertise that can help employees do their jobs more effectively. A commitment has been made not to terminate any employees as a result of these productivity studies. Reductions are made through attrition only.

## TOTAL QUALITY MANAGEMENT IN MADISON

In 1982, the city of Madison, Wisconsin[18] (population 170,000), had a stale economic base due in the main to a slowly growing population, a large service economy, the University of Wisconsin, a few large manufacturing firms, the state capital and the county seat. In 1983, the university experienced lower enrollment due to the baby boom having passed through, fewer customers were available for local businesses and citizens became cost conscious in the light of California's Proposition 13. As a result, in 1983 a group of local business and government leaders began to turn to the teachings of W. Edwards Deming relative to quality improvement. This led in late 1985 to the formulation of a community-based organization, the Madison Area Quality Improvement Network (MAQIN). The purpose of MAQIN was to support local quality improvement efforts and to provide leadership to make continuous quality improvement the pervasive management method in Madison.

The Madison quality efforts grew into a widespread community effort with twelve key elements as follows:

1. Energetic champions
2. The right mix of people, including those with
   • Power or access to power
   • Education in quality management
   • The willingness to take risks
   • Collaborators versus competitors
   • Perseverance and commitment
   • Anti-parochialists
3. Synergy building
4. A need, frustration or opportunity
   • Problems
   • Gaps
   • Resources
5. A vision
6. A strategy for involving others
7. Something visible or concrete that will be successful
8. An event
9. Publicity
10. Money
11. Interaction with other people and communities
12. Chamber of Commerce involvement

As mayor of Madison from 1983 to 1989, Joseph Sensenbrenner used the total quality management approach to deal with a number of city problems,[19] which included the following:

1. City services were in a steady decline. For example, in the city garage, repair delays and equipment unavailability were major problems. Based upon personal investigation, the mayor found that the source of the downtime problem was in the relationship the city had with its suppliers, not the point at which the worker couldn't find the missing part. The problem was a flaw in the system, not a flaw in the workers. As the mayor put it: "There was a major failure of a city service whose symptoms, causes and solution were widely known, but that had become chronic because government was not organized to solve it." From that point on, the city wrote vehicle and equipment purchase specifications so that they included a warranty and addressed the ease of maintenance, the availability of parts and the resale value over time. Finding the solution also required teamwork, breaking down barriers between departments and including

front-line employees in problem solving. The result of the changes in the system was a reduction in the average vehicle turnaround time from nine days to three days at a savings of $7.15 in downtime and repair for every dollar invested in preventive maintenance. The annual net savings to the city was $700,000.

2. After setting up a city-wide quality and productivity program at all levels, including unions, and hiring an administrator for it, the city took on projects in the streets division, the health department, day care and data processing. A second wave of quality initiatives worked wonders in morale and improved productivity, improved customer service and saved money.

When Mayor Sensenbrenner left office in 1989, the Madison city departments were involved in twenty to thirty quality improvement projects at one time. As the mayor said at the time: "If businesses insist on quality, offer their expertise, share their training programs with governmental officials . . . the payback can be substantial."

## THE TYLER, TEXAS, EXPERIENCE WITH PRIVATIZATION

Tyler Texas, a city of 80,000, began to look at privatization about five years ago. Its old landfill was full and the city began to explore new locations. Then a private hauler proposed that the city enter into a partnership in a regional landfill. The hauler would operate it. "The initial reaction was skepticism," said Tyler City Manager Gary Gwyn. "The city wasn't sure it would save money. But the more we talked, the better it looked."

The private hauler offered the city a large concession on the tipping fee. Tyler's rate would be one-half of the regular rate. "It was such a positive thing for the city that we couldn't walk away," said Gwyn.

There is a downside, however. Ownership of the landfill changed and the new owner announced that the landfill will accept sludge from a sewage authority in New Jersey. The community is concerned about the possibility of future environmental problems. The large volume of waste exported from New Jersey will reduce the life of the landfill by three to four years. The city learned from the experience. "We won't allow the owner to import such waste under a new contract without the approval of City Council," Gwyn said.

Tyler has also contracted out collection and disposal of restaurant waste. Traditionally, waste from grease traps was dumped into the sewage treatment plant. This is no longer permitted. Rather than cope with the new regulations, the city identified companies that handle such waste and contracted with one of them. "The charges are higher, but that is a function of the new regulations, not privatization," Gwyn said. "Service is probably better than with a city-run operation and it's a problem area that the city doesn't have to fool with anymore."

Tyler will continue to privatize. The city is considering whether to contract out residential curbside recycling and the operation of an obstetrics clinic. One unexpected benefit of contracting out has been its effect on city departments. "The city owns three cemeteries. We tried to bid out the maintenance, but didn't. Our own parks department underbid the private contractors. Their bid came in under their previous year's budget. The threat of privatization brought the department to life. It is now very entrepreneurial," Gwyn noted.

## A CONSOLIDATION MODEL: AUSTIN/TRAVIS COUNTY, TEXAS

After eighteen months of work and deliberation, the Joint Commission on Metropolitan Government of Austin/Travis County, Texas,[20] concluded that "delivery of governmental services in the context of geographical and jurisdictional boundaries is no longer meaningful; that units of government and methods of service delivery that were designed to resolve immediate problems are no longer suitable for the long-range health of the metropolitan region."

### Background

The Joint Commission was established in January 1985 by resolutions of the Austin City Council and the Travis County Commissioners Court. These resolutions had their genesis in growing concerns about the cost and quality of service delivery in an environment of rapid population growth, accelerated proliferation of governmental units, and the perceived duplication of effort among governments providing services in the metropolitan area.

The seventeen-member Joint Commission on Metropolitan Government was established to study service delivery alternatives, including the feasibility of creating a metro government structure for Austin and the other cities in Travis County. The commission was broadly representative of the citizens of Travis County. Five of its members were appointed by the Travis County Commissioners Court, seven by the Austin City Council, two by the other incorporated cities within the county, and two by the Travis County legislative delegation. Travis County and the city of Austin provided funding and excellent staff support for the efforts of the commission.

The findings and recommendations presented in the joint commission's report are based on eleven written reports prepared for the commission by a team of outside consultants, ten on specific service functions and one on metropolitan governance structures and on numerous presentations made by officials, staff and citizens at the commission's twenty-six public meetings. The commission's report is the result of more than eighteen months of detailed study of the present operations of Travis County's local government entities and the governance strategies used in other U.S. areas.

### Commission Objectives

The consensus objectives of the commission were to accomplish the following:

- Reduce layers of government in Travis County and the reliance on single-purpose governmental units
- Improve efficiency and reduce costs in the delivery of services
- Provide superior regionwide comprehensive planning and coordination of delivery of services
- Ensure equity in financing services, provide adequate service to all areas and prevent inequitable taxation or subsidies
- Improve the fiscal health of the region through unified financial planning, upgrading cumulative bonding capacity and reducing overlapping debt
- Ensure improved accountability of government

The commission's efforts, and those of its research staff and consultants, were directed toward formulating policy recommendations to realize these objectives.

### Approach to the Study

The joint commission collected data about present and planned services and service delivery approaches within the Austin/Travis County metro area in several ways. These included the following:

1. Meetings with department heads from Travis County and from cities and other local jurisdictions within the county to hear presentations on their areas of responsibilities and to gather reactions to alternative service delivery approaches.

2. Study and discussion of detailed research reports prepared by the commission's consultants on ten service delivery areas and various consolidation alternatives. Service areas covered in the reports included purchasing; management of vehicles and equipment, building and property; information and communication systems; law enforcement; fire protection and rescue; traffic; transit and roads; health services; land use planning; water and wastewater services; and human services.

Consolidation alternatives covered in the research reports included partial/functional consolidation, establishment of a metro government entity to operate certain functions, full consolidation of the governments of Austin and Travis County and privatization of certain functions and services.

3. Presentations by students and practitioners involved with metropolitan government administration.

4. A series of public hearings held throughout the metropolitan area to give individual citizens and groups a chance to voice their opinions.

### Findings and Recommendations

After extensive study and deliberation, the joint commission recommended that regionwide consolidation of local governments be the long-term objective of the city of Austin and Travis County. The commission recognized that regionwide consolidation is a complex process that must be phased in over a substantial period of time (Exhibit 11–1). Although the commission identified five phases, the process is a continuum with numerous intermediate steps. It will require adjustments and refinements en route to the ultimate goal. The joint commission noted that changes to the existing structure would demand the commitment and willing participation of the elected officials and staff of the city of Austin and Travis County and recommended that other incorporated cities and governmental entities be included but not be required to participate.

**Exhibit 11–1**
**Summary Chart Regionwide Comprehensive Planning**

| | |
|---|---|
| Phase I | Operational improvements and partial consolidation of certain governmental functions through interlocal contracts |
| Phase II | Delivery of certain services on a metro basis, including |
| | —Land use planning |
| | —Water and wastewater |
| | —Parks and recreation |
| | —Health services |
| | —Human services |
| | —Solid waste collection and disposal |
| | —Traffic, transit, and roads |
| Phase III | Delivery of other services on a metro basis, including |
| | —Law enforcement |
| | —Fire protection |
| Phase IV | Consolidation of the city of Austin and Travis County |
| Phase V | Consolidation with neighboring counties |

### PHASE I

During its deliberations, the joint commission identified numerous specific methods for improving service delivery or reducing costs. These are important first steps toward full consolidation and can be accomplished with few legal constraints. Its recommendations included operational improvements and partial consolidations through interlocal contracts of all ten governmental functions that were the topic of the previously described research reports. The commission also recommended that efforts be made to consolidate other services when it is allowed under existing state law. One such function identified by the commission was elections administration.

Most of the recommended improvements or consolidations do not require any changes to existing state statutes. The major exception is zoning and building standards ordinance-making authority for Travis County. Certain changes to existing statutes would also help simplify consolidation of purchasing water and wastewater services.

## PHASE II

During Phase II, the commission recommended that many of the basic services provided by local governmental entities be consolidated under one metro government entity. The services recommended for metro consolidation included land use planning, water and wastewater, parks and recreation, health services, human services, solid waste collection and disposal and traffic, transit and roads.

Although the commission recognized that creating a third entity may not be desirable, it viewed the entity as a possible short-term step toward full consolidation. Alternatively, these services could be administered by an existing entity, which would provide services to the metropolitan area composed of the city of Austin, the unincorporated areas of Travis County and, on a voluntary basis, the other incorporated areas within the county and possibly areas in other counties. Implicit in either option is the concept of reducing the cost and thereby the taxpayer burden of administering these services.

## PHASE III

In this phase, two other services, law enforcement and fire protection and rescue, would be added to the metro government structure. Given the critical nature of these services to the life and safety of citizens, the commission believed the consolidation would require more extensive planning than Phase II services. Consolidation would occur only after the structure established in Phase II is operating effectively. It should be noted that the commission believes it desirable to continue the role of the volunteer fire and rescue departments to the maximum extent feasible.

## PHASE IV

This phase involves full consolidation of the city of Austin and Travis County into a single governmental entity. Metro services from phases II and III, with the possible exception of water and wastewater, as well as the other services either entity now provides would be handled by the consolidated entity. The city and county judiciary would also need to be revamped. Regardless of the structure elected, this phase would require substantial changes to existing state laws.

## PHASE V

Since the city of Austin now extends beyond the boundaries of Travis County and since metro-type growth now extends into neighboring counties, the commission recommended that consolidation with neighboring counties be pursued in this final phase. Changes to existing state law are likely to be required, depending upon the desired powers and authority of the consolidated governmental entity.

The commission also recognized that statutory and constitutional authorization of new financing techniques would be required when certain services are provided on a metro basis to allocate the cost of such services equitably among users. If different areas of the county (e.g., heavily urbanized areas and sparsely populated unincorporated areas) required and were provided different levels of service by a metropolitan entity, a uniform tax rate would be unfair. When user charges are the financing mechanism, this creates no problem (i.e., the cost of service varies among users according to level of use). However, the uniformity clause of the Texas state constitution precludes levying variable property tax rates based on levels of service. It was the commission's judgment that if tax-supported services are to be delivered on a metro basis, the state legislature would have to authorize variable tax rates for different areas based on the level of services provided.

The joint commission also recommended that its own existence be continued to provide an oversight function and even expanded to include members from neighboring counties. It also recommended that regionwide comprehensive planning be emphasized throughout the process, using existing entities such as the Capital Area Planning Council (CAPCO) to assist in the planning effort.

### Conclusions

In an effort to address issues of rapid growth and governmental proliferation in the Austin/Travis County area, the Joint Commission on Metropolitan Government developed a comprehensive blueprint for eventual governmental consolidation. The reception to the commission's recommendations by local groups such as the League of Women Voters and by the local media was excellent. The commission's report also received favorable initial comment from several local officials. The slowdown in the Texas economy resulting from the sharp decline in oil prices, with a resulting decrease in sales tax collections (which constitutes a significant revenue source for Texas cities), provided a climate conducive to proposals designed to improve the efficiency and reduce the cost of local government services.

A positive direction has been established by the joint commission's report. Efforts since have included follow-up on work to begin to implement selected functional consolidations. However, it remains to be seen whether a more logical approach to the provision of governmental services will overcome a local rights orientation of the electorate and their elected officials in the Austin/Travis County area.

## A MIDDLE ROAD TO REFORM: THE ATLANTA/FULTON COUNTY ALTERNATIVE SERVICE DELIVERY EXPERIENCE

The last few decades have witnessed vigorous opposition to most attempts at large-scale governmental consolidation and annexation in major metropolitan areas. Such efforts have encountered adverse reactions from public officials and citizens alike, to the extent that the basic issues of fragmentation and fiscal inequities are obscured or even ignored. As a result, virtually all major service reorganizations have taken the form of piecemeal transfers of individual functions while leaving intact the basic structure of the existing service delivery system. With the persistence of fiscal pressures and taxpayer dissatisfaction in both central cities and suburbs, local governments will continue to be pressed to find workable and effective solutions to mitigate structural deficiencies in their service delivery systems.

An initiative in Atlanta/Fulton County, Georgia,[21] took a "middle road" approach that produced some potentially sweeping reforms while stopping short of the major surgery associated with metropolitan consolidation or annexation. The Atlanta experience offers some valuable lessons in pragmatic reform within the constraints of big city politics. The achievements of the blue-ribbon Atlanta/Fulton County Study Commission compare favorably with other governmental reform efforts in Rochester, N.Y.; Tampa, Florida; Portland, Oregon; and Denver, Colorado. The multiservice tax district proposal adopted by the commission stands as one of the most significant reforms in large city government in the last few decades.

The commission's far-reaching recommendations relative to local service delivery and financing won the early approval of the Georgia General Assembly and the governor.

The Atlanta/Fulton County experience points to the following conclusions:

• Proponents of metrowide governmental concepts will find support in neither core cities nor suburbs

• Local control is the crucial concern to citizens in those services that most directly affect personal life-styles (e.g., police, zoning authority) and efficiency and effectiveness are secondary considerations in such instances. However, they are key concerns in reorganizing other municipal services

Historically in the United States, cities have delivered "hardware" services such as public works, police, fire and public utilities. Counties, on the other hand, have been responsible for the "softer" functions such as public health and welfare. During the 1960s and 1970s, however, these traditional distinctions broke down as many federal social service programs were aimed directly at municipal governments. Meanwhile, county governments have assumed more traditional municipal functions in order to serve rapidly urbanizing areas. These trends have led to problems of governmental service duplication and public outcries of fiscal inequities. One solution to the problem is through complete city/county government consolidation such as the Nashville/Davidson County and Jacksonville reforms during the 1960s. Another frequently advocated solution is the annexation of urbanized unincorporated county areas by the central city. However, such major surgery invariably stirs adverse political repercussions that often spell doom for such efforts before the necessary momentum is achieved.

Citizens of Atlanta and Fulton County, Georgia, as in many major metropolitan areas, have been concerned with local government reorganization for at least the past thirty to forty years. The 1952 Plan of Improvement was intended to provide a permanent and rational reallocation of service responsibilities between city and county governments. The plan at once tripled the size of the city of Atlanta and permitted automatic future annexation of unincorporated county areas when they reached a prescribed level of urbanization. However, in 1969, a Georgia court ruled this provision unconstitutional, a decision that effectively terminated the opportunity for further territorial expansion of the city and paved the way for increased participation by Fulton County in the provision of municipal services.

As in the case of many counties surrounding large central cities, Fulton County had evolved into a full-service urban government, delivering most traditionally municipal services to its residents in unincorporated areas. Since most such services are financed by the county's general

fund, two-thirds of which are derived from Atlanta taxpayers, charges
by Atlanta of fiscal inequity through double taxation had become rampant. Fulton County retorted with accusations of inequity resulting from
its provision of services at Grady Hospital in downtown Atlanta to a
clientele overwhelmingly composed of Atlanta residents. Despite several
city, county and state attempts, no viable resolution to these differences
was forthcoming. By the end of a decade, an imposed settlement by the
rural-dominated Georgia General Assembly appeared to be a real possibility. The governor, furthermore, believed that continued city/county
friction posed a major threat to the passage of other legislation proposed by his administration. These conditions set the stage for a con-
certed effort to resolve the problem.

The governor appointed the Atlanta/Fulton County Study Commission, a blue-ribbon group of nineteen members representing business,
civic and governmental interests at the local and state levels. The governor charged the commissioners to undertake a thorough and objective
analysis of the delivery of governmental services and associated revenues of Fulton County and its municipalities, including the city of Atlanta, to ensure that their citizens shall receive adequate services at an
equitable cost.

The commission appointed a small staff and adopted a proposal from a
team of outside researchers. The eight-month research agenda consisted
of three major components:

1. Description of the present governmental service delivery system
2. Analysis of current and projected problems in the existing system
3. Design and evaluation of alternative service delivery system

At one of its first meetings, the members of the commission identified
the key issues to be considered in the study: questions of service delivery
and cost inequities, financing public hospital and health services, public
housing, social services and tax assessment and collection practices. The
commission also decided to hold two sets of public hearings, one at the
start of the study to gain citizen input on service delivery and financing
problems and a second set at the conclusion of the study to report on its
work and recommendations. It also decided that each public service should
be studied separately, without constraints imposed by a predetermined
model delivery system.

Working papers and memoranda were prepared by the researchers
and distributed to the appropriate working committees. These papers
described the existing service delivery arrangements, their financing and
major strengths and weaknesses. The committees reviewed the papers,
requested supplementary information and used the data as a basis to

evaluate alternative service delivery options and financing schemes. This was supplemented by interviews with local officials, comparative budget analyses and an analysis of the crucial "subsidy issue." After completing the service-by-service analyses, the committees brought specific recommendations to the full commission for discussion and action. After adoption by the full commission, draft legislation was prepared for each recommendation and eventually submitted by the governor to the Georgia General Assembly.

During the eight-month study, the full commission met thirteen times and each of the three committees met at least nine times. The high level of sustained interest and participation by the commissioners was a reflection of the importance placed on the study by the governor and the public; it was widely perceived to be the last real opportunity for many years for local determination of the extent and nature of governmental reform in Atlanta/Fulton County. The commission's final recommendations for change are shown in Exhibit 11–2.

**Exhibit 11–2**
**Atlanta/Fulton County Study Commission Recommendations**

| Service | Key Recommendation |
|---|---|
| *General Government* | |
| —Code enforcement | Mandate uniform codes |
| —Elections | Clarify office qualifications |
| —Planning/zoning | Increase coordination across jurisdictions |
| —Tax assessment/collection | Revise qualifications of assessor and appeals process |
| | |
| *Physical/Environmental* | |
| —Libraries | Transfer entirely to county |
| —Solid waste | Transfer disposal to county |
| —Traffic engineering | Have city contract to other jurisdictions |
| —Water and sewer | Merge city/county systems |
| | |
| *Public Protection/Health/Welfare* | |
| —Adult probation | Have state assume greater financial role |
| —Emergency medical services | Support integrated statewide system |
| —Hospital | Have state assume a portion of the costs of the major regional hospital |

| —Fire services | Create fire districts throughout County |
| —Recreation | Support increased city/county cooperation |

*Financing*

Create tax service districts for all area-specific services

*Annexation*

Prohibit without consent of the annexed population

*Service-No Recommendation*

| —Business licensing | —Data Processing |
| —Public housing | —Agriculture services |
| —Aviation | —Electricity/gas |
| —Street lighting/cleaning | —Coroner/medical examiner |
| —Corrections/jails | —Courts |
| —Police | —Public health |
| —Social services | |

Of the twenty-six services studied in detail by the committees and reviewed by the full commission, thirteen received recommendations for change. In some instances, the recommendations had few, if any, immediate cost impacts. For these, not unexpectedly, little resistance to passage was encountered.

A second group of recommendations called for greater involvement by the state in financing the services. After resolving questions of feasibility, these recommendations received quick approval by the commission.

A third group of recommendations urged or mandated greater city/county coordination and cooperation. No functions were actually transferred and fiscal impacts were negligible. This group of recommendations also received quick approval by the commission.

A fourth group of recommendations presented the greatest challenge for the commission. These recommendations would have direct impact on allocation of service responsibility and/or financing:

• County assumption of library and solid waste disposal functions.

• Expansion of a fire district concept already existing in two unincorporated areas to all the remaining unincorporated areas of the county. This shifted fiscal responsibility to those direct recipients of the service. Accompanying this was a recommendation for centralization of fire training and investigation.

• Eventual merger of city and county water and sewer systems and equalization of rates charged to all customers. A nine-member board would be created to oversee the development of a comprehensive long-range plan for the distribution of new water lines. Disputes would be arbitrated by a majority of the active judges of the Superior Court of Fulton County. This recommendation encountered considerable opposition from the county due to its investment in plant and equipment, but the plan eventually passed the full commission.

- Expansion of tax service districts to include all those services for which recipients are area specific. This was the most hotly contested of all of the commission's recommendations. In a final compromise, the commission agreed to tie the tax service district recommendation to a companion recommendation that would effectively eliminate the possibility of future annexation of unincorporated areas by the city of Atlanta. Also included was a phase-in period of five years to help offset the expected nine to thirteen mill tax increase that would impact unincorporated areas. Overall, this was viewed as a major step forward in resolving the long-standing "subsidy" debate.

A last service, police, is especially noteworthy because *no change* was recommended. Substantial research and debate concentrated on this activity. In the final decision, the demand for local control overwhelmed considerations of efficiency, effectiveness and economies of scale. Despite the strong evidence in support of some centralization (e.g., training, special investigations, laboratory work), no strong advocate stepped forward to promote such changes. The result was a unanimous vote for no change.

With the exception of education, the commission addressed all major services in the eleven jurisdictions within Fulton County. In some cases, it recommended changes in operation and finance; in others, it recommended the implementation of general principles to redress significant inequities and build the foundation for future changes. The commission operated for the most part at the general policy level; it had neither the time, resources nor mandate to perform a series of management reviews or performance audits of individual operating departments in every governmental jurisdiction in Fulton County. By so limiting itself, the commission was able to concentrate on the major comparative aspects of service delivery across jurisdictions and to seek to answer questions of broad significance to all citizens of Fulton County.

The experiences of the Atlanta/Fulton County study commission point to a middle road to reform that appears more palatable to all concerned parties than the more drastic options of large-scale consolidation and annexation. Much of the work of the commission is directly transferable to other cities and counties across the country that are plagued with similar fiscal inequities and organizational inefficiencies and that seek a politically acceptable and effective service reorganization option.

## NOTES

1. Tharon J. Green, "Self-Managing Teams in the Human Resources Department," City of Hampton, Virginia, January 1990, p. 1.

2. Michael Monteith, "Hampton's Electronic Real Estate System," City of Hampton, Virginia, January 1990, pp. 1–2.

3. Terry Brandt, "From Japan with Quality," *Western City*, May 1981, pp. 13–14.

4. "Quality Circles at Ramsey County Human Services," Ramsey County, Minnesota, 1981, pp. 1–2.

5. "Quality Circles in the City of Dallas: A Summary," City of Dallas, Texas, December 1981, pp. 1–3.

6. "Productivity Report: Mechanics Quality Circle," City of Fort Collins, Colorado, April 1981, pp. 1–9.

7. Gordon Prentice, "Productivity Improvement Program Narrative," Hennepin County, Minnesota, 1981, pp. 1–3.

8. Clarence L. Smith, Jr., *Final Report: Improving Local Governmental Productivity Through Application of Participative Methods Improvement Techniques (Quality Circles)* (Raleigh: Productivity Research and Extension Program, North Carolina State University, 1981), pp. 1–18, appendices.

9. Letter from D. W. Hartman to author, July 1, 1981.

10. Michael G. Miller, "Team Management Case Histories or a Tale of Two Cities and One City Manager," City of Council Bluffs, Iowa, 1981, pp. 1–8.

11. James L. Mercer, *Quality Circles: Productivity Improvement Process*, Management Information Service Report, vol. 14, no. 3 (Washington, D.C.: International City Management Association, 1982), p. 6.

12. Cam Caldwell and Frank Seaver, "Quality of Work Life for Cities: A Management Concept for the Eighties," City of Garden City, Michigan, 1981, pp. 1–4.

13. C. H. Huckelberry, "The Quality of Working Life Experience at the Department of Transportation and Flood Control District," Pima County, Tucson, Arizona, May 1981, pp. 1–25.

14. "Florida Launches QCs," *Florida Productivity Reporter* (Tallahassee: Florida State University, August/September 1981), pp. 1–2.

15. Letter from L. Wayne Etheredge to author, June 2, 1983.

16. Tharon J. Greene, "Leadership Challenges," City of Hampton, Virginia, January 1990, pp. 1–5.

17. Tharon J. Greene, "Organization Development in the City of Hampton," City of Hampton, Virginia, January 1988, pp. 1–7.

18. Joseph Sensenbrenner, "Quality Comes to City Hall," *Harvard Business Review*, March–April 1991, pp. 64–65, 68–70, 74–75.

19. James L. Mercer, "Privatization: Alternatives in Delivering Services," *Municipal Attorney*, vol. 32, no. 2 (March/April 1991), p. 21.

20. John A. Gronouski and James L. Mercer, "A Consolidation Model: Austin/Travis County, Texas," *National Civic Review*, vol. 76, no. 5 (September–October 1987), pp. 450–454.

21. James L. Mercer and Allen L. White, "A Middle Road to Reform: The Atlanta/Fulton County Experience," *Western City*, January 1979, pp. 13–15, 27.

# Selected Bibliography

## BOOKS

Beuhler, Vernon M. and Y. Krishna Shetty, eds. *Productivity Improvement Case Studies of Proven Practice*. New York: AMACOM, 1981.

Davis, Stanley M. and Paul R. Lawrence. *Matrix*. Reading, Mass.: Addison-Wesley, 1977.

Dewar, D. L. and J. F. Beardsley. *Quality Circles*. Cupertino, Calif.: International Association of Quality Circles, 1977.

Herzberg, Frederick. *The Motivation to Work*. New York: Wiley, 1959.

Kerr, Clark and Jerome M. Rosen, eds. *Work in America: The Decade Ahead*. New York: Van Nostrand Reinhold, 1979.

Levine, Charles H., ed. *Managing Fiscal Stress: The Crisis in the Public Sector*. Chatham, N.J.: Chatham House, 1980.

Mali, Paul. *Improving Total Productivity: Management by Objectives Strategies for Business, Government, and Not-for-Profit Organizations*. New York: Wiley, 1978.

McClelland, David Clarence. *Motivating Economic Achievement*. New York: Free Press, 1967.

McGregor, Douglas. *The Human Side of Enterprise*. New York: McGraw-Hill, 1960.

Maslow, Abraham. *Motivation and Personality*. New York: Harper and Row, 1970.

Mercer, James L. *Strategic Planning for Public Managers*. Westport, Conn.: Quorum Books, 1991.

Mercer, James L. and Edwin H. Koester. *Public Management Systems*. New York: AMACOM, 1978.

Mercer, James L. and Ronald J. Philips, eds. *Public Technology: Key to Improved Government Productivity*. New York: AMACOM, 1981.

Mercer, James L., Susan W. Woolston, and William V. Donaldson. *Managing Urban Government Services: Strategies, Tools and Techniques for the 80's.* New York: AMACOM, 1981.

Michael, Stephen R., et al. *Techniques of Organizational Change.* New York: McGraw-Hill, 1981.

Miller, Ernest C. *Advanced Techniques for Strategic Planning.* New York: American Management Associations, 1971.

Nolan, Robert E. *Improving Productivity Through Advanced Office Controls.* New York: AMACOM, 1980.

Ouchi, William G. *Theory Z: How American Business Can Meet the Japanese Challenge.* Reading, Mass.: Addison-Wesley Publishing Company, 1981.

Pascale, Richard Tanner and Anthony G. Athos. *The Art of Japanese Management: Applications for American Executives.* New York: Simon & Schuster, 1981.

Pfeiffer, J. William. *Strategic Planning Selected Readings.* San Diego: University Associates, 1986.

Pfeiffer, J. William, Leonard Goodstein, and Timothy M. Nolan. *Applied Strategic Planning: A How to Do It Guide.* San Diego: University Associates, 1986.

Steiner, George A. *Strategic Planning.* New York: Free Press, 1979.

Szanton, Peter. *Not Well Advised.* New York: Russell Sage Foundation, 1981.

Washnis, Georgie J., ed. *Productivity Improvement Handbook for State and Local Government.* New York: John Wiley, 1980.

## ARTICLES AND REPORTS

Beardsley, Jefferson F. "Training is the Heart of the Lockheed Quality Control Circle Program." *Transactions*, 29th Annual Conference, American Society for Quality Control, 1975, Milwaukee, Wisconsin.

Beasley, David. "On the Job, Yet Right at Home." *The Atlanta Journal/The Atlanta Constitution*, December 16, 1991, pp. C1, C7.

Brandt, Terry. "From Japan with Quality." *Western City*, May 1981, pp. 13–14, 22.

Bryson, John M. and William D. Roering. "Applying Private-Sector Strategic Planning in the Public Sector." *Journal of the American Planning Association.* Chicago, Winter 1987.

Caldwell, Cam and Frank Seaver. "Quality of Work Life for Cities: A Management Concept for the Eighties." Unpublished paper. City of Garden City, Michigan, 1981, pp. 1–4.

Cole, Robert E. "Made in Japan-Quality-Control Circles." *Across the Board*, November 1979, pp. 72–78.

Deming, W. Edwards. "What Happened in Japan?" *Industrial Quality Control*, August 1967, pp. 89–93.

Dewar, Donald L. "Measurement of Results—Lockheed Quality Control Circles." Paper presented at the American Society for Quality Control Technical Conference, Toronto, Canada, May 1976.

"Florida Launches QCs." *Florida Productivity Reporter.* Tallahassee: Florida State University, August/September 1981, pp. 1–2.

Gottschack, Earl C., Jr. "U.S. Firms, Worried by Productivity Lag, Copy Japan in Seeking Employees' Advice." *The Wall Street Journal*, February 21, 1980, p. 40.

Gray, Daniel H. "Uses and Misuses of Strategic Planning." *Harvard Business Review*, January-February 1986.

Greene, Tharon J. "Achievement Award Program in Hampton." City of Hampton, Virginia, January 1990, p. 1.

———. "Leadership Challenges." City of Hampton, Virginia, January 1990, pp. 1–5.

———. "Linking Executive Compensation to the Organization's Mission." City of Hampton, Virginia, January 1990, p. 1.

———. "Organization Development in the City of Hampton." City of Hampton, Virginia, January 1988, pp. 1–7.

———. "Organizing for Effectiveness." City of Hampton, Virginia, January 1990, p. 1.

———. "Self-Managing Teams in the Human Resources Department." City of Hampton, Virginia, January 1990, p. 1.

Gronouski, John A. and James L. Mercer. "A Consolidation Model: Austin/Travis County, Texas." *National Civic Review*, vol. 76, no. 5 (September-October 1987), pp. 450–54.

Hanley, Joseph. "Our Experiences with Quality Circles." *Quality Progress*, February 1980, pp. 22–24.

Harned, Ellis W., et al. "Development of a Strategic Management Process: A Case Study of the Pennsylvania DOT." Task Force on Strategic Planning Process, Harrisburg, *Transportation Research Record No. 1028.*

Howard, Mark. "Successfully Establishing a Strategic Planning Process." Metropolitan Transportation Authority (New York), December 1986.

Huckelberry, C. H. *The Quality of Working Life Experience at the Department of Transportation and Flood Control District*. Pima County, Tucson, Arizona, May 1981, pp. 1–25.

Ishikawa, Kaouru. "The Cause and Effect Diagram." *Quality Circle Application, Tools and Theory*. Milwaukee: American Society for Quality Control, 1976.

Juran, J. M. "International Significance of the Quality Control Circle Movement." *Quality Progress*, November 1980, pp. 18–22.

Kauffman, Jerome L. and Harvey M. Jacobs. "A Public Planning Perspective on Strategic Planning." *Journal of the American Planning Association*, Chicago, Winter 1987.

Konz, Stephan. "Quality Circles: An Annotated Bibliography." *Quality Progress*, April 1981, pp. 30–35.

Larson, Thomas D. "Our Future By Choice." Symposium on Strategic Planning for State and Local Transportation Agencies, Transportation Research Board, Colorado Springs, September 1985.

Marks, Charles H. "Managing Industrial Projects." *Automation*, February 1979, p. 70.

Mercer, James L. "Cutback Management Florida Style." *Quality Cities*, February 1991, pp. 28–31.

———. "Growing Opportunities in Public Service Contracting." *Harvard Business Review*, vol. 61, no. 2 (March/April 1983), pp. 178, 186, 188.

————. *The Mercer Group, Inc., 1990 Privatization Survey*. Atlanta: The Mercer Group, Inc., 1990, pp. 1–46.

————. "Organizing Around Critical Success Factors: The Structure of the 1990's and Beyond." *Texas Town & City*, March 1991, pp. 10–11, 40.

————. "Organizing for the 80's—What About Matrix Management?" *Business*, July-August 1981, pp. 25–33.

————. "Privatization: Alternatives in Delivering Services." *Municipal Attorney*, vol. 32, no. 2 (March/April 1991), p. 21.

————. *Quality Circles: Productivity Improvement Processes*. Management Information Service Report, vol. 14, no. 3. Washington, D.C.: International City Management Association, 1982, pp. 1–14.

Mercer, James L. and Roxan E. Dinwoodie. *Study of Privatization Practices in State Rehabilitation Agencies: Executive Summary*. Atlanta, Ga.: Georgia Division of Rehabilitation Services, 1990, pp. 1–9.

Mercer, James L. and Allen L. White. "A Middle Road to Reform: The Atlanta/ Fulton County Experience." *Western City*, January 1979, pp. 13–15, 27.

Mercer, James L. and Susan W. Woolston. "Setting Priorities: Three Techniques for Better Decision Making." *Management Information Service Report*, vol. 12, no. 9. Washington, D.C.: International City Management Association, 1980.

————. "Urban Strategies for the 80's." *Western City*, October 1980, pp. 12–14, 16.

Meyer, Michael D. "Strategic Management in a Crises-Oriented Environment." Massachusetts Department of Public Works, Transportation Research Board, Washington, D.C., January 1987.

Miller, Michael G. "Team Management Case Histories or a Tale of Two Cities and One City Manager." Unpublished paper, City of Council Bluffs, Council Bluffs, Iowa, 1981, pp. 1–8.

Monteith, Michael. "Hampton's Electronic Real Estate System." City of Hampton, Virginia, January 1990, pp. 1–2.

*New Worlds of Service II—Local Government Strategies*. "Excerpts from the Report of the International City Management Association's Committee on Future Horizons." October, 1979, *National Civic Review*, vol. 19, no. 2, February, 1980, p. 73.

Nobles, Gregory H. "The Homeless Become Target of Scapegoating." *The Atlanta Journal/The Atlanta Constitution*, December 17, 1991, p. A25.

Nutt, Paul C. and Robert W. Backoff. "A Strategic Management Process for Public and Third-Sector Organizations." *Journal of the American Planning Association*, Chicago, Winter 1987.

Pflaum, Ann M. and Timothy J. Delmont. "External Scanning—A Tool for Planners." *Journal of the American Planning Association*, Chicago, Winter 1987.

Phillips, Julian R. and Allan A. Kennedy. "Shaping and Managing Shared Values." Unpublished McKinsey & Company Staff Paper, United Kingdom, December 1980, pp. 1–55.

Prentice, Gordon. "Productivity Improvement Program Narrative." Unpublished paper, Hennepin County, Minnesota, 1981, pp. 1–3.

"Productivity Report: Mechanics Quality Circle." City of Fort Collins, Colorado, April 1981, pp. 1–9.

"Project Management: Past, Present and Future: An Editorial Summary." *IEEE Transactions in Management*, August 1979, p. 49.

*Quality Circles: A Dynamic Approach to Productivity Improvement*. Executive Action Series #256, Bureau of Business Practices, Inc., Waterboro, Connecticut, June 1981, pp. 1–64.

"Quality Circles at Ramsey County Human Services." Unpublished paper, Ramsey County, Minnesota, 1981, pp. 1–2.

"Quality Circles in the City of Dallas: A Summary." Unpublished paper, City of Dallas, Texas, December 1981, pp. 1–3.

*The Quality Circle Program of the Norfolk Naval Shipyard*. Office of Personnel Management, April 1981, pp. 1–17.

Reiker, Wayne S. "Quality Control Circles—Development and Implementation." Paper presented at the American Society for Quality Control Technical Conference, San Diego, California, May 1975.

Sedam, Scott M. "Quality Circle Training Process Should Cover Relating, Supporting, Problem-Solving Skills." *Industrial Engineering*, vol. 14, no. 1 (January 1982), pp. 70–74.

Sensenbrenner, Joseph. "Quality Comes to City Hall." *Harvard Business Review*, March-April 1991, pp. 64–65, 68–70, 74–75.

Smith, Clarence L., Jr. *Final Report: Improving Local Governmental Productivity Through Application of Participative Methods Improvement Techniques (Quality Circles)*. Raleigh: Productivity Research and Extension Program, North Carolina State University, 1981, pp. 1–18 and appendices.

*Strategic Planning for State and Local Transportation Agencies*. Outline of Videotape Presentation. Washington, D.C.: Transportation Research Board, 1988, pp. 1–35.

Swartz, Gerald E. and Vivian C. Comstock. "One Firm's Experience with Quality Circles." *Quality Progress*, September 1979, pp. 14–16.

Usilaner, Brian L. "Productivity Incentives." *Proceedings*, Fall Industrial Engineering Conference, 1981, pp. 553–39.

Ward, Bernie. "Managing Change." *Sky*, July 1987.

Wechsler, Barton and Robert E. Backoff. "The Dynamics of Strategy in Public Organizations." *Journal of the American Planning Association*, Chicago, Winter 1987.

Wilkins, Alan. "Organizational Stories as an Expression of Management Philosophy." Ph.D. dissertation, Stanford University, Palo Alto, California, 1978.

"Will the Slide Kill Quality Circles?" *Business Week*, January 11, 1982, pp. 108–9.

Yager, Ed. "Examining the Quality Control Circle." *Personnel Journal*, October 1979, pp. 682–84, 708.

# Index

**About the Author**

JAMES L. MERCER is President/CEO of The Mercer Group, Inc., an Atlanta-based management consulting firm that he founded. He is a certified management consultant (CMC) and is a widely published author. He is the author of over 200 articles and reports for such publications as the *Harvard Business Review* and has authored *Strategic Planning for Public Managers* (Quorum Books, 1991), and has co-authored three other books dealing with management in the public sector. He has been widely quoted in the *New York Times*, the *Boston Globe*, the *Washington Post*, *Forbes*, the *Los Angeles Times*, the *Wall Street Journal*, and in many other national and international media.

# The Best Castle Ever

By Harriet Ziefert
Illustrated by Carol Nicklaus

**A Random House PICTUREBACK® READER**

Random House 🏠 New York

Text copyright © 1989 by Harriet Ziefert. Illustrations copyright © 1989 by Carol Nicklaus. All rights reserved under International and Pan-American Copyright Conventions. Published in the United States by Random House, Inc., New York, and simultaneously in Canada by Random House of Canada Limited, Toronto.

*Library of Congress Cataloging-in-Publication Data:*
Ziefert, Harriet. The best castle ever / written by Harriet Ziefert ; illustrated by Carol Nicklaus. p. cm.–(A pictureback reader) SUMMARY: In arguing over who contributed the most to building the best sandcastle ever, Lewis, Steffy, and Angel accidentally destroy their handiwork. ISBN: 0-394-81997-7 [1. Sandcastles–Fiction.] I. Nicklaus, Carol, ill. II. Title. III. Series. PZ7.Z487Bi 1989 [E]–dc 19 88-26317

Manufactured in the United States of America 1 2 3 4 5 6 7 8 9 0

American made 7690. 829

"Let's make a castle,"
said Lewis.

Lewis dug.

Angel dug.

Steffy dug.

They all dug
lots of sand.

Lewis dumped.

Steffy dumped.

Angel dumped.

They all dumped
lots of sand.

Lewis got water.

Angel got water.

Steffy got water.

# They all got lots of water.

Dig…

dump…

pour.

Pour...dump...dig.

"Look!" said Lewis.

"I made a moat."

"Look! Look!" said Steffy.

"I made a boat."

"Look! Look! Look!" said Angel.

"I made a flag."

"This is the best castle ever," said Lewis.

"And I made it the best!"

Angel was mad.

He pushed Steffy.

Steffy was mad.

She pushed Angel and Lewis.

# Everyone pushed and pushed.

SEVILLE TWP. LIBRARY - 398
6734 N. Lumberjack Rd.
Riverdale, MI., 48877

# They all fell down.

# They fell on the castle.

The moat was gone.

The boat was gone.

The flag was gone.

The castle was gone.

Everyone was sad.

But Lewis knew what to do.

"Let's make a castle," he said.

"The best castle ever!"

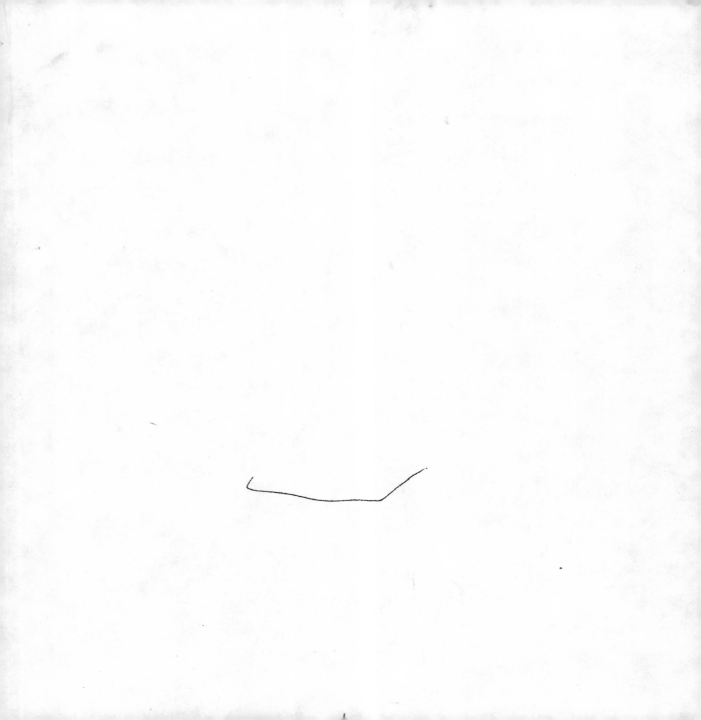